An Essay for Ezra

Thinking Theory
Grant Farred, Series Editor

AN ESSAY FOR EZRA RACIAL TERROR IN AMERICA

Grant Farred

Thinking Theory

University of Minnesota Press
Minneapolis
London

The University of Minnesota Press gratefully acknowledges financial support for the publication of this series from Cornell University.

Frontispiece: Self-portrait by Ezra Farred, age 8.

Portions of the text are adapted from "The Terror of Trump: Through the Body of a Child—An Essay for Ezra," *Journal of British Cultural Studies* 25, no. 1 (2018): 11–23.

Published by the University of Minnesota Press
111 Third Avenue South, Suite 290
Minneapolis, MN 55401-2520
http://www.upress.umn.edu

ISBN 978-1-5179-1179-9 (hc)
ISBN 978-1-5179-1180-5 (pb)
A Cataloging-in-Publication record for this book is available from the Library of Congress.

Printed in the United States of America on acid-free paper

The University of Minnesota is an equal-opportunity educator and employer.

28 27 26 25 24 23 22 21   10 9 8 7 6 5 4 3 2 1

This essay is dedicated to my son,
Ezra Glynn Juffer Farred.
With love, Nip, for you, always.

It is necessary to live in terms of terror.
—Alexandre Kojève, *Introduction to the Reading of Hegel: Lectures on the "Phenomenology of Spirit"*

Because, *for man to be redeemed from revenge*—that is for me the bridge to the highest hope, and a rainbow after long storms.
—Friedrich Nietzsche, *Thus Spake Zarathustra*

Contents

1 November 2016

Wednesday morning, November 9, 2016, assumed its usual routine. Except it was nothing like a normal morning in our household. Nothing like it at all.

Following the pattern of mornings, my wife, Jane, got up around 6:00 a.m. with our son, Ezra, who was then eight years old. As is their practice, mother and son sat down to breakfast. I write late, Jane prefers to work in the morning, so I normally rise about an hour later. For her part, Jane is generally in bed by 10:00 p.m. That part of our domestic routine was business as usual. What was not normal was everything that happened after Jane had her first cappuccino and Ezra picked his way through an assortment of offerings. For Ezra, breakfast could be anything from a randomly chosen cereal to freshly prepared mac and cheese. Mac and cheese might be his first meal. On a good day.

Ever since Donald Trump announced his candidacy for president, Ezra has listened carefully to Trump's pronouncements. It is a habit, I am glad to say, that he retains to this day. At home, whether we are watching television news (almost always of the cable variety), he is scrolling through sites on his iPad, or he and I (or he and Jane) are listening to National Public Radio in the car on our way to or from school, Ezra pays unusual attention to what Trump has to say. In the buildup to the 2016 election, Nip (my nickname for Ezra) was especially tuned in to Trump's pronouncements as they concerned race—or, more precisely, racism—and gender. "Trump hates women," Ezra said after several stories broke about Trump's behavior in relation to women who had worked with him in business, been contestants in his beauty pageants, or been involved in his TV shows. Ezra's distaste for Trump's misogyny intensified as the *Access Hollywood* tape became public. I think Jane and I managed, just barely, to ensure that Ezra was not exposed to that moment of obscene white male privilege.

Trump was graphic: "And when you're a star, they let you do it. You can do anything." In the spirit of locker-room jocularity, the *Access Hollywood* host, Billy Bush, was quick to express wonder and amazement:

BUSH: Whatever you want.
TRUMP: *Grab 'em by the pussy.* You can do anything.[1]

Jane and I tried, as far as it was possible, to spare Ezra these lurid details. At the very least, the more than usually crude ones. Ezra has linguistic facility enough. No need to fine-tune it. And now, at the time of this writing, he is possessed of a preadolescent imagination—this means an extended vocabulary and an aptitude for just the right turn of phrase. At the age of eight he certainly did not need to be introduced to language of the "Grab 'em by the p—y" variety. No matter, Ezra—like many of the kids at his school, where Trump was, and remains, viscerally disliked—clearly grasped the gist. In the age of the internet, it has become impossible (for good as well as ill) to shield one's child from a presidential candidate's—and then a president's—boorishness and vulgarity. In any case, since Ezra has, as just mentioned, his own iPad, supplemented, since 2019, by a smartphone, which he wields with a disconcerting proficiency, he can lay eyes on all the information his heart desires.

Worst of all, Ezra is far more adept than I am at finding his way around internet sites such as YouTube and TikTok—and who knows what else. Ezra can access sites that recount Trump's latest transgressions with no difficulty at all. It is all readily available, everything from stories about Trump's alleged assaults on women to his early-morning, unfiltered tweets—id of the purest variety, Freud might say. All of this is exacerbated by Trump's standing as the septuagenarian who boasts the world's shortest attention span; one wonders if Freud might be able to explain how, not if, the two are linked. To say nothing of Trump's mindless rants and his blatant lies (more than nineteen thousand and counting as of June 2020).[2] To say nothing of his blatant racism.

For Ezra, it is this last propensity that disturbs the most. This all came to a head, in the most personal way, in the spring and summer of 2020. The ways in which violence against black bodies unsettles Ezra was brought home as a visceral truth in the period following the murder of George Floyd, an African-American man, by a white Minneapolis police officer, Derek Chauvin, as three of Chauvin's colleagues looked on. Officers Thomas Lane, J. Alexander Kueng, and Tou Thao watched as Chauvin kept his knee on George Floyd's neck for nine minutes and forty-nine seconds.

While we live in Ithaca, New York, Ezra's two older brothers live in Minnesota: Alex, the eldest, lives in St. Paul, and Anton, as well members of our extended family, lives in Minneapolis. And not just in any neighborhood, but in the Longfellow neighborhood in South Minneapolis. Anton lives, literally, just a few blocks from East Thirty-eighth Street and Chicago, which is in the adjoining Powderhorn neighborhood, where Floyd's murder took place. Not *our* neighborhood, as such, but our home away from home. So, yes, in an expansive, proprietary sense, *our* neighborhood.

Every year, we spend at least a couple of weeks of our summer vacation in the Longfellow neighborhood. We shop at the Target—just this side ("our" side) of the railway tracks that separate Longfellow from Powderhorn—that was ransacked and left a burned-out shell; it has since been rebuilt into an upscale store, more Whole Foods than Target, if you can believe that. We ride our bikes down Lake Street, past the police station that was gutted by the protesters, in order to enter the Greenway, a pleasant, winding bike path that leads to downtown Minneapolis. The corner of Minnehaha Avenue and Lake Street is home to the Third Precinct, which, as we are by now all too aware, is arguably the worst police precinct in all of Minneapolis. We patronize the local bowling alley, Memory Lanes. We order takeout from our favorite Indian restaurant, Gandhi Mahal (also, sadly, a victim of the protests and gone for good). From time to time, Ezra, Anton, and I check out the fancy bikes at a store called The Hub, which has all the trappings of a hipster joint.

On May 25, Memorial Day, 2020, from our home in Ithaca, we watched the video. Derek Chauvin's knee on George Floyd's neck. Until Floyd died. We watched it, replay after replay, endlessly. We watched in horror, understanding the anger of the protests that followed Floyd's killing. Nevertheless, we were still aghast as "our" part of the country erupted into flames. Death, black death, police brutality, destruction, looting, carnage. Anger.

Our response—Ezra's, Jane's, and mine—was visceral. It could not but be. We *know* this neighborhood. Our family lives there. We live part of our ordinary lives there. There is for us a geopolitical intimacy with, an affective bond with, the ways in which the Black

Lives Matter movement achieved a new national intensity (as well as an international resonance) and the Defund the Police movement found its first voice.

We have walked these South Minneapolis streets. We will walk these Longfellow and Powderhorn streets again. As a diasporic black man who is father to a black son, to watch the George Floyd–derived spectacle unfold in South Minneapolis is to know terror as a dull, immediate fear. This is how terror induces helplessness; this is how, in destroying a life, lives, terror threatens to vacate psychic intimacy—how it can throw one's place in the world into question.

In our Ithaca living room, huddled together out of an unspeakable vulnerability, the three of us watched Dave Chappelle's Netflix special titled *8:46*. (Eight minutes and forty-six seconds was the originally reported duration of Chauvin's kneeling on George Floyd's neck.) The time *to* death is everything. (Because of time, what else could Chappelle's special have been named?) Alex sent us the link to *8:46* and so Jane, Ezra, and I watched Chappelle. A key figure in this essay, Chappelle held forth on, inter alia, police brutality. We watched in desperate, disenfranchised, silence. We watched it again, and again. We watched *8:46* because Chappelle understands. What is more, Chappelle *understands* in a critical Heideggerian sense. That is, Chappelle's (to) *understand* encompasses both *verstehen,* to make something stand in the open, and *Verstand,* which signifies Reason, or reason—what we take to be common sense or a "general understanding" of what is, or should be, "obvious" to all.[3] Again, we could peg this, in some ways at our peril, as "common sense."[4] (As such, Chappelle departs from Heidegger because the latter insists on a strict separation of one definition from the other. So much so that Heidegger dismisses the second definition as not philosophically useful.) Chappelle conflates these renderings. More than that, however, he utilizes both in order to mobilize *verstehen* and *Verstand*'s different but, for his purposes, mutually reinforcing meanings. For Chappelle, *understand = verstehen + Verstand.* (For Kant, as we know, the distinction is clearer. Kant offers *Verstand* as "understanding" and *Vernunft* as Reason.) In order to achieve distinction (in the course of which we are doing violence to Heidegger's concept), if not clarity, let us name it *Ver-stehen.*[5]

Chappelle integrates *verstehen* and *Verstand* into a Heideggerian compound so that he can bring to light what it means to *understand* the black community's response (or the responses of the various constituencies within the black community) to George Floyd's murder. Chappelle starts from the premise that to *understand* is to know what is self-evident, apparent, and commonsensical. Things are as we see them; they are as they appear to us, and, because of this, everyone should be able to grasp "how it is"; how it belongs, that is, to Reason—that is, things are as they appear, and, as a consequence, how we process what appears produces, out of its constitutive logic, a "reasonable conclusion."

Chappelle also relies on Heidegger's *verstehen* in order, over the course of eight minutes and forty-six seconds, to lay things bare. Chappelle grapples toward the truth of *what is* by seeking to bring the violence to which black life is subject out into the open, producing a "clear grasp of [the] thing as a whole."[6] Through *Verstand* Chappelle meditates his way—*8:46* is nothing less than a thinking of racism, a thinking that emerges out of the urgency of the now, an intense reflection on *what is* in the United States; as such, *8:46* is a Chappelle special sui generis, only superficially like his other work—to the more rigorous realm that he crafts as *verstehen* so that the former adds critical ballast to the latter, rather than, as in Heidegger's distinction, hierarchizing and, in so doing, refusing *Verstand* as a mode of critique.

These Streets Will Speak for Themselves I

Approach the matter analogically. It is all quite simple, really. I promise. In order to understand what is happening to and in America in the wake of the death of George Floyd, white America must consider things analogically. The "thing" that is black America's response to the murder of a black man in broad daylight, a police officer committing this act of violence in full view of his colleagues, indifferent to the onlookers recording him on their cell phones.[7] Some of the bystanders implored Chauvin to stop, to treat Floyd's (black) life as though it had value, some value, just enough value that would allow Floyd to keep breathing. To treat the other as though he were human. Instead, as the senior officer, Chauvin exercised his authority to the point of death. Chauvin's was an act so blatant in its disregard that it rises to the charge of sadism. Unmoved by all around him, most of all the dying man beneath his knee, Chauvin committed an act of cruelty as though it were a matter of no consequence. Took a human life as though it were simply another act performed in the line of a duty rooted in violent indifference to black life, and death. The route to white *Verstand* runs through white (police) sadism. As such, to watch George Floyd being killed is to recoil because of the intense fear and anxiety that it provokes. The work of terror is to make immanent the fragility of black life, always subject to the predations of white force. Black life can be snuffed out at will. Black life depends on the forbearance of white force.

And should we have any difficulty understanding the propensity for white police sadism, all we need to do is turn to Chappelle. He just happens to have the perfect analogy.

If white America wants to understand black America and its response to George Floyd's killing by a white policeman on a Minneapolis street, all white America has to do is think like the Los Angeles Police Department. (There is, of course, another alternative. White America could think a mimesis of the self. That is, it could seek to comprehend those individuals, those constituencies of white America, who are publicly supportive of the black struggle against injustice. Those white Americans who participate in protests, those white Americans who lead movements in areas where there are no significant black populations. In the summer of 2020, white people in the city of Portland, Oregon, the state of Utah, and other venues showed themselves ready to struggle for a transcendent principle, which we could name "justice," "equality," or simply the determination to make their voices heard for what might be called, commonsensically, "doing the right thing." Self-reflection on the order of the white self addressing its—intellectually delinquent? morally abject?—white self: Why do other whites have the capacity for *Verstand*? Is there something to be learned not from those Americans who are "unlike" me but from those whom I resemble in racial profile, if not in the ability to understand?) To be specific, all white America has to do is emulate the mind-set of the four hundred members of the LAPD who hunted down and killed Christopher Dorner, a black man who had previously worn the uniform of the LAPD.

Dorner was born in New York City and raised in Southern California. From 2002 to 2013, he served as an officer in the U.S. Navy Reserve. In 2007, he joined the LAPD, a short-lived tenure. He was fired from the LAPD in 2008—in Dorner's view, an act of retaliation for his having filed a complaint about a fellow cop (Teresa Evans) for using excessive force while arresting a suspect suffering from dementia and schizophrenia. From the time of his dismissal in 2008 through 2011, Dorner appealed his firing to various institutions, beginning with the LAPD and going all the way to "the Superior Courts and California Appellate courts." None of it met with any success. Finding himself out of options, in February 2013,

Dorner posted his "manifesto," as the document became known, to his Facebook page. In his "manifesto" Dorner named forty police officers he intended to kill. He alleged that the LAPD remained, despite the turmoil of the 1992 riots, intensely racist, and that the department had not changed at all since the "Rampart and Rodney King days."[8]

From February 3 to February 12, Dorner killed four people. His victims were two police officers, a young woman named Monica Quan, and her fiancé, Keith Lawrence (who was African-American). Monica Quan was the daughter of Randal Quan, the attorney who had represented Dorner in his lawsuit against the LAPD. According to Dorner, Randal Quan, who had been the first Asian-American captain in the LAPD, was sympathetic to the department and so had not provided the kind of counsel his case required.

The LAPD tracked Dorner to a cabin in the San Bernardino Mountains near Big Bear Lake. The police surrounded the cabin, and after Dorner failed to comply with their demand to surrender, law enforcement bulldozed the building and fired pyrotechnic tear gas canisters into it. According to the coroner's account, Dorner died of a self-inflected gunshot wound to the head.

Chappelle, whom Dorner names a "genius" in his manifesto, has a different account of Dorner's demise. (Dorner affords comedian Kevin Hart the "genius" honor as well, much to Chappelle's chagrin. It is, however, chagrin of the most endearing variety.) Chappelle starts *8:46* slowly, relating the events of Dorner's death. For the most part, he maintains, for the length of the scene, a staccato style, with short, punctuated bursts of speech, culminating in an emphatic eruption. By the end of the "Dorner" scene, Chappelle is literally spitting out his words:

> They found him. Big Bear. Hiding in a cabin.
> When they found out what this nigger was, no less than four hundred police officers showed up and answered the call. And boy let me tell you something, they swiss-cheesed this nigger.
> He is dead as dead can be. And you know why four hundred cops showed up?
> Because one of their own was murdered.
> So how the fuck can't they understand what going on in these streets?
> We saw ourselves like you see yourself.[9]

To make sense of the protests that shook the nation after May 25, 2020, requires nothing other than a basic grasp of mimicry. Call it empathy, if you insist; or not, as you wish. *Verstand* would do as well. Just practice the political act of "feeling like." Of feeling like black America. Of feeling like, if not someone other than you, then some white person—or a collection of white persons (LAPD officers intent on avenging their own)—who is not you but whose outlook Chappelle presumes you to share. Chappelle asks white America to see itself as another, heavily armed, version of itself. To imagine itself as an LAPD officer who has lost a colleague to a dismissed and, needless to say, bitter former colleague. Chappelle asks white America to imagine that. Just for a moment.

We can all agree. This is simple, a not in the least bit difficult thing to do. If white America can transcend itself for a moment, then Chappelle's analogy will be crystal clear. The protests that followed George Floyd's death were—if the turn of phrase might be permitted—no different from the response of four hundred LAPD cops showing up outside a cabin in Big Bear. How could white America *not* understand? Chappelle's analogy is (disproportionately) biblical in its simplicity: an eye for an eye, a tooth for a tooth. Except that on this occasion that single tooth (Dorner) had to endure a force (LAPD officers) four hundred times larger. Except that the entire history of whites in America is one of disproportionate force.

But let us not lose sight of Chappelle's analogy, because what happened on the streets of Minneapolis, New York, Los Angeles, Chicago, placid suburbs in Utah, and struggling postindustrial towns in central Pennsylvania in response to George Floyd's killing is the—racially—inverted image of what took place in the San Bernardino Mountains. Chappelle enjoins white America to (try to) draw from the same psychic well. To summon up, from somewhere in the entanglements of its (white) self, the depths of LAPD anger. Chappelle asks white America to tap into its considerable reservoir of (racial?) resentment. Make the effort, Chappelle urges white America, to recall those fierce feelings of loyalty to one of its own.

Having commanded that response, or those responses, white America now has to think itself in relation to the indigenous population (not only were the colonists armed with superior weaponry, but they were also not averse to low-tech but deadly biological warfare, such the distribution of blankets contaminated with smallpox) and in relation to the enslaved Africans and their descendants (again, guns, whips, all forms of corporal punishment, as *Uncle Tom's Cabin*, the blues, jazz, and *Roots,* from their different vantage points, remind us). A pattern that continued through Reconstruction, that marked the battles for civil rights (Bull Connor is but the most emblematic figure in this regard; snarling dogs, protesters, the late John Lewis included, marching fearful but undaunted across the Edmund Pettus Bridge) and continues into our moment. The story of America for its black population, the reality for minorities in this country, is one reign of terror after another, with nary a Robespierre in sight, reaching our moment as the terror of Trump. We have reason to pause, to brace ourselves and wonder if it is this, surely it is not this, that Alexandre Kojève means when he enjoins us, "It is necessary to live in terms of terror."[10] What good can terror, in any form, do for disenfranchised America? It has already done so much violence to the black body and psyche. Still and all, Kojève's injunction unsettles. It unsettles because it appears haunted by the possibility that it contains within it another, more ominous, understanding.

After all, it took six Baltimore police officers to "subdue" a black man, Freddie Gray, and get him into the back of a "paddy wagon." The history of whites in America is the history of a stacked deck. The numbers always disproportionately favor white America.

The odds are on your side, white America. Through the Chappelle-inspired Heideggerian neologism, Chappelle is asking white America to *Ver-stehen* this. Grasp, white America, what is common sense. White America, subject your historic advantages to the critique of Reason. *Understand, Ver-stehen,* your political inheritance.

White America should date itself as follows: May 26, 2020. This date, if the crisis of racism is to be taken as an opportunity for thinking the history of white supremacy, must mark the moment of white self relocation. (The imperative tone matters: *must,* not *should* or *could.* The time for the conditional is "8:46" too late. If, that is, we understand eight minutes and forty-six seconds as a historical evocation made out of the present that is violently indebted to the past. And is, moreover, a time that threatens to repeat itself, ad nauseam, in the future. Can the clock that is white supremacist racial violence be stopped at "8:46"? One doubts it, very much, and with historical good reason.) The moment of white psychic readjustment, at least as it pertains to an America rethinking itself in the afterlife of George Floyd. Out of black death, the birth of white *Ver-stehen*?

No Más

Nip, growing up in apartheid South Africa, this is what racial inequity, allowing for the geopolitical differences, felt like. White South Africa, my son, always had the numbers that mattered. The apartheid regime had the repressive apparatus, the military arsenal (police vehicles, army tanks, rubber bullets), and the law on its side. Nip, as your mother and I tried to explain to you as we watched *8:46*, the social unrest that followed Floyd's death is the inversion of that trend. For a long moment, following Floyd's killing, white America got a different view of things. Nip, for the first time, maybe, they got a glimpse of what it looks like and what it feels like when the force of the "jackboot" simply becomes too much.

Ezra, this is what America is made to look like when the police, firm in the belief that they have a license to be brutal and that no one will hold them accountable for their actions, kill one black man or woman too many. It is, of course, always one too many. But no one, least of all police officers, sadistic and otherwise, knows just when black America will scream, in the spirit of Roberto Durán pummeled into submission by "Sugar" Ray Leonard, "No más." (I watched that fight on tape-delay in Cape Town, Nip, in November 1980. Billed the "Super Fight," it was a little *loco,* spiced with plenty of controversy because no one could believe that Leonard had inflicted quite that much punishment on Roberto "Manos de Piedra" Durán, especially because their first fight, in June 1980, had been so brutal. Turns out that the "Manos de Piedra," the "Hands of Stone," belonged to Leonard, not Durán.) No one knows when black America will scream so loudly that white America will have no choice but to hear the primal depth of that "No más," echoing down the decades, in its own menacing register, from the cauldron that was the Louisiana Superdome in November 1980.

In a moment such as George Floyd's murder, it is not (simply) a matter of black America seeing itself being, literally, put to death. Of white America seeing black America being put to death. It is something fundamentally different. It is that moment when black America decides, in a public declaration that resonates across the length and breadth of the country, a declaration whose asynchrony and unity cannot be fully explained (a secret, as Jacques Derrida might have it, hidden even from itself), that it no longer wants to see itself as white America sees it. That is, dying from the excessive force that white America so regularly uses against black America. There are times when black America sees what it is white America does, and in its turn black America, unable to bear the pain, the disgust, and the helplessness, retreats into itself. Once more. There are other times when black America sees what it is white America does, and it fights back as best it can. And then there are times, such as this one, when black America sees what white America does, and in response black America summons up the deepest reserve of its strength. In that moment black America accesses all of its *ressentiment* and, as James Baldwin would insist (as we will see momentarily), its love and its hopelessness, determined to marshal its resources to the best of its abilities. It reaches out to its allies for their support. In that moment black America resists, it struggles, it fights, with all its might. In that moment black America stands against all the repressive forces of white America.

And when that happens, as we have seen, the effect of black resistance is cataclysmic. Black America confronts white America for what it is, for what it has done to black America, and, most important, for how white America continues to act against black America, with an impunity that goes back centuries (slave owners, overseers, Jim Crow advocates, unreconstructed segregationists, sadistic cops, vengeful federal marshals). This is white America's hatred for black life. This is the disregard for black life that is at the very core of the idea named "America." Black America taking to the streets in the wake of George Floyd's murder is the sound of black fury. With that fury, when Baldwinian love finds itself under threat, black America turns the world of white America upside down. White America has left black America no choice. Black America must take its stand. It must take its stand against racism, injustice, police brutality, and a racist president's race-baiting, or it will continue to die. Continue to die one police knee at a time, one too-easily discharged police bullet at a time, one Driving While Black arrest at a time, one excessive, premeditated police chokehold at a time. There is nothing to do in such a situation except to say "No más," and to struggle with all one's might against that which is.

White America has left black America no choice but to make white America, once again, as if for the first time, recognize the depth of black suffering and degradation. Once more, white America is called upon to confront the reservoirs of black anger and the highly incendiary admixture of futility, love, and hope—against hope—that is black life.[11] (It would, of course, be infinitely better for black America if it could *compel* white America—through some force, coercive, moral, or otherwise—into such a confrontation. Best of all, an absolute impossibility, it would seem, would be white America's taking up this work of its own accord, with the understanding that this task is girded by a requisite set of difficulties— history, violence, and so on—that white America must engage.)

These Streets Will Speak for Themselves II

In *8:46* Chappelle speaks as the streets (speak) when he issues his analogical injunction to white America. See. See black life. See what black America sees, sees every day. See how black America sees white America. See, listen (attune yourself to), and think the streets.

The event of George Floyd is how black America and its allies— white, Asian-American, Latina/o-American—speak when they take to the streets. This is how black Americans make the streets speak. The streets speak in such a register that white America cannot ignore its history of violence, its systemic racism, the lawlessness that is the police force in cities and towns the nation over, and the too-close relationship among police, prosecutors, and the American judicial system.[12]

Through the resonant anger that emerges from black protests, black America shows white America how powerful the streets can be. Chris Dorner wanted, desperately, to clear his name. As he states in his manifesto:

> I have exhausted all available means at obtaining my name back. I have attempted all legal court efforts within appeals at the Superior Courts and California Appellate courts. This is my last resort.[13]

For its part, black America is in search of a new name, a name that is autochthonous to the streets.[14] And these streets, as white America well knows, are most likely to be streets that, until Memorial Day 2020, white America claimed, unthinkingly, as its own. From Seattle's Capitol Hill Autonomous Zone, or CHAZ (a brief but nonetheless memorable occupation), to San Francisco's redecorated precincts to the Third Precinct in Minneapolis, black America has staked its claim to the nation's streets.[15] In Portland, white mothers, white combat veterans, and children surround a federal building in solidarity with antiracist struggles. The intention is to hold the streets for as long as possible. In the name of the streets, where black life is routinely, violently snuffed out, black America intends to make white America remember Memorial Day (2020) as white America has never remembered Memorial Day before. Black America has memorialized Memorial Day (2020) as George Floyd Day. A day of black death.

"Trump's America"

The effect of George Floyd's murder on Ezra was that it left him with a badly shaken sense of physical safety. Police brutality against black bodies was brought home to him in the late spring and summer of 2020 with a proximity, a force, and a deep sense of geosocial familiarity. Ezra *knows* now, as he did not before, that streets familiar to him are the very streets that brings death to black bodies.

As we walked our dog in Ithaca one morning in June 2020, talking about the uproar on America's streets, Ezra offered a pithy insight, one possessed of piercing clarity: "This is Trump's America, Dad."

I wanted to say to Nip that in "Trump's America" you are threatened, my son. Threatened, my son, as you have never been threatened before. That was the thought I formed. But I held my tongue. Ezra was eleven years old then, some two months shy of his twelfth birthday. I was silent because it seemed to me that in that moment Nip already had plenty to deal with; not only rampant racism but also, beginning in the spring of 2020, the spread of COVID-19, which put paid, abruptly, to his in-person school year and introduced him to virtual learning. As such, there was no need to heighten his fears about Trump.

What is more, George Floyd, Ahmaud Arbery (Atlanta), Breonna Taylor (Louisville), and Rayshard Brooks (Atlanta) were all murdered by police in the spring and summer of 2020. That seemed to me lesson enough for Nip. Or too many lessons. Or not enough lessons. I could not tell which. I still cannot.

I am drawn hither and thither because violence, the prospect of violence, intimidation, the prospect of intimidation—each demands its own particular mode of preparation. With the proviso, of course, that it is impossible to prepare properly or fully for any of these modes. All the while we know that they all provoke fear, uncertainty, and an existential anxiety in the black self. After all, terror is a versatile phenomenon. Throughout the black self's life, the form that terror takes might mutate, but its presence remains, in and of itself, ominous, omnipresent, and seemingly indestructible. To be lived with; to be lived with and struggled against. To be lived with in order to outlive terror, in all its forms, in its every articulation.

Chappelle's Magnanimity

For all its resonance, thinking analogically has its limits. So much so that we could say that Chappelle's question about apparent white incomprehension (*nicht verstehend*, or, to render our Heideggerian neologism in the negative, *nicht Ver-stehen*), even as a declarative, misses the mark. At best, Chappelle's critique is misleading. The question, such as it is, is not "So how the fuck can't they understand what going on in these streets?" No. That line of inquiry will not do.

Chappelle's question must be replaced by an indictment and proceed from there into a call that exceeds politics. (Offered as an indictment, the question would have to be: How could white America not understand—*Verstand*?) To be clear, white America *understands*. It both grasps the nettles of *Verstand* and comprehends—*verstehen*—the violence that lies before it, that is committed in its name. Of that Chappelle, and all historical minorities, is sure. White America has always understood, in registers philosophical and vernacular, what is offered here as a neologism, *Ver-stehen*. For four hundred years white America has acted with intent. White America has been living easily with—cohabiting at leisure with, enjoying the benefits of—this country's "Original Sin." Since at least 1619, and who knows how long before that, black subjugation was already under way as a political project. It was an economic ambition to be fulfilled. The body and labor of the other were the means through which colonialist mastery of America could be achieved. White Manifest Destiny began with the desire for and visions of indigenous subjugation (and extermination, if possible; genocide, if necessary) and black enslavement. How could this be forgotten? Who could forget this?

It is quite easy to forget, suggests the Algerian-born French philosopher Jacques Derrida, a Jewish thinker who lived the anti-Semitism of Vichy France. Under the rule of Marshal Philippe Pétain, who headed the Vichy government, Jews in Algeria were disenfranchised, an event that affected Derrida's family and left a lasting imprint on the boy then known as Jackie. Memory of atrocity, and what follows in its aftermath, how to live this condition, would prove critical to Derrida's work, especially later in his life.[16]

Writing about forgiveness, a radical mode of being in relation to the other, which we will take up in relation to Baldwin (and in some measure through Derrida), Derrida explains how historical amnesia is critical to erasing the role of violence in the establishment of nation-states. The deliberate writing out of violence, Derrida argues, exceeds forgetting: "This foundational violence is not only forgotten. The foundation is made *in order to* hide it; by its essence it tends to organize amnesia, sometimes under the celebration and sublimation of the grand beginnings."[17] Amnesia, as such, is neither an accidental loss nor the failure of memory. The violence inherent to the nation's founding is "sublimated" to the force of origin. "Grand beginnings," as such, are structurally "organized" to indemnify the "founding" against what is "hidden" in and by it. The "foundation" of the nation is designed as an immunizing psychopolitical architecture, sealing off the originating violence from public memory and embellishing this founding with festivals of "celebration." Except, of course, that we know all "foundations" to be subject to the wear and tear of time (sometimes ruinously so), and, because of this "natural" force, the violence of the nation's founding inevitably begins to seep through the architectural cracks.

Try as it might, then, white America's violent founding permits of no historical amnesia. Of the long-term (genocide, slavery) or the short-term (police brutality, disenfranchisement) variety. In just the last century or so, white America enacted, in thirty-six states across the Union, Jim Crow legislation. Right alongside the usual suspects, Alabama, Mississippi, Louisiana, the Commonwealth of Virginia, and the Carolinas, we find California, Oregon, Massachusetts, Nevada, Washington, and Utah. Across the Union, Jim Crow laws were a consistent political decision. Discriminatory state laws were not a legislative aberration. White America condoned and tolerated, both implicitly and explicitly, lynching—a practice that has not yet, as we head into the third decade of the twenty-first century, been fully eliminated. To overturn Jim Crow legislation, African-Americans had to undertake the struggle for Civil Rights. Today, as always, the determination to disenfranchise African-American voters remains a constant threat.

The effects of income inequality, underresourcing of school districts, and redlining, to name only three, remain in need of urgent address. This "foundational violence" is America's history, unforgettable. Which white American can possibly claim not to know it? How can white America possibly insist that it owes its newly acquired antiracist consciousness to the sadistic spectacle of George Floyd's death? That would be perverse. It would be perverse because designating George Floyd's murder a road to Damascus moment (a conversion event, shall we say, that instant when the truth becomes inarguable) is tantamount to making an offering of thanks to Derek Chauvin. It would be no less than declaring, "Were it not for Chauvin's brutal act, white life would have gone along in its usual unperturbed way."

No wrong has been righted in this country's history without a struggle in which black Americans have borne a disproportionate share of the burden. A struggle, at least as it pertains to race, that has always required black leadership and large-scale black sacrifice. Harriet Tubman, Frederick Douglass, Martin Luther King, Fannie Lou Hamer, Rosa Parks, Jackie Robinson. Armies of men, women, and children who braved white America's antipathy, anger, and violent reprisals. And, yes, death.

For black Americans it has always been reign of terror after reign of terror. Racial terror in the era of Trump has been simply the latest installment of this bloody and violent saga.

Because black Americans will confront this violence, it remains the privilege of white America to treat this history as if it were a series of matters long since rendered obsolete. Racism, structural inequality, routine encounters with police brutality—white America considers these matters entirely resolved and of no consequence today, no matter that the threat to black life continues into our precarious present. Only white America can afford not to know what this means. Only white America has to be reminded of these struggles, has to be reminded every time racism manifests itself, one more time, and black bodies lie dead. Routine discrimination, inadequate resources, acute economic vulnerability in the face of the COVID-19 pandemic. The struggle begins again, as if for the first time. As if for the first time with George Floyd. As if George Floyd were the first time.

For the moment, and a good thing it is too, it appears that there will be no more calls from black and antiracist America, except in the most institutional locations, for "police reform."[18] No, Rodney King, Michael Brown, Freddie Gray, each of their deaths showed conclusively that police departments in America cannot be reformed. They are entrenched in their repressive modes of behavior. They regard black life as expendable. Police departments across the United States have no fear of the law because they are shielded by the law. Not only that, but worse, they take their actions to be the law. Police actions, whatever they might be, enact the law. All police actions are, regardless of the furor that follows, and then subsides, above reproach by the law. In Kristy Parker's succinct phrase, what police sadism on the order of Chauvin and his ilk has long since produced is "lawless policing."[19] "Lawless policing" cannot be reformed. It must be dismantled, in its entirety. Time to begin again, this time with the intention of outlawing, entirely, police brutality, the recognition of which cannot but put policing itself—the police force, structures of command, the history of policing—in the dock.

Failure to do so will ensure that police actions continue to be, as the phrase goes, "above the law." The law can be broken with impunity. By the police. A white police officer can kneel, in the presence of amateur videographers (that is, anyone with a cell phone), in the presence of other police officers, on a black man's neck until he dies and fear no repercussions. The pessimism about police reform hangs heavily over Angela Haverty and Earl Smith's work on police violence. They began their writing, they reflect, "after Trayvon Martin and Mike Brown were murdered, but before Philando Castile was shot and killed at point-blank range, around the time that Freddie Gray was given the police van ride that ended his life. It was, and still is, difficult to imagine a time when the violence, the policing of Black bodies, will stop. We have trouble imagining when it will slow down."[20] Ahmaud Arbery was murdered on February 23, 2020; George Floyd, May 25, 2020; and Rayshard Brooks, June 12, 2020. Freddie Gray was killed on April 12, 2015, just eight months after Michael Brown on August 9, 2014.[21] No wonder, then, that Haverty and Smith "have trouble imagining when it will slow down." They are by no means alone.

A black man can appeal for relief, "I can't breathe," or, as in Freddie Gray's case, he can "request an asthma inhaler"; a black man can even, in desperation, beseech his dead mother for help ("Mama"), it makes no difference to a white cop.[22] Black life does not matter. Black life has no value. Black lives do not matter because they have no value. A black man's death is a matter of no consequence. Just another day in the Minneapolis, Baltimore, Ferguson, Atlanta Police Department. Living under the condition of "Life under Suspicion"— or "Guilty until Proven Innocent."[23] "Thug life," Trump might have it, is expendable. Snuff out their last breath. Even if it takes eight minutes and forty-six seconds. Even if their last words are a plea: "I can't breathe."

This was Chauvin's reality, this is how he took himself to be. Free to terrorize black bodies, all the while understanding himself to be, quite simply, doing his job, going about his business. To reconceive Hannah Arendt's famous anthropological description for our moment: Chauvin is nothing other than the "banality of terror." Like Adolf Eichmann, Chauvin was simply doing his job. He certainly did not expect to find himself facing third-degree murder charges. He did not see what he was doing as in any way different from what the cops who killed Gray in the back of a paddy wagon in Baltimore (Brian Rice, Caesar Goodson, Alicia White) did, or what Darren Wilson, the cop who shot and killed Brown in Ferguson, Missouri, did when Brown announced his submission, "Hands up, don't shoot," or what those Staten Island brothers in blue were doing when they ignored Eric Garner's vulnerability: "I can't breathe," Garner cried out, but Daniel Pantaleo just kept right on choking. Three Louisville PD cops, Jonathan Mattingly, Brett Hankinson, and Myles Cosgrove, secured a no-knock warrant, and in the ensuing shoot-out that occurred between Breonna Taylor's partner, Kenneth Walker (a licensed gun owner), and the cops, Taylor was shot, eight times.

Not only does black speech have no value. It can be ignored because it has no veracity. Guilty until proven, well, guilty. Every black man in handcuffs or with his hands above his head either remains a threat, restraints notwithstanding, or he is a trickster—capable, no doubt, of magically freeing himself from handcuffs so that he can attack an armed officer. As such, the black man must be killed. No black man tells the truth. Ever. "I can't breathe" and "Hands up, don't shoot" are coded black resistance, a code indecipherable to white law enforcement. Blacks lie. All the time.

Chauvin, as it were, drew the short straw. "All" he did was act according to the code made universal by white police officers—Brian Rice, Darren Wilson, Daniel Pantaleo, Jonathan Mattingly . . . Brutal bureaucrats of terror. These were the terms in which Chauvin acted, knowingly, chauvinistically, if you will permit the pun (low-hanging fruit, I grant), adding an entirely more sinister, Minnesota PD edge to "garden variety" police violence. Chauvin's murder of George Floyd was simply too much for black America. One knee too many. Chauvin imagined he would go home that Memorial Day evening, enjoy a cookout with his family, go to bed, and wake up the next day and just go on with his life. As if nothing extraordinary had happened. That he had taken a life might not even have registered with him. Not in such a way as to make him act differently in the moment when he was exerting maximum force on the most vulnerable part of the human anatomy, anyway.

By murdering George Floyd, Derek Chauvin concatenated Staten Island to Baltimore to Ferguson to Atlanta. George Floyd's death, horrific, intensely public, brutal and shameless in its execution, gave, as Chappelle might have it, the "streets" their voice. For his part, Trump was not listening. As always, the president who has spent a lifetime trafficking in white supremacy was too preoccupied with the sound of his own voice to hear black anguish. Black anger he denounced forthwith.

Trump, Long Since a Racist

Trump is impervious to critiques of racism, I explained to Ezra. "Trump's racism goes back further than you might imagine," I said to Nip one night in the summer of 2018 as he readied for bed. "What he is doing now is only the latest such act and, because he is president, it is getting more attention." After all, we know that Trump's long history of racism dates, first, to 1973, with further evidence of it again in 1978, when his company was investigated for housing discrimination. In both cases the U.S. Department of Justice sued Trump for his bias against African-American renters.[24] His stance on the 1989 Central Park jogger case—in which a white woman, Trisha Meili, was brutally assaulted and raped and for which five black and Latino young men were wrongfully accused, tried, and sentenced to jail, only to be released in 2002 after a convicted rapist (Matias Reyes) admitted to the crime (in 2001)—remains, at the time of this writing, unchanged.[25] Trump's racism, then, has never been latent. It has always been explicit.

Donald Trump has spent decades building up his armory of terror. Yet no one could have predicted its unplumbable depths. Just when you are sure that he has hit racist rock bottom, as with his propagation of the totally discredited "birtherism" theory (that President Barack Obama was not born in the United States), he surprises you yet again. With Trump, no nadir is ever truly a nadir. Each racist articulation, from 2016's "Mexican rapists" (that infamous New York escalator moment) to 2017's "good people on both sides" (Charlottesville, "Jews will not replace us"), from his description of Haiti and other black-majority countries as "shitholes" to his attack on the late Elijah Cummings's black-majority district in

Baltimore as a "rat and rodent infested mess," is nothing but a temporary placeholder for the next new subterranean level he is drilling down toward.

For this reason, if for no other, I am glad that Ezra has always been possessed of a keen racial consciousness. However, perverse as it may seem, I do wish he could learn antiracism from a more thoughtful racist source. There simply must be more articulate, more intelligent, and less narcissistic racists in the world. Racists who do not put one in mind of other institutional racisms. Racists who practice a racism that does not cut so close to the paternal bone.

"Will We Have to Move?"

"Will we have to move?" With this question Nip raised the specter of my apartheid childhood. Then, decades ago, in a very different place, in an entirely removed historical moment, I experienced Nip's ontological anxiety. What my son gave voice to as a nine-year-old, I lived when I was seven. My family was deracinated from a liberal, racially mixed neighborhood in one of Cape Town's less affluent southern suburbs. (We knew it as Black River. It has since taken on the altogether fancier moniker of Rondebosch East.) We were forced, by law, to move to Hanover Park, a then still-under-construction distant township designated exclusively for the coloured (mixed-race) community. This rude uprooting was the outcome of the Group Areas Act, which decreed that all South Africans must live exclusively within the areas designated as theirs according to four racial categories: white, black (or "African" or "native"), coloured, and "Indian" (those South Africans who traced their roots to the Asian subcontinent).

So when Nip began to worry about the safety and sanctity of our home, when he wondered about the building of a wall that would separate the United States from Mexico, as he continues to do, a select group of specters began to haunt me.

I was taken aback because who could have imagined that this type of political scenario would ever come back into vogue? And certainly not in America, where I have now lived for more than thirty years, at least not in so unvarnished a form as to stir the ghosts of apartheid racism. My apartheid psyche, reawakened; my historical encounter with enforced racial separation brought back to life, raised from its dormancy. My history, with its origins on the far side of the Atlantic Ocean, across a generation, inherited by Nip, against his will and mine. This memory is the gift of my political unconscious and my body to his (one mixed-race body to another). Or less a gift than a historical imposition, infusing my son's psyche and body with the burdensome memory of my political past. Because of Trump, the politics of deracination became plural in our family; Trump made deracination, within our household where the diasporic and the native (Jane is an Iowan) convene, a multigenerational reality. What the psyche and the body remember is what the psyche and the body, like it or not, pass on. That which can be recalled is that which is bequeathed to the next generation. Memory haunts the psyche and the body, lives (on) in it, passes through the psyche and the body, against all historical odds. The further we move from the site of the "original" deracination, the more determinedly that memory, that history, follows us. It refuses to let our psyches and our bodies out of its grasp. The hold of memory is eternal, resilient enough to survive three decades and a transatlantic crossing.

This is how we might define low-level terror: knowing what it is to be afraid just when we thought we were done being afraid. A fear that was thought to have been overcome resurfaces. This is not only low-level terror. It is to know trauma—the triggering back into life of that which was imagined as submerged. Safely. Think again.

Nip's question opened a small sluice gate of memories, memories of other political psyches and bodies that I had barely thought of in a long time. Listening to Trump promise, "We're going to build the Wall," I felt like it was 1988 Europe all over again. Only this time the role of Erich Honecker, the last East German communist determined to keep his people (including one Angela Merkel) safe from the ideological predations of their cousins on the other side of the Wall, was being played out almost three decades later by a lapsed Presbyterian—of German stock—from the outer New York borough of Queens.

Ezra's fretting, and then some (Jane and I constantly having to reassure him that we would remain in our home, no matter a Trump victory; a fear that has since subsided, but not entirely), is the sort of existential concern that really should not preoccupy an intensely active and wonderfully creative child. Sometimes, when he was around eight, Ezra struggled to get to sleep because Trump was the last subject that he engaged at night. He went to bed ready to remember. Jane and I hope that his sleep will not be too full of today's and yesterday's memories. Our wish for him is Shakespearean, free of tragedy—that Nip might know what it is "to sleep, perchance to dream" of childlike things. A strange and ironic thing it is to quote Hamlet in the hope that today's existential terrors might be banished. Better a tragic Shakespearean hero than a live, artificially tanned, orange-haired ogre.

Deracination

American, diasporic African, African-American, black, white, Nip's body stands as the physical embodiment of his white mother and his black father. With his mop of very long hair (until the spring of 2020, when he was shorn of his locks by his brother; Nip's hair, a victim of shelter-in-place, you might say), his dark eyes, and his gangly physique, he looks a fair approximation of Jane and me. When I remark that he is "beautiful," Ezra protests, no doubt in reference to the many times his long hair has caused him to be mistaken for a girl. He insists that he is—as he so unabashedly puts it—"handsome." The fluidity of Nip's gender identity—how he looks to the world, how he looks at the world, much of it in response to how the world looks at him, of course—has Ezra-imposed linguistic limits. "Handsome" is permissible, embraced, if only dialectically; "beautiful" is rejected. However, while Nip proclaims his heteronormativity, he is not above performing something altogether less heteronormative when the mood takes him.

The specter of forced removal, then, American-born and -raised as he is, should not be a concept that forms part of Nip's political repertoire. Not so for me.

I know that deracination turns on political fears about the physical spaces that the body can rightfully occupy; that is, spaces it can safely move about in without fear of legal transgression and its concomitant legal penalties. Deracination limits, as a matter of law, where the body, where the child, where the child's body, can be. An issue entirely implicated in proscription: where the body is not allowed to be. (It does no less damage to the mind, I hasten to add. On that matter I have written elsewhere.)[26] Where, the issue has now become, the black body—Nip's body, and those of his parents, white mother, black father—is *verboten,* prohibited from being. What it would be like . . . to be a body without fear of being uprooted. To be safe in this place, your home, that you consider yours. What a historical conjuncture ours is . . . to be in this moment where the black boy's entire being is rendered precarious. Rendered, precisely, to be even more precarious than a black boy's life already is. To be in this time. Heidegger ringing in my ears, demanding a transcription: *in dieser Zeit sein.*

The *Being/Sein,* or *Dasein* (which is closely related to *Being* but must also be understood as "being there"), to use Heidegger's most famous term, of Ezra's body concatenates for me as individual memory, political memory, and confrontation. (In this essay I use *Being* and *Dasein* interchangeably and to designate the essence (truth; essence of truth)—*Wesen*—of what it means be in the world. *Wesen* marks the "quintessence" or the "essence" that constitutes the inner principle or nature of a thing. For the purposes of this essay *Dasein* is distilled to something on the order of "essence of truth," incorporating as it does *aleitha*—"truth." That is, a multivalenced and specifically purposed *Dasein* rendered as the "essence of the truth of *Being.*" Of course, such a designation does not account for the many complexities that Heidegger offers in his several workings of *Dasein.* This working definition also means that "being," uncapitalized and unitalicized, is employed in its everyday English-language usage; that is, as a foundational verb without the philosophical weight of *Being/Dasein* but that cannot but evoke notions of "essence," "truth," and what it means "to be in the world." In those moments when both being—the ontic—and *Being*—the ontological—are at work, this "duality" is marked by a slash; on the other hand, when there is such proximity as to presume a conflation, then the ontological *Being* instantiates both. Lastly, the working distinction between being and *Being* is that the former is concerned with, shall we say, human beings in their everydayness (that which is experienced as being to hand), while the latter stands as the "study of beings as such." We will turn, shortly, to the political memory. In part because I want to stay it, leave political memory in its place, a while longer. It is a body politic, a body that was all politics, and so it is a place I want to keep at bay. If only for a little longer.

Such a goal is beyond my capacity because soon enough the memory will abut, intrude upon, the confrontation. The memory will grow out of the confrontation, repeatedly. No matter. Let us keep them from each other a moment longer.

In thinking this confrontation that so disconcerts me, I am put in mind of Roland Barthes's contemplation of the "Photograph" at the very end of *Camera Lucida.* The photograph, Barthes postulates (it is not a question, as such; it is pure declarative), is either "mad or tame? . . . Such are the two ways of the Photograph. The choice is mine: to subject its spectacle to the civilized code of perfect illusions, or to confront in it the wakening of intractable reality."[27]

My "choice" is clear. It would be an act of willful dissembling to pretend civility with Nip. It would amount to malfeasance if I were to disabuse Nip of his fears without explanation. I must not. I must not because his fears are real, to him as much as to me. Not so much that they will be realized—that they will come to pass and we will be forced, by some decree or law, to move out of our house—but they are real, possessed of political substance, in the sense that how his psyche and his body understand themselves in the world will have to change. Nip will now have to live with being exposed to Trump-induced vulnerability.

Because Trump won in November 2016, I must do away with the "perfect illusion" of psychopolitical stability. The child's psyche and body can no longer draw on old patterns of behavior. Because Trump won, I must commit to "confrontation" on the order of "intractable reality." I must find the language that speaks of Ezra's psyche, of how his body is in the world, so that such a "confrontation" is politically apposite to this "spectacle" of race-baiting, or worse, that will, sooner or later, present itself to Nip. Present itself to him as, no doubt, something like—I fear, I hope that I am wrong—an existential threat.

According to Barthes, it is "morality" rather than "ethics" I must teach Nip. For Barthes "morality" stands in exact contradistinction to "ethics." In that inimitable "autobiography" *Roland Barthes by Roland Barthes,* he writes, "*morality* should be understood as the precise opposite of ethics (it is the thinking of the body in a state of language)."[28] Barthes gives "substance" to both "thinking" and "language." Barthes apprehends both "thinking" and "language" from the location of the "body," which lends both a certain immanence. Leaving "ethics" undefined, Barthes gives us to think "morality" as that mode of being/*Being* in the world that emanates from the "body," that emerges from the "body" as it "thinks" its way in, through, and because of "language." "Morality" is how the "body" conducts itself in the world. Prosaically, in Barthes's terms, "morality" is how the body acts and speaks, announces, articulates, and produces in the world. "Morality" is, didactically phrased, what we say and do in the world. (It is, of course, also how we say and do in the world.) It might even be, and this is no philosophical stretch, who we are. For Barthes there appears to be, in terms of "morality,"

no difference between "language" and thought, nothing that separates word from action.

However, that Barthes is so specific and decided in his argument
should give us, briefly, pause. His argument, after all, hinges on
"thinking." It is only through "thinking" that the "body" can command both the necessary—"moral"—"language" and actions. "Morality" turns on "thinking," which in its turn sets the tone of the
body's "moral" action and "language." We are, following Barthes,
asked to pin our faith on that mode of "thinking" that permits of a
break or rupture between what it is we say and what it is we do; how
it is we say things and what it is we do.

Caution about Barthes's seamless continuum is advised, in no
small measure because of that most political of warnings that
Heidegger issues in *What Is Called Thinking? (Was heißt Denken?)*.
Conventional political wisdom (such as that found in the Epistle
of St. James, as we will see when we turn our attention to Baldwin)
would have it that, following Heidegger, "What is lacking . . . is action, not thought": we think too much and act too little.[29] Heidegger, as we know, disagrees: "It could be that prevailing man has
for centuries now acted too much and thought too little."[30] This
is Heidegger's mantra, his slogan for doing politics/being in the
world: Always, think first. Always, think what it is we say. (Think
how it is we say it.) We must "make" language in such a way that
language can bear thinking. To "make" language as such is to use
language with precision, always attentive to etymology, heeding,
that is, Heidegger's opposition to *verstehen*. Through our fidelity to
language, we demonstrate our commitment to never presuming an
inevitable commensurability between what it is we think and what
it is we understand ourselves to be saying.

Subject all language to thinking. That is, understand language
as the struggle to find a language in which we are able to think. We
must recognize that the language in which we struggle to think is
the self-same language against which, for very good reasons, historical and philosophical, we might have to struggle. We must be
skeptical of the language in which we think so that we subject all
actions, beginning with our deployment of language, to thinking.
Solid political advice, especially as it comes from a philosopher
(Heidegger) who knows only too well how (National Socialist; his
National Socialist) words can produce catastrophic actions.[31] The
Holocaust, the Shoah. Six million dead bodies. "Sixty Million and

more," by Toni Morrison's account, the number that stands as the dedication to *Beloved*.[32] Let us commit ourselves to thinking more, to acting only when it follows thinking.

Amid all my contemplation, a voice breaks in. A voice that, in its political acuity, sides decisively with Barthes over Heidegger. A voice that makes its case with startling brevity. A short, incisive, philosophically disruptive question.

"Why is Trump a racist, Daddy?" Ezra asks. "Why does he hate black people?"

In Ezra's encounter, there is no distinction between the white body and the white mind, between the ways in which this (one, overweening) white male body has metonymically come to dominate his consciousness, and that of an entire nation (and the world's, too), and the language that body puts into circulation. Language and action, action that follows or precedes language. Mexicans are "murderers and rapists." A disabled reporter from the *New York Times* is ridiculed before the nation's press corps. A Mexican journalist is forcibly removed from a press conference. A white female TV reporter is singled out because of her diminutive stature. A white Trump supporter physically assaults a black man in full view of the predominantly white audience at a Trump rally. Trump's chief of staff assaults a journalist. Protesters at George Floyd rallies are "thugs." "White Power" issues from the mouth of a geriatric Trump supporter living in The Villages, a central Florida retirement community, a visceral response to the raw (white) political anger that followed George Floyd's murder.[33] All this with impunity; and every day, we are assured of the threat of more to come. How do we think our actions under these conditions?

Perhaps, in order to confront our moment, we can amend Barthes. Make him read as follows: "Acting is the body in a state of language." The body speaks, speaks its racism, its misogyny, its many phobias, in its actions. This speaking, regardless of whether it is considered inarticulate or unthinking, stands, nevertheless, as the speaking of what, and how, it is the—*this*—white body thinks.

2 Martin Luther King and White People

We have chosen each other
and the edge of each other's battles
the war is the same
if we lose
some day women's blood will congeal
upon a dead planet
if we win
there is no telling
we seek beyond history
for a new and more possible meeting.
—Audre Lorde, untitled

In January 2012, when he was three and a half years old and in only his second semester at one of the local Montessori schools in Ithaca, Ezra came home one day and regaled Jane with an account of his very first Martin Luther King Day celebration. Trying to encourage his enthusiasm for racial justice, Jane—a political activist since her late teens, currently working with "illegal immigrants" detained in Batavia, an upstate New York facility (detention center)—remarked on how much King had done for African-Americans. Without missing a beat, Ezra offered a wonderfully insightful rejoinder: "Yes, Mommy, and for white people too." Touché. An Audre Lorde moment, I wonder? Jane, Nip, and I, "We have chosen each other / and the edge of each other's battles / the war is the same."

Sometimes, however, Nip might have been suggesting, while "the war is the same," we must all nudge each other farther in, as it were, from the "edge of each other's battles," closer toward the center of the "battle." Or, perhaps, more pointedly, Nip was suggesting that the "war" is not always the "same." The war operates on one set of terms for him and me, on another for Jane. Perhaps all these possibilities, and countless others, hold, each in its own moment, or in some variable combination with each other. Regardless, Nip's incisiveness gave Jane and me, in the best possible sense, a reason to pause, a moment to ponder the effects—consequences—of our having "chosen each other."

Little wonder then that Jane and I exchanged proud glances at Nip's MLK corrective. Ezra was articulating a politics, a sharp-edged politics on the order of the dialectical. What Nip established through his retort, "and for white people too," was a dialectic concerning the racialization of Martin Luther King—champion of Civil Rights, sure, but when King is so situated he is made to bear "the burden of over-representation" in that he is mainly understood as advancing the cause of black freedom; that is, struggling to end black subjugation in America.[1] Obscured, conveniently or not, by the failure to render King as a champion of universal liberation from the practice of American racism are the effects of racism, ethical and otherwise, that extend well beyond the black community. This is not to undermine the force of King's address to, both directly and implicitly, those principally responsible for, inter alia, black disenfranchisement, economic destitution, suffering, and vulnerability, but to recognize that King cannot be circumscribed into blackness. At least not without "moral" consequences, as Barthes might have it.

King offers us King as figure of universal liberation memorably, of course. He warns, "None of us are free until all of us are free." And yet the universality of that caution is invoked only as critique. In articulating the "power of nonviolence," King gives full voice to Civil Rights as the project of "universal" liberation—at the very least, "universal" as implicating all of America, a consistent feature of his thinking. "The struggle," King makes clear, "is between justice and injustice, between the forces of light and the forces of darkness. And if there is a victory it will not be victory merely for fifty thousand Negroes. It will be a victory for justice, a victory for democracy."[2] The Negro "struggle" is the catalyst for procuring—and securing—"justice" in America, and, in so doing, it extends its accomplishment into the enshrining of American "democracy" for all Americans, not just for the benefit of "fifty thousand Negroes," urgent as that project is. Justice and democracy, regardless of who "struggles" for them, no matter who sacrifices most, are indivisible—gifts, of the historically oppressed to their oppressors.

In the Civil Rights movement's striving to secure the franchise, King echoes the call that had earlier been issued by figures such as Du Bois. (Most famously in the classic 1903 work *The Souls of Black Folk,* in which Du Bois states plainly his opposition to Booker T. Washington's willingness to forgo the universal franchise in exchange for separate, black economic advancement—"In all things that are purely social, we can be as separate as the fingers, yet one as the hand in all things essential to mutual progress.")[3]

In this regard, Nip clearly throws in his lot with the King–James Baldwin "far" side of the dialectic. Not so much King as appealing, in Lincoln's famous words, to America's "better angels," but King as freed from the shackles of identity (however necessary that containment and mobilization of self might have been understood to be) and released into a universalist discourse about rights, responsibilities, and the political effects of injustice.[4]

Releasing the (racial/-ized) self into a historic relation to the other is a singular kind of work, a difficulty central to the thinking of Emmanuel Levinas. "The task," in Levinas's resonant phrasing, "is to conceive of the possibility of a break out of essence."[5] This is what Nip offered to Jane, whose work on migration (especially as it pertains to violence against the other) is influenced by Levinas. It may be, however, that Nip's response was more than an offering, that it was more than the act of (in)advertently giving advice to his parents. It may be that Nip's speaking constituted an ethical violence. By refuting the dominant representation of King as the icon of the "Negro struggle," Ezra broke his mother "out of her essence." And me, black onlooker, silent witness, too. Out of Nip's offering emerged a Du Boisian moment in which America's second-oldest "burden" (America's Original Sin) was redistributed once more.[6] ("The problem of the twentieth century, is the problem of the color line.")[7] Redistributed within a narrow domestic sphere, to be shared, unequally, as all burdens are, by all: son, mother, father.

As Rendered by Ezra, the Dialectic

The dialectic, as has been well established by now, is a concept crucial to the thinking of this essay. There are several "valences" to the dialectic drawn upon in this work.[8] Sometimes the dialectic is of the negative variety, as given to us by Theodor Adorno; in other moments we come to Adorno through the thinking of Fredric Jameson.[9] In still others the dialectic is "mediated" (itself a problematic term in some dialectical circles) by Georg Lukács (whose work is entwined in this essay with that of Maurice Merleau-Ponty), and there is Lukács in conversation with other thinkers of the dialectic, among them Bertolt Brecht (especially pertaining to the notion of the "contradiction" and the specific role it performs in the functioning of the dialectic).

However, it goes without saying, neither Jane nor I had instructed Ezra in the finer points of the dialectic. He came by that honestly. In any case, "Hegel," "*negative dialektik*," and "determinate negation," all critical to Adorno's project, and "contradiction," the cornerstone of Brecht's, constitute a philosophical vocabulary with which no three-and-a-half-year-old should be even vaguely familiar. Ezra, mercifully, isn't. Or, I should say, he wasn't then and isn't now, at the time of this writing, a twelve-year-old who threatens to tower above his parents.

It is difficult to say how Nip came by his complicated understanding of race, racism, and the ubiquity and specificity of their effects. Or to account for his ability to express his understanding with an evocative pithiness (bringing Du Bois to life through King). Part of the explanation may very well turn on Nip's understanding of himself, a topic of discussion in which the three of us engaged as soon as Jane and I thought him capable of being able to comprehend what it meant to have a white mother and a black father. That may be why Civil Rights, by Ezra's account, can only be apprehended—must only be apprehended—as universal in its impact. What Du Bois agitated for, what Martin Luther King sought to do, what King's "dream" turns on, is a fundamental shift in the way all Americans, black and white, think their relation to each other (a truth that holds all the more painfully now, in the wake of the murders of Breonna Taylor and George Floyd). Each of these figures is, in turn, entrusted with the work of, simultaneously, if at all possible, "conceiving of the possibility of a break out of essence."

Thinking King through Fredric Jameson's Dialectic

In light of the focus of our discussion (racism in America, gnomically phrased), Jameson's essay "Wagner as Dramatist and Allegorist" (in which Jameson draws on Adorno) hardly seems the most likely place to turn. However, Jameson's critique of the tendency to think in exclusionary or compartmentalized terms is especially insightful as a hedge against exclusionary thinking. (As such, it is also a caution against the circumscription of archives, no matter the rationale. "Ezra's dialectic" stands as its own refusal of circumscription.) To follow compartmentalization as a critical mode, Jameson argues, amounts to the "reification of whole zones of our subjectivity."[10] That is, the effect of "reification" is to locate certain aspects of our being/Being in the world—"whole zones of our subjectivity"—beyond the reach of thought. As a consequence, crucial political events (such as Civil Rights, sans Ezra's dialectic, indulgently phrased) run the very real political risk of being designated, for ill much more than good, as *verboten*—or other, if you prefer. Restricted to our "essence," everything that is not designated as belonging constitutively to "us" is what we condemn to that "zone" we consider outside our purview, beyond our remit. In so doing, we refuse it any purchase on our "subjectivity." Everything that has not been "reified" is something that can, at best, touch us only, shall we say, rhetorically—which is to say, not or hardly at all. Ezra's refusal to contain King is a clear rebuttal to any proclivity that reduces self to essence.

With good reason.

King's focus, the spirit of his critique, was always universal. And King's was, as we know, a political ethos that began and ended in love: "*Agape* is understanding, creative, redemptive good will for all men."[11] ("Agape," love beyond love, or, grace, will constitute a crucial element in relation to our discussion of Baldwin and the question of forgiveness.) Even if, as needs must, King began from an overdetermined, intensely racialized, ("first") ground that was the (African-)American condition. For this reason, at its core, King's struggle was for absolute equality, absolute equality before the law, and, of course, the oneness of humanity before God—"redemptive good will for all men." A oneness, moreover, that derived from nothing less than the biblical magnificence of God. "The ringing testimony of the Christian faith," King declares, "is that God is able."[12] "Able," and indeed dedicated, to save "all men." God can. God can save "all men," without exception. That is the promise.

As such, King worked to effect change in the entire nation's political consciousness, a change that would, out of sheer historical necessity, have to begin simultaneously in the nation as a whole and within the individual moral bearing of each and every American. No one could—or can, as we learn from Harriet Tubman, Sojourner Truth, John Brown, Du Bois, King, Baldwin; the list is long, and always incomplete—ever be absolved of responsibility. (This responsibility, as we shall see, is a mode of thinking taken up and distilled by Baldwin in such a way as to apprehend us in our presuppositions.) The law, above all Civil Rights legislation, marked, importantly, only the beginning of this process. "The habits, if not the hearts, of people have been and are being altered every day by legislative acts, judicial decisions, and executive orders. Let us not be misled by those who argue that segregation cannot be ended by the force of law."[13] The determination to achieve a morally reoriented nation, a nation worthy of its "better angels," requires a system of dual power, to invoke Lenin's famous political strategy in the buildup to the Bolshevik Revolution: the "force of the law" and the ability to change "hearts." Jameson, in his reading of Lenin's dual power, proposes representative democracy (which Jameson would have us be done with, completely) and utopia as the two tracks.[14]

King's judgment at this specific moment in this particular essay, "On Being a Good Neighbor," speaks more of a "liberal realpolitik" than of Leninist revolution. ("Liberal realpolitik," if the contradiction might be permitted, so as distinguish King's "realpolitik" from the trenchancy of Bismarck's.) Nevertheless, this turn to realpolitik is out of character for King. In fact, it is at odds with the overall tenor of the essay. However, it is precisely because of King's ability to recognize that the Civil Rights struggle would have to be conducted, simultaneously, on two fronts, the law and the Law (that is, God's Law), that his articulation achieves such salience—and Lenin resonates with us. The enshrining and protecting of Civil Rights and moral self-reflection were equally important to securing one more step in the direction of justice.

King's position is, of course, more in line with his observation that "man-made laws assure justice, but a higher law produces love," so the exceptional ascription that is the "force of law" comes as a sharp reminder of the need for a struggle founded on a Christian modality of dual power.[15] In place of Lenin's "government of the bourgeoisie" and the soviets (workers' councils), King offers the sacred and the profane, if you will, lending special credence to that instance in which the emergence of justice precedes the human capacity for universal love.[16] Love follows the law, most likely slowly, in a process to which King (as well as Baldwin, as we shall see) is, in all philosophical probability, averse—indeed, that he generally abjures. Ideally, for King, the order of things would be reversed: the law should follow love.

After all, King's struggle was for a higher moral purpose; for King, above the law that was enshrined in the U.S. Constitution was always the Law. God's Law, in part Mosaic, fierce and dogmatic, in part messianic, filled with the possibility of redemption—through forgiveness, which is for him "not an occasional act; it is a permanent deed."[17] In the main, however, King took his inspiration from the New Testament. Out of these twenty-seven books (the four canonical Gospels, the Acts of the Apostles, the fourteen Epistles of Paul, the seven catholic Epistles, and the book of Revelation), King crafted a message steeped in the teachings of Jesus-the-Christ, a prophetic call to arms imbued with love, forgiveness, and the promise of the salvific for all Americans, if we understand King narrowly (which is to say, within the confines of the United States as a nation-state) for a moment.

Ever the probing, nuanced dialectician, Jameson in this context—this time in his attempt to explicate the multiplicity that is "Wagner"—serves to remind us why King can signify so distinctly these many decades after his assassination. "'Wagner,'" writes Jameson, "means multiple positions which are scarcely reducible to each other and which cannot really be synthesized into a single history."[18] "Martin Luther King," the "Civil Rights movement," the black nationalist struggle, the women's movement (with its racial striations, about which Lorde has a great deal to say), we are free to speculate, have devolved into such a Wagnerian array of narrative and political possibilities. Because "multiplicity" is the order of the day, because there are visible "edges" as well as distant centers, it means that for all the universalist vision of King's politics (remarkably powerful when stripped down to its barest Christian essentials: "The answer is simple: feed the poor, clothe the naked, and heal the sick"), the struggle for racial and economic equality (among other struggles—"The church must be the conscience of the state") remains beyond the capacity of such a "synthesis," a "synthesis" that would amount to the triumphant account that is a "single history."[19] Such a process, the "single history," could emerge only out of the "elevation" of "multiplicity" into singularity, the result of which would be the "battle" forfeiting its (political) "edge." Hardly a development for which to wish—a political and philosophical outcome that should never be desired. After all, every dialectic produces not a "resolution" as such but an entirely new series of conflicts.

Our political reality, as we are intensely aware, functions (continues to function) in terms that are "scarcely reducible to each other."

Ours, then, is the (continued, continuing) heterogeneous moment of racial antagonism, antagonism spoken (loudly, all too loudly; violently, all too violently; unjustly, all too unjustly; brutally, all too brutally) and unspoken (in part because it is unspeakable, in no small measure because any speaking risks the self, which makes it all the more important as well as all the more fear-inducing to speak in the name of this risk). Of course, ours is a political conjuncture that demands any (thoughtful) speaking that we can conceivably command. Precisely because ours is a racially charged moment that is at once all too articulated (and voluble), technologically ubiquitous (made inescapable by the ever-present political front that is social media), and unspeakable, we are charged with the need to produce a language that can speak, simultaneously, in the specific registers that each requires, what is readily spoken and what is all too unspeakable.

After all, American presidents such as George W. Bush and Trump have shown a determination to roll back the legislative force of many Civil Rights laws. The acts enshrining equality, the universal right to vote, fair districting, and other such democratic rights are apparently what must be excluded from this country's "single history." (Trump has also promoted a program of "patriotic education," which would downplay America's history of genocide and slavery.)[20] White Americans of a certain ideological stripe, it would appear, are enamored of one "Wagner" only, and would prefer to "reduce" everything to that single account. (With good political and philosophical reason, there are some who would find the allusion to "Wagner" as such entirely appropriate.) Of course, Bush and Trump are only the most recent examples. Lest we forget, there was also Ronald Reagan, with his full-fledged attack on unions, his denigration of the social safety net that he and his British counterpart Margaret Thatcher represented as the "nanny state," his vilification of African-American women as "welfare queens," and his hypersexualization of African-American men as "young bucks" feasting on "T-bone steaks." All this is to say nothing of the recently discovered tapes of conversations between then president Richard Nixon and Reagan, the latter then in his capacity as governor of California, in which Reagan denounces Africans as "monkeys"—a Darwinian trope invoked by "the Gipper" because African countries at the United Nations had the temerity to oppose America's Cold War policies. These Africans. How dare they. Such impudence. In Reagan's racist logic, Nixon failed to put uppity Africans, no doubt presumed to be flush with newly achieved sovereignty, in their place at the United Nations.[21] The place in question being, it is fair to presume, the one assigned to simians.

In the era of Trump, presidential racist logic came full circle, again, with the reappearance of a button from Reagan's 1980 campaign. "Reagan '80," the top inscription on the button reads, followed by, horror of horrors, "Let's Make America Great Again." The more things change, the more . . . The ideological intent is always the same, with Nixon, with Reagan, with Trump: "Make America Great Again" stands as the most obvious code for "Make America White Again." Or, more specifically, "Keep America White." Better still, "Keep White America in Charge." Let us not mince words: "Make America Great Again" = "White Power."

Martin Luther King, as Rendered by a Three-and-a-Half-Year-Old

In Ezra's unmediated, visceral response to Jane, there is something politically salient. Our (then) three-and-a-half-year-old's sense of justice is grounded in something on the order of racial largesse. A sense of magnanimity: "for white people too." However, in terms of racial politics there is more to it, as I will argue shortly. Nip's critique of the gift that King made America in August 1963 at once echoes King's higher calling, recalibrates the racial scope of King's "Dream," and serves as a reminder to us in our moment of how King's vision has been thwarted. We can attribute this to, just for starters, the gutting of Civil Rights legislation and the coagulation (if not the ossification) of the Civil Rights struggle into an annual celebration that is dispensed with by the third Monday in January. ("Martin Luther King Day"—irony of charismatic ironies; remember MLK for a day, and all commitment to justice, equality, and workers' rights is done and dusted.) All this buttressed now by the continued assault on black life (as well as minority, indigenous, Muslim, and immigrant life) that so routinely mars the everyday American experience for those who are not white.

The road ahead, then, seems steep. What is more, it seems that at least as long and difficult a climb awaits as when King addressed America on the National Mall in Washington, D.C., on August 28, 1963. The immediate cause, of course, is Trump and the white supremacist forces he has unleashed. However, as has been argued, the attack on black life, indigenous life, women's lives (reproductive freedom being not the least among those rights under attack, especially with a now pro-life Supreme Court), and minority and immigrant life precedes Trump. Nonetheless, our conjuncture has its particularities, a moment marked by its specific, (as ever) intense, mode of racial strife. Unlike in the 1950s and 1960s, this time the white state's animus extends to every other. Most determinedly now, in addition to its attack on black, Latino, and immigrant life, the white state's targets include those refugees held captive, with little chance of legal redress, on the U.S.–Mexico border or in the various detention centers that dot the American landscape. (As Walter Benjamin reminds us, "Not even the dead will be safe from the enemy, if he is victorious.")[22]

This must be the reason, then, that I grasp at the semblance of political possibility in Ezra's "correcting" Jane. (As we well know from Adorno's work, semblance, *Schein,* coexists with truth, *Warheit,* so in all likelihood I'm holding on to something like a semblance of the truth; or, I'm holding out for something that I hope resembles the truth. In truth, what I want is some political scenario in which truth wins the day.)[23] Unlike Jane and me, Nip has the advantage of youth. Young as Ezra was in 2012, he was untouched (that is to say, he could "only" be phantasmatically affected by the curse of history, but that is true of most of us) by the bitter battles that marked the turbulent moment that was the Civil Rights–black nationalist era. However, the more Ezra learns about Martin Luther King, the more the politics, racial sensibilities, and cultural stakes of the 1950s and 1960s leave their mark on him.

Nip, in his perspicuity, in his ability to make Jane and me wonder at the sharpness of his insight, inclines toward Kojève. Via Martin Luther King, Ezra introduces us to his own pedagogical mode, a bracing blend of King and Kojève, of instructing his parents into how to "live in terms of terror." Nip's three-and-half-year-old speaking uprooted Jane and me from our routine domestic discussion—inquiring into Ezra's day—and confronted us with a hardly recognized truth: "and white people too." A three-and-a-half-year-old's perspicuity can be a terrible, if not quite a terror-inducing, thing. Especially when the parents find themselves made into Civil Rights students by the toddler's simple, but piercing, statement of political truth.

Nonetheless, a certain paradox obtains. As much as Nip is still unburdened by the Civil Rights past, he seems, for reasons unknown to us, to have imbibed something foundational to the spirit of Martin Luther King. (A benefit, no doubt, of the annual celebration. So MLK Day is due a rethink on my part.) In that famous 1963 speech on the Mall, King simultaneously expresses his faith in America and challenges it to be felicitous to itself: "I have a dream that one day this nation will rise up and live out the true meaning of its creed: 'We hold these truths to be self-evident, that all men are created equal.'"[24] Ezra's rendering is, as we have learned, less poetic, and much more direct: "and for white people too." Nip's comprehension (his precise rendering, the pithy precociousness of his language) of King's vision—about which there is, as already suggested, undoubtedly a messianic edge, so that we might name it his life's "mission"—shares King's commitment to equality, and yet Nip's is distinct, in part because it is so unvarnished, its animating force deriving from a declarative simply phrased. What girds both King's proclamation and Nip's declaration is a trenchant truth, a truth birthed by dialectics, the antinomies of black and white, right and wrong, "justice and injustice, the forces of light and the forces of darkness," for starters. For his part, Adorno argues that "profundity, as Hegel did not fail to note, is another element of dialectics, not an isolated trait."[25]

Under no circumstances would I pronounce Ezra "profound," but Adorno's critique of dialectics draws us up short when he reminds us, via Hegel, that inherent to the dialectic—it is "not an isolated trait"—is the propensity for penetrating insight(s); "profound" from *profundus,* "deep and vast," "entering deeply into subjects of thought or knowledge."[26] Let us hope that Hegel was not too picky about the source of the dialectical "profundity," or, for that matter, the age of the bearer of such (an) insight or the domestic context in which the dialectic came to life. Regardless, Nip's critique must be recognized as demanding a "deep" engagement with "subjects of thought or knowledge."

In taking up, first in this register then that, the path along which Ezra's "subjects of thought or knowledge" wends, I am reminded of Heidegger's "Letter to a Young Student." The thinking of *Being,* Heidegger writes to Mr. Buchner in June 1950, is most likely filled with error. In itself, of course, error (as a parent, as a thinker, as a teacher) is inevitable. What matters, Heidegger ends the letter, is that we make the other audible to us. "Everything here is the path of responding that examines as it listens," Heidegger writes. "Any path always risks going astray, leading astray. To follow such a path takes practice in going. Practice needs craft. Stay on the path, in genuine need, and learn the craft of thinking, unswerving, yet erring."[27]

Nip, you tease me about many things. My fandom of the Knicks is, as you know, difficult because it is impossible to refute. In relation to my work, however, your single refrain is always "So, Daddy, are you thinking about thinking?" Followed by a laugh that always has more of the feel of a satisfied smirk. Followed by a joke about Heidegger, especially about how "funny" he looks on the covers of his books.

In response, son, I offer you this: in order to "listen" to you, to hear what it is you are saying to me, in order that I might "respond," especially in the moment of record, I trust to nothing so much as thinking. Only if I think can I "examine" what you say, and only if I "examine" what you say, so that I might glean its veracity, can I "respond" to you in and with truth. The "risk," Nip, is significant. I could, in following this line of thinking rather than that one, easily find myself having "gone astray." I would hate to do that. However, my son, the nature of thinking is such that I must commit to following that "path" called "thinking." It is what I "practice," in this way or that, with an inkling of insight or none at all; I have long since committed myself to this "thinking." My "need" for thinking, Nip, is "genuine," my dedication to this "craft" absolute. I am sure that, contrary to Heidegger's urging, I have been guilty of "swerving"; that is, I have not followed the "path" as strictly as I should have.

However, every misstep, my son, is itself worthy of thinking. As is every "erring."

Your teasing is always affectionate. I know this because when ATrane and I did our Heidegger sessions over the summer of 2020, you listened. Sometimes you stole in when my focus was on this passage or that. Sometimes you were simply being disruptive. But there were moments, as you told me, when you just wanted to "listen."

I cherish those moments. Not only for me, but for you too. I want for you to "stay on the path." To think. That is a good way to live. Thinking is what leads us to *Being*. And *Being* is at the core of Mr. Buchner's question and it is at the sharp end of Heidegger's "response." Heidegger is "practicing his craft" in "listening" to the "young student." I want to "listen," Nip, to what surrounds us, and I want you to "listen" to that too, to "listen" so that we are never in error about the terror of our world.

I love when you listen to me thinking about thinking. If I did not think, if your mother and I did not, each in our own way, commit to thinking, we would not have been able to "examine" your powerful declarative.

Heidegger's enjoining me to think enables me to "listen" to your incision, to your succinct but memorable—or memorable because succinct—declarative on the work of Martin Luther King.

"And for white people too."

For Ezra, the truths to which King appeals are indeed self-evident. In his response to his mother, there is a deeper resonance. Nip would never reproach Jane—he loves his mother far too much for that—but there are other ways in which he will, without thinking, annoy her. (He annoys me too, only to a far greater extent.) Nip offers a clear reminder that Martin Luther King must be apprehended as an antiracist figure, as a champion for all humanity, albeit as an apostle of and for freedom who makes different demands of different constituencies.[28] Racializing King's struggle, representing it as the struggle *for* blacks exclusively, does nothing but undermine—demean, even—the vision for which King lived and, tragically, was assassinated. On the matter of truth as universally legible (and, in Derrida's sense, a call to political responsibility that owes much to the Abrahamic as a form of "irresponsibility"), Adorno is clear to the point of poetry: "The need to lend a voice to suffering is a condition of all truth. For suffering is objectivity that weighs upon the subject; its most subjective experience, its expression, is objectively conveyed."[29]

In a word, what Adorno is calling for is politics, at least if we understand politics as, in one way or another, deriving from and tending toward representation. (That is, what Jameson stands four-square against in "An American Utopia.") Not only does politics demand a "voice," its own voice, if you will, but it also insists on a "voice" that is distinct and unique to politics. However, this is a "voice" overwritten by a historic burden, matched only by the historical responsibility it demands: "suffering." As such, "suffering" is that "condition" which impresses and imposes ("weighs") itself on every thinking subject. The ethical subject in history, as Levinas might argue, is the subject who knows "suffering," the subject who knows what it is to suffer injustice, oppression, wrongful death (which makes the other, those intimate to the deceased, suffer—suffering extends from self to other), discrimination in any form.

To suffer is, in King's rendering, to know how to outlast the other: "We shall match your capacity to inflict suffering by our capacity to endure suffering"—to endure beyond that with which the subject is afflicted, to endure beyond that to which the black body and psyche are subjected.[30] To suffer, then, is to know—or, at the very least, to be acquainted with—pain (to have endured it; to have had it inflicted upon the self or those intimate to the self), to have known injury (to have been the victim of an act intended to harm), or to have been subject to a transgression (without, we might speculate, any possibility of adequate redress). To suffer, as such, is be instructed into how justice works precisely because justice has—historically—failed the subject. Justice has, in fact, often failed entire constituencies, leaving these collectivities vulnerable to all manner of "suffering." And, in so doing, testing the limits of what the subjects are made to endure, sometimes exceeding what they can endure. Justice is learned, in King's terms, through negation, so that we might speak of a negative justice.

Coming to justice through negation is possible, as King makes manifest, precisely because the black experience of "suffering" is deeply ingrained within the history of the black self. Out of this "suffering" has emerged not only resistance (predating, by centuries, the Civil Rights movement) but also the capacity to endure (as, for example, the Harlem Renaissance poetry of Langston Hughes and Countee Cullen, or Zora Neale Hurston's novels, gives "voice to") and to produce, through these struggles against injustice, the "truth." (Suffering—pain, love, loss, economic destitution—is, as we know, the very stuff of the blues. It is made audible by Robert Johnson, Lead Belly, B. B. King, Muddy Waters; it aches all the way through the oeuvres of Coleman Hawkins, Charlie Parker, Miles Davis, Sarah Vaughan, Billie Holiday, John Coltrane, Ella Fitzgerald, and Thelonious Monk, among others.) Not only to produce the "truth" of black life but also to hold up this "truth" as the self-evident failure of America's promise to itself. To "suffer," in Adorno's terms, is to bear the burden of truth-making. It is to assume the Samsonian task of holding up the pillars of truth in a decrepit temple overrun by seething violence and moral turpitude.

Whether such an imposition is evenly distributed or not (and we know, from Marx as much as from any other source, that the "suffering" inflicted by the machinations of capital always afflicts some and not others; at the very least, some are afflicted more—much more—than others), the "need" makes itself apparent to all. Understood outside of Adorno's privileging of the "object" over the "subject" (in Hegel, of course, the reverse is true), the substantiality of the "object" makes itself politically manifest. The "object" does no less than "weigh upon" the subject. As such, what "suffering" alerts us to is negative dialectics (*negative dialektik*) itself: the interface among concepts, objects, ideas, and the material world. Through politics ("suffering," in this case, which we must designate as "negative," in no small measure because of its inherent dialectical potentiality, which owes everything to the limits that history has thrown up), Adorno reveals negative dialectics as that intervention into the world that opens up the possibility of achieving something greater ("truth," specifically) by way of negation; the parts, "suffering," "truth," the "object," and so on, are sublated (*Aufhebung*) into something greater—again, the emergence of "truth" through politics; "truth" coming into the world through the antinomic working of history. Phrased in its most banal but by no means unimportant iteration, "truth" is what we arrive at through recognizing our responsibility to "suffering."

This is the kernel of unadorned truth that Nip's declarative, "and for white people too," revivifies. It is a reproach, if not specifically to Jane, then, certainly, it has resonances far beyond our domestic space. Listen, again: "and for white people too." Martin Luther King did not work only on behalf of black people. Preordained limitation is not how the messianic (or the call issued by "suffering") works; the messianic is never circumscribed, even if it is, as Benjamin might describe it, only a "weak messianism" struggling against considerable odds to sustain itself. To wit: no one in history is transformed into radicalism by "suffering" as much as Jesus-the-Christ. In King's sonorous account, "Jesus lifts his thorn-crowned head and cries in words of cosmic proportions: 'Father, forgive them; for they know not what they do.' This was Jesus' finest hour; this was his heavenly response to his earthly rendezvous with destiny."[31]

The messianic cannot be restricted, not by this thing and certainly not by that one. Messianism, as we know from the monotheism that is Christianity, is pretty much a zero-sum game. Save one, save all. The Gospels of Matthew (18:12–14) and Luke (15:3–7) teach this through the parable of the lost sheep. Save one, save the one that is lost, and the dedicated shepherd "forsakes" the ninety-nine so that he may find the one who makes whole the ninety-nine who are already safely ensconced in their pens. To save (the lost) one, the lost one above all, then, is to save all—is to make the overwhelming majority complete. Surely, this decision, to save the one, is the shepherd's "finest hour." The messianic, even in its "weakest" form, is always inscribed with the authority of an injunction. In Christianity it is the unjust proscription that is nonnegotiable. The Son of God must die. (As such, it is the Word. The Word has been written: the Innocent, Son of God, must die so that all others might live. His "earthly rendezvous with destiny" is what secures eternal life for all.) This is the messianic logic under which the Son is sacrificed. The lesson is unambiguous. Die for one (as the shepherd saved the one), die for all, regardless of each individual's moral worth.

"For God so loved the world that He gave His only begotten Son."

It is difficult, then, to take issue with Ezra's rendering of King's logic. There is nothing to do except acknowledge that "white people" too are welcomed into Martin Luther King's embrace. And, what is more, King's love—"forgiveness is not an occasional act; it is a permanent deed"—is, like Jesus-the-Christ's, without condition. God's love and forgiveness, as offered to "white people" by King, does not depend on white people's repenting for their failure to "rise up and live out" the "true meaning" of America's "creed."

This is a truth capable of instilling mild—or great, who can be sure?—terror in the black self. To forgive white transgression, again and again. "Forgiveness is a permanent deed."

God's grace is of such an order that it, we might speculate, releases everyone—"white people" in this particular instance—into the freedom to determine if, and how, they will assume the "weight of suffering." And whether they must do so without delay. They must ask whether too much time has already been lost. White people alone can—must—decide if they are to open themselves to the possibility of a "come to Jesus" moment.

"White people" must grapple with whether they will—and, if so, how they will—assume the "weight of suffering" for which they and they alone are historically responsible. Redemption of the self, redemption of every self, white no less than black, is the possibility that King, true to scripture, holds out, without exception. Is one (even) possible without the other? No, emphatically so, King pronounces: "Their [white people's] destiny is tied up with our destiny and they have come to realize that their freedom is inextricably bound to our freedom. This offense we share mounted to storm the battlements of injustice must be carried forth by a biracial army. We cannot walk alone."[32]

"Practice needs craft": Can the white self face terror? Can the white self confront the terror that emanates from within itself? Is it capable of responding to the terror it has let loose in the world? Can it stay true to the "path" to thinking, a "path" strewn with the possibility of error, a series of errors that have their origin in the "practice" that is white terror?

These questions obtain with a rare force. What will become clear, however, through our discussion of Baldwin, is that—for all its eloquence, rhetorical force, and historical resonance—King's stands as but a "weak messianism" in comparison to the radical act of forgiveness that Baldwin, in the most painful tones, offers to white America.

The promise of redemption is the political and spiritual possibility that King holds out for "white people." In itself, such a possibility is, a priori, a searing moral and political indictment, succored by the enduring presence of love. For King, however, it is not at all clear that Ezra's "white people," who have oppressed and continue to oppress and denigrate black life, are more in need of, shall we say, redemption than those whom they have oppressed. (Questions persist. Do they indeed "suffer"? And, if so, how do they "suffer" for the "suffering" they cause? How do they produce a "voice" that can tell of the "suffering" they have imposed? Is it possible to learn how to "suffer"? What is the white self's "subjective experience" of the "suffering" it has visited upon black bodies? And a question that poses particular difficulty for those who have endured, endure still: Are black people to offer forgiveness to whites? And if so, under what conditions? To address these last two questions, we will turn, in part, to Derrida and Vladimir Jankélévitch, in their work on forgiveness. In addition, of course, to Baldwin.) King offers "white people" the chance to "rise out" of the moral quagmire entirely of their own making (four centuries in the making) and out of the violence it has bred. What would it mean to cause "suffering" no more? To say, "The other will no longer suffer because of me"? The promise that Adorno holds out is, as we have established, "truth." Through "suffering" the "truth" of both self and other, the other who has "suffered" so because of the (white) self reveals itself.

3 The Farceur

Derrida, in his reading of Levinas (not the Levinas text to which we will turn later), reflects on the relationship between self and other in what Derrida names the "extradition of sovereignty" from self to other. "*This* extradition," Derrida writes, "in which responsibility for the other delivers me over to the other. No grammatical markings as such, no language or context will suffice to determine it."[1] Is this the only way to close the circle of "suffering"? The circle of "suffering" is closed in that moment when the (white) self, through assuming "responsibility for the other," is "delivered over to the other"; in that moment "sovereignty" is "extradited" so that, if we follow Derrida's argument, it becomes possible to imagine both self and other as "sovereign" subjects. (Or, through negation, to imagine both self and other as "nonsovereign" subjects, denuded of "sovereignty" by each other, by standing one before the other, entirely without "sovereign power"—that is, without power over self or other.) In *On Cosmopolitanism and Forgiveness,* in a statement to which we return later, Derrida contemplates, hopefully: "What I dream of, what I try to think as the 'purity' of a forgiveness worthy of its name, would be a forgiveness without power: *unconditional but without sovereignty.* The most difficult task, at once necessary and apparently impossible, would be to dissociate *unconditionality* and *sovereignty.* Will that be done one day?"[2] The question is raised, then, as it must be, can there be a "forgiveness without power"? From whom or from whence does this "power to forgive" derive? What is its source? Is such a forgiveness enforceable, or can it manifest itself only in that realm of the beyond toward which King argues?

In a different scenario that is this encounter between self and other, self and other emerge as equal on the far side of "suffering," made equal by "suffering." Self and other, we might go so far to propose, become "sufferers"—if only for the moment after (all) "suffering" ceases—indistinct from each other. And as a result, we might propose, all "sovereignty" is subsumed into/as fraternal equality—the condition of universal freedom, to repeat King's argument, is that no one is free until all are. The ethical is realized in that moment that sameness obtains if we understand sameness as the dissolution of sovereignty while retaining, out of sheer historical necessity, the possibility of a(/an ethical) subject that knows itself capable of suffering in order to secure justice. The opposite proposition, of course, also presents itself. That is, the dissolution—the sheer destruction, effected in Derridean terms—of sovereignty is the absolute precondition for the ethical subject.

"Suffering," if we think Adorno and Derrida together, is the first principle of the non- (or even anti-) "sovereign" self. "Responsibility," then, is that act of forcibly uncoupling the self from "sovereignty" in order to relocate—move, displace—the self into the realm (psychopolitical space) of the other. In disenfranchising itself, which is what "extraditing sovereignty" amounts to (relieving the self of the burden of "sovereignty"—the source of injustice?), the self begins the political work of "responsibly" thinking what stands between self and other.[3] This act, as Derrida acknowledges when he accedes to the uniterability of "delivering the self over to the other," is a constitutively deficient one (sans "grammatical markings, language or context"), a process that is fraught with uncertainty. Daunting, in fact, because this political act of ceding "sovereignty" is a priori indeterminate—it might be able to mark a putative beginning, but it cannot, under any circumstances, determine where or how this process will unfold or end. Such an opening onto the forswearing of "sovereignty" (is such an act even possible?), of course, runs the risk of the undoing of the self. The indeterminate, then, demands a singular political thinking. It requires that we apprehend the indeterminate as if it were the very first thought of politics, the very first act that politics must undertake. The indeterminate as politics sui generis, as that politics to which (all) politics must aspire.

The indeterminate stands in sharp contrast to the violence (through which the "sovereign" self defines itself against the other) that white America continues to breed afresh (the August 2020 shooting of protesters by a white teenage vigilante in Kenosha, Wisconsin, being but one instance among many), here as we stand on the precipice of the third decade of the twenty-first century. (Let us remember the Trump caravans, pickup trucks bearing flag-waving, gun-toting white Americans, that have menaced cities such as Portland, Oregon, and small towns in North Carolina. That is the voice of "sovereignty," understanding itself as racially threatened, defining itself defiantly against the other, precisely without the possibility of "deliverance.") King's "Dream," in its most vivid and uplifting articulation, offers "white people" the opportunity to, by forming a "biracial union," escape that nightmare (George Wallace: "I say segregation now, segregation tomorrow, segregation forever") in which they have cocooned and cossetted themselves.[4]

James Baldwin, a black visionary (and maybe even a messianic) of a very different stripe, is like King and Derrida in that he, as we will see in the next section, is also dedicated to the "extension" of the self in the direction of the other. Baldwin, as I will argue, goes a step further in that he advocates absolute forgiveness, in a gesture that is at once politically counterintuitive and redolent with the teachings of a radical Christianity. Baldwin's Christianity, to massively oversimplify his position, begins and ends with loving those who oppress you. This radical self-expectation could easily stand as his founding principle.

"Shooting up schools is a white kid's game."

We'll get to Baldwin shortly, and give him full treatment. But for now I'd like to turn to Dave Chappelle again, this time Chappelle as farceur. The concept of the "farceur," a term that derives from the Middle French *farcer*, "to joke" (to crack a joke, to be the author of a farce), is invoked here to designate Chappelle, first, as a provocateur—the comic who jokes, but often with a series of ruthless, philosophically inflected iterations. That is, Chappelle operates in the Socratic–Platonic and Foucauldian traditions of thought insofar as he repeatedly takes up the question of self, principally as it might be understood to signal the turn to care of the self. The word "farceur" can be traced to the Latin *farcire,* "to stuff." In this etymological way the farceur functions as the (comic) figure who arrests—or apprehends—the joke in its tracks. That is, "to stuff," which resonates with the possibility of being overfull, is to "stop" the joke in order to explicate how the joke's essence—its truth—is being "upheld." By holding the joke in place we can see how the joke thinks the relationship of the self to itself. It also then becomes possible to critique how care of the self functions in relation to the farceur and to critique what constitutes the proprietary relationship of self to itself.

Figured as a singular farceur, Chappelle is invoked here to, inter alia, trouble, echo, complicate, challenge, contradict (himself as well as others), and shed a comic light on the arguments (philosophical and otherwise) that run through this essay. As such, Chappelle is the farceur who has given the notion that African-Americans are (or might be) responsible for whites—an idea that he shares with King and Baldwin—a fair amount of thought.

It is in this farceuristic vein that Chapelle critiques the epidemic of school shootings. Reflecting on this violence, Chappelle finds himself with no other option than to conclude:

> I don't see any peaceful way to disarm America's whites.
>   There's only one thing that gonna save this country from itself, the same thing that always saves this country: African-Americans.
>   And right, and I know the question that all of y'all have in your minds is, "Should we do it?"
>   Fuck yeah, we should do it. . . . It is incumbent upon us to save our country.
>   And you know what we have to do. We have to be serious.
>   This is an election year, and every able-bodied African-American must register . . . [dramatic pause]

Chappelle uses this narrative break, created by the silence he has orchestrated, to ramp up the predictable liberal-democratic expectation. Every politically responsible member of the audience is waiting for Chappelle to play the role of advocate for democracy. The injunction the audience is waiting for is to act like a responsible, committed citizen. That is, everyone should register to exercise their democratic right to vote. Chappelle destroys that expectation:

> . . . for a firearm license.[5]

Liberal-democratic presumption exploded, if such an incendiary pun might be indulged. *The* liberal-democratic verity, the franchise, as it pertains to minority constituencies, African-Americans foremost among them, dismissed. Not raised to the level of farce, as such, representative democracy is nonetheless dealt a telling blow.

Liberal-democratic expectations confounded (if African-Americans are going register for anything, it should be to own a gun, not to vote), Du Bois's struggle during his NAACP tenure, the Civil Rights movement's very raison d'être, rings hollow, if only for moment (and possibly longer, we cannot be sure). A sick joke? The farceur's revenge on liberal-democratic pieties? Faith in the franchise dismissed in favor of an act that enables African-Americans to commit violence, legally.

Chappelle, exploiting the role of farceur he has crafted for himself, has managed to, rudely, put a "stop" to liberal-democratic expectations. Or, he has translated *farcire* into a colloquial English (that is, as pertaining to the United Kingdom) phrase: the farceur has "stuffed" liberal-democratic expectations. He has beaten them. He has beaten the audience, both by delaying the punch line and by confounding expectation. (The phrase, aggressive in intent even when delivered playfully, is often rendered as "I/We stuffed you." Undoubtedly dated now, it resonated with braggadocio in the late 1960s and early 1970s, especially in cricket.)[6]

However, when Chappelle explains his preference for gun registration over voter registration, his preference reveals itself to be, simultaneously, an ominous threat to the U.S. state and white Americans as well as a quite brilliant proposition. African-American gun registration as realpolitik, black "pragmatism" as showing up the soft underbelly of state institutions. The farceur as canny political operator, one who would make Bismarck proud. Especially with a denouement such as this:

That's the only way they'll change the law.

Hoisting white America by its own petard. This is the solution to gun violence in America. The only way in which the Second Amendment loses all ideological force is if the legal right to own a gun is exercised by all African-Americans. A constitutionally armed black America, a black America acting within the bounds of the law, armed and willing to exercise its Second Amendment rights, will pose the gravest threat to every ideological argument made by white America in favor of the right to bear arms. Arguments made in the U.S. Congress in defense of gun ownership in the wake of Columbine, Sandy Hook, Parkland; arguments funded by the National Rifle Association; arguments mobilized on the bumper stickers, at least one of which is a Confederate flag, of pickups driven by poorly groomed, tattooed white men in battle fatigues ("camo," in the current aesthetic argot) or grimy tank tops; the right to kill school-children defended relentlessly, all the way to the Supreme Court, if necessary. All of these arguments embellished by political observers of a certain vintage, by the visage of a frail Charlton Heston, former NRA president, waxing lyrical and promising to uphold the Second Amendment against the threat that was "Mr. Gore": "From my cold, dead hands . . ."[7] So speaks the spirit of "Moses."

All these arguments, Chappelle suggests, are vulnerable to the specter of mass, legal black gun ownership.

The Second Amendment will die not because of mass shootings in suburban schools (to name, again, only the most spectacular: Columbine, Sandy Hook, Parkland) or mall movie theaters (Aurora, Colorado; Lafayette, Louisiana; and so on).[8] It will, instead, perish on the altar of (potential, legal) African-American gun ownership.

Ever the strategic pragmatist-farceur, Chappelle enjoins African-Americans to apply, today, if possible, for their gun licenses. African-Americans should swarm gun shows in those states where it is legal to buy a gun on-site, no questions asked.

In twenty-nine states it is possible to purchase a firearm at a gun show, courtesy of what is known as the "gun show loophole," a fact that makes Chappelle's political advocacy at once oddly redundant and profoundly threatening.[9] In America you cannot vote without registering, but you can buy a gun without a license. If this is how the United States functions institutionally, then it would be much more effective for African-Americans to purchase guns in order to produce political change than it would be for them to register to vote, run for political office, or even win political office. America is a gun owner's utopia.

By acquiring their guns legally, African-Americans will fulfill the farceur's pledge. African-Americans will, once more, save America by saving white children from gun violence at school.

Since this is the state of things (once more, it is capital that counts, even if it is dressed up as a constitutional amendment), African-Americans should be lining up to attend gun shows in those twenty-nine states, more than half the nation, as they would, to invoke a famous Chappelle sketch, outside liquor stores after collecting their "reparations checks."[10] In advocating for an entirely unexpected form of political action, Chappelle provides an insight into how difficult it is, in real political terms, to "extradite sover-eignty to the other."

Registering to vote is for suckers. Or, worse, black Americans unwilling to exercise their Second Amendment rights. Change will come only through mass African-American gun ownership. Armed black America. Armed to scare white America straight.

In the white political imaginary, the only thing worse than whites having their guns taken away is African-Americans exercising their constitutional right to own guns.

"From my cold, dead, white hands..."
    As many guns as possible, if you please. As many as African-Americans can afford.
    As many semiautomatics as possible, to be precise.

We can laugh because of, we can even laugh at, the (seemingly preposterous, perverse, tragic) proposal that Chappelle makes. But Columbine, Sandy Hook... this, and the Pulse nightclub... Parkland... Dayton... Thousand Oaks... and those to come are no laughing matter.

As always, America's political vectors remain constant—fatally so, when it comes to gun violence. Can America's racial and moral calculus be undone by Chappelle's denouement? By his provocation that the other's legal right to gun ownership constitutes, in an axiomatic logic of the most perverse variety, the only means through which to save white America from itself, from its own children, those gun-toting white kids who come to school armed and intent on exacting violent, scattershot revenge? The innocents who get caught in the crossfire are, well, collateral damage.

The farceur has, then, happened upon the only way to save some white American children from other white American children. And who knows, it might be precisely because of the threat of large-scale black gun ownership that some other children—some others' children—too might be spared.

There is no gainsaying Chappelle's argument: "I don't see any other way to disarm America's whites." Disarm them to save their children. From them. From their pathological attachment to the Second Amendment. It is only the threat of African-Americans exercising their constitutional rights that holds out the prospect of saving white Americans from themselves—of saving their children, white children, in too many instances. That is, saving white children across the country from the gun violence of other white children.

The truth is inarguable: "Shooting up schools is a white kid's game."

Time for African-Americans to step up and save the white children.

By any means necessary. That is, by the most legal means.

Dave Chappelle has revealed the perverse autoimmunity of the Second Amendment.

The "gun show loophole" is, when all else fails, white America's only hope.

As long as it is neither white adults nor white teenagers who are the ones buying the guns.

Stand back, white America, and let the African-Americans get their hands on those guns.

And then, only then, maybe, will law address the epidemic of gun violence.

Black America's work, macabre, perverse, "self-sacrificing" as it may be, is never done. The manner of the other's salvific work, the form it will be asked to assume, is infinitely malleable. But beyond the call of duty? No, for the other nothing—as it pertains to the salvific—is beyond the call of duty. Not even being asked to venture into the predominantly white, militaristic, and racist space that is the American gun show.

4 Deracializing MLK

I doubt not God is good, well-meaning, kind,
And did He stoop to quibble could tell why
. . .
Yet do I marvel at this curious thing:
To make a poet black and bid him sing!
    —Countee Cullen, "Yet Do I Marvel"

No matter the indifference to biblical injunction or degradation of the American polis, in his refusal to garrison King as a figure solely of and for black liberation, Nip is onto something. With economy of phrase, he has yanked King (his message, at any rate) out of his over-determined blackness and into universality. Nip insists that Martin Luther King speaks to, and for, all of America. King may not be, as I have said, audible in the same register to everyone, but there can be no doubt that, at every rhetorical level, King appeals to, as I have already mentioned, what Abraham Lincoln called in his first inaugural address America's "better angels." Trying to hold together a nation on the brink of civil war, Lincoln appealed to his fellow citizens: "We are not enemies, but friends. We must not be enemies. . . . The mystic chords of memory . . . will yet swell the chorus of the Union, when again touched, as surely they will be, by the better angels of our nature."[1] Lincoln's attempt to forestall catastrophe failed, as we well know. With his reference to the "mystic chords of memory" he was surely reaching out to the wrong constituency (southern whites), because Lincoln returned this self-same constituency to a new form of violence and racist oppression. What Lincoln should have sought, in this regard, was not the "chords of memory" but dis-cord. Lincoln ought to have severed the "memory" of historic transgression from the Reconstructionist present (the present that was, of course, the future Lincoln did not live to see) in order to make the present stand as a judgment against the toxicity of all such "memory." Despite its failure—Jim Crow is only one of many names for it—Lincoln's appeal continues to echo into our very moment. Surely it is high time for those "better angels" to do active battle, to engage, with ferocity and determination, the persistence into this present of those devilish "memories."

Ezra, without a moment's hesitation, is clearly of the opinion that we should liberate King into full American belonging. Why restrict his political effect to blackness? Is that not itself a kind of exclusionary tendency bordering on racism, the particularization of King so that he derives all his historical force from racial overidentification, and thereby the very antiracist struggles that he waged are neutralized? Not to put too fine a point on it, but this is how political oppositionality is denuded, robbed of its integrity and impact. To paraphrase the Harlem Renaissance poet Countee Cullen, this amounts to "making a prophet black, and keeping him so, regardless." Surely the God of Cullen's sonnet is "wiser," and one hopes, "better," than that? Why else "bid" such a poet into song?

Insisting on the apostle of peaceful resistance as black amounts to a kind of strategic racial essentialism. A singularity, if you will, in that it makes him racially univocal. So rendered, King is remanded to speak in one voice, with one voice; there is no recognition that although his speaking begins with him (blackness), it does so out of a historical necessity that chafes against precisely his particularization. King's is a speaking intent on exceeding its speaker. King's is an appeal to every American's "better angels," although some Americans have long since banished those "angels." (In any case, there is really only one "bad angel" of note, and it took John Milton to recuperate him from perdition while giving him literary life.)

To so "racialize" Martin Luther King is to limit him—against his will, against his every Christian straining—to blackness. If such an act of violence against King is no longer permitted, what emerges is the possibility of the self delivering itself (over) to the other. That is the political prospect for which we must strive: all selves inclining toward the other.

The effect of this strategy—again, "racializing" MLK—is to let the most powerful, historically transgressive constituencies off the hook. Inadvertently or not, Nip has correctly identified this constituency: "white people," before and above all others. It is imperative for "white people," I take Nip to be saying, to completely rethink their understanding of the Civil Rights movement and Civil Rights legislation (the need for its preservation, strengthening, and constant reinvigoration). They must begin this process with how it is they apprehend Martin Luther King and how it is they have taken their political distance—political irresponsibility, decidedly not of the Derridean variety—from him and the material benefits they have reaped from their alienation.

Out of the mouths of babes. Or, out of the unmediated mouth of a three-and-a-half-year-old.

To cast the pop group En Vogue's early 1990s lyrics in the discursive register of Ezra's Martin Luther King: "Free your mouth, and the truth will follow."

Race Is Everything, Race Matters Not at All

Out of the direct address that is Nip's "and for white people too" emerges political depth and complexity. But then again, I am glad to say, complexity is at the core of Nip's racial thinking.

It is one thing, of course, to suggest that Ezra's racial consciousness derives from an innate savviness. True as that might be (or not), Nip's aptitude has the benefit of being grounded in a racial reality. In a word, it is his birthright. Nip has a white American mother and a black diasporic father. Because of our son's lived reality, he has always had to negotiate race as, simultaneously, of grave import and of little consequence. On the one hand, in our everyday domestic life, race is, as the aftermath of Trump's 2016 electoral victory made clear, a critical factor, the stuff of serious conversation; sometimes Jane and I would wish it different. On the other hand, there are far more moments in which race has no discursive purchase at all.

Life has its natural rhythms. There is Jane's work, there is my work. For both of us that amounts to teaching, grading, writing— the everyday stuff of institutional academic life. For Nip there is his school life at Montessori, his iPad, his friends, and, since the fall of 2019, basketball. Turns out he can play. Jane and I try to keep track of Nip's interests, a difficult thing because they appear to be ever changing and, needless to say, ever expanding: music (which includes constantly updating his playlists and practicing, always with reluctance, his instruments—guitar, drum, keyboards), riding his scooter at the skateboard park, and more. And, of course, Jane and I ferry him to and from his various basketball activities. Some interests, such as his love for music and his enthusiasm for the skateboard park, are sustained; other pursuits, as in that line from T. S. Eliot, "come and go" (although, I hasten to add, as a family we never talk of Michelangelo). For her part, Jane is a lifelong, die-hard Chicago Cubs fan and follows the team religiously; she is also an activist with a particular interest in immigration issues. I have the fortunes of my beloved Liverpool F.C. to keep watch over.

Nip has two white brothers and a black sister. They are all older than Ezra and live far from us. His brother Alex is a writer in St. Paul, and his brother ATrane (Anton) lives in Minneapolis. His sister, Andrea, is part of the managerial team at a midsize bank just outside Seattle. Within our family, then, the dynamics of race are fluid and unpredictable, and, as such, occupy a complex place in our lives. Race is at once unavoidable, that facticity (onticity) that must be thought, and insignificant. In this regard, ours is a life that can, at a moment's notice, be disrupted out of its everyday routine into a confrontation with the racial realities of our time. Our lives, like those of everyone else, are lived at the mercy of contingency. We are subject to the "thrownness" (Heidegger's term) of the world because everything can change in a heartbeat, depending on who knows what. The latest tweet, a new outbreak of racial violence, legislation that Congress might take up. A playground incident, an untoward comment at school. Any of these have the potential to affect the household. *C'est la vie.*

What the Athletic Body Is to Ezra

Because of his racial lineage, Nip has developed an acute awareness of his body. After he has hit the heavy bag at our local YMCA for about two minutes (if that), he will flex his muscles and pronounce himself "jacked." I nod in acquiescence, stopping just short of public agreement. However, what preoccupies Ezra most about his body is its "color."

Nip insists that he is "black." Well, he is not. He is a shade, just a shade and barely that, darker than cream, if that. His concern with his skin tone—a language with which I am distinctly uncomfortable and, as such, something that I will address more fully shortly—has produced in Nip a quest for public allies. He is always on the lookout for those who speak against Trump, or seem likely to, and he is always watching for those who look like him. What Nip is hoping to find, Jane and I have decided, is affirmation for himself in those musicians (Chance the Rapper, Lil Nas X, Breakbot, and Travis Scott are current favorites, but there is an ample assortment of others, such as Bach, Miles Davis, and Bill Evans, which makes me happy) and athletes. Musicians and athletes who are able to perform—to borrow a Latinate phrase from C. L. R. James's *Beyond a Boundary* in his discussion of the wonderful Trinidadian batsman Wilton St. Hill—*in excelsis*, with excellence. (James feels a real surge of pride at the talent of his fellow Trinidadian, describing what he is to black West Indians thus: "I know that to tens of thousands of coloured Trinidadians the unquestioned glory of St. Hill's batting conveyed the sensation that here was one of us, performing *in excelsis* in a sphere where the competition was open.")[2]

For Nip the skin color he claims for himself is a source of pride. It is how he affirms his budding racial self-consciousness. It is racial affirmation mimetically reflected and absorbed. Taken into the (young) self. Taken as the (young) self's own. Appropriation (of the self) to politically unimpeachable ends. The body in search of a fellow other, the body that recognizes itself in a fellow other; the body of that fellow other is the body that has raised the possibility of Ezra thinking his body affirmatively, no matter the obstacles that he confronts and is, undoubtedly, still to encounter. In this search for the fellow other, there is, of course, no guarantee of a lifetime prophylaxis. No matter, because of this other body there is an affirmative device in place that can (provisionally, momentarily) protect the self. This is an affirmative device, I am glad to say, that can provide some insulation against what Shakespeare names, in that most famous of soliloquys (from *Hamlet,* needless to say), "the slings and arrows of outrageous fortune." "To sleep, perchance to dream." "To dream" another world, that world where "outrageous fortune's" barbs are less likely to be active.

In part, Ezra finds his "dream" in athletes, not least of them the former Liverpool player Philippe Coutinho and seven-time Formula One (Fᵢ) racing champion Lewis Hamilton. It is through figures such as these that Nip derives a sense of how to carry himself in the world. Ezra will never score an outrageous goal from a free kick thirty-two meters away, but he understands, I intuit, that what the Brazilian international Coutinho gives him, a mixed-race boy in

Ithaca, New York, is more valuable than even that precocious skill. And it is a precocious skill—Coutinho accomplished amazing feats when he was at Liverpool. (At the time of this writing, Coutinho is back at F.C. Barcelona after plying his trade in Germany for Bayern München, where he spent the 2019–20 season on loan. He left Liverpool for F.C. Barcelona in January 2018, but his first stint there came to a disappointing end in August 2019.)

I have tried, thus far with no success, to alert Nip to the talents of Trent Alexander-Arnold, a native Scouser, as Liverpudlians are called. I am smitten with Alexander-Arnold, that singular player who is a footballer rather than a player defined by his position—Alexander-Arnold cannot be described as a defender, his nominal position, except out of logistical necessity. (TAA, as I've dubbed him, was born in October 1998 in West Derby, just a short distance from Melwood, which used to be Liverpool F.C.'s training ground until they moved to their new facility in Kirkby.) Like Nip, Alexander-Arnold has a black father and a white mother. But Nip is not biting on TAA. Who said mimicry is everything?

Adorno's negative dialectics is activated for me in Nip's refusal to align with Alexander-Arnold. Negative dialectics gives us the capacity to understand that the concept (the *Begriff,* let us name it "race," no matter that it functions here not as an absolute but on the order of gradation for Ezra) and the object or subject matter (*Sache,* Ezra, specifically, in this instance) are not equivalent. Nip does not "see" himself in TAA in the ways that he identifies with Hamilton or Coutinho, producing a contradiction between what we might expect of the concept and what it actually delivers—the very instantiation of "nonidentity," one of the most crucial terms in Adorno's critical armory. Or *Vorrang des Objekt* Nip, if you will—the "priority of the object" that is Nip.

Swagger, audacity, intense discipline, and absolute self-belief are characteristics that Nip's other hero, Lewis Hamilton, Formula One champ, embodies. Born in a housing estate (British public housing, also known as "council estates," roughly equivalent to American "projects") in Stevenage, England, to a white English mother and a black Caribbean father, Hamilton won his first championship with McLaren in 2008, becoming the first and only black driver to do so. Since then, he has won six F1 championships with the Mercedes team (2014, 2015, 2017–20), thus making of Nip a Mercedes fan. Now that he has equaled German racer Michael Schumacher's record for world championships (seven apiece) and surpassed Schumacher's record for grand prix titles (winning his ninety-second in October 2020, taking him past Schumacher's ninety-one), Hamilton is the most successful driver in the history of F1 racing.[3]

For his ninth birthday (at the end of July 2015), I get Nip an early present. I buy tickets (for him and me) to the 2017 Canadian Grand Prix at Circuit Gilles Villeneuve in Montreal. Jane, who has no appetite for fast cars, goes with us, but she wants no part of the race.

We leave Ithaca early on the Saturday morning before the race (all F1 races, I should note, take place on Sundays). It takes five hours to drive from our house to Montreal. We stay with friends in an idyllic little lakeside town on the western tip of the Island of Montreal—just twenty-five miles from downtown. On Saturday afternoon Nip, Jane, and I take a stroll through the town, Sainte-Anne-de-Bellevue, situated on the shores of Lake Saint-Louis, at the "confluence of the mighty Saint Lawrence and murky Ottawa Rivers" (as our hosts describe it). Jane wants coffee. We find a charming two-story store that stocks a delightful assortment of jams, to say nothing of the upscale selection of clothing, household furniture, and various higher-end knickknacks for sale.

While Jane strolls through the lower level, Nip and I goof around in the furniture section upstairs. One of the white sales assistants approaches and asks if she can help us. I politely decline. However, wherever Ezra and I turn, there she is. Nip notices this and asks, "Why is that woman following us?"

It's time, I realize, to explain something to Ezra.

"We're black," I say, "and so she thinks we're going to shoplift."

"What?" Nip looks at me quizzically. "She thinks we're going to put a big chair in our pockets?"

He is being, at once, funny and quite serious. He's right, of course. The physical impossibility of it.

"It's what black people have to deal with routinely," I say. "We're always suspected of shoplifting in stores." Especially stores where the assistants do not think we can afford the merchandise, I deliberately do not add.

Ezra is not letting this go.

The moment is now.

His racial nous kicks in: "I bet that if Mommy were with us that woman wouldn't follow us."

"You're right," I say.

This is how you tell your son the truth about how race works in the world.

This, to be poetic (which is to say that I rage against the post-lapsarian), is how, so un-Miltonically, innocence is lost. This is that moment when (your son's) innocence is lost: "The bud disappears in the bursting-forth of the blossom." On the one hand, of course, Hegel holds out the promise that truth "bursts forth" out of the fast-disappearing "bud." On the other hand, I really would like to treasure that "bud" for just a moment longer. Alas. Poor Yorick.

The moment is now.

Because of Ezra's critique, I can no longer indulge my affinity for—my inclining toward—the "bud" (of innocence). This is the moment that cannot be struggled against. This is the moment whose time has come. Nip's logic entirely negates my inclining toward innocence; Nip's demand, I am forced to acknowledge, is grounded in an irrefutable racial arithmetic. His is a rather straightforward equation: one black father and one black son do not, in this picture-perfect little lakeside town, equal one white mother. Arithmetic is not Nip's strong suit, but he knows the formula for this racial/racist logic: $2 \neq 1$. In this racialized scenario, the political calculations are clear: two black (male) bodies (with no allowance made for the disparity in age) do not equal one white (female) body. Such is the gendered nature of this racial/racist arithmetic. It is only the white mother who can provide black father and son with the necessary prophylaxis against racialized suspicion. The white mother alone can insulate "her" black bodies and the (overdetermined) pathologies that attach themselves to all black bodies. (In 1970s Britain this approach—the black body is guilty until proven otherwise—was known as the "sus laws," an obvious abbreviation for the "suspicion" to which all black bodies were subject. In America, this law enforcement tactic, known as "stop and frisk," was put into practice in New York City by then mayor Michael Bloomberg. It is a practice about which Bloomberg, when he unsuccessfully ran for president, dissembled, claiming not to have known that "stop and frisk" was in fact racial profiling. That "stop and frisk" targeted mainly young African-American and Latino men somehow escaped Bloomberg's grasp. "The mayor doth protest too much, methinks.")

In this bucolic scenario, the small political drama playing out on the shores of Lake Saint-Louis, everything turns on the white mother/wife. Her absence alone is what matters; her presence is definitive. Despite her absence, the white mother is phantasmatically present for son and father; through her absence, the white mother/wife makes herself phantasmatically present, the only "object" that can stay the psychosocial assault on black male bodies. Whiteness cannot be excised. The white mother/wife is the political phantasm that brings home to "her" black bodies the realization that their vulnerability can, to phrase the matter negatively, be undone only, and then only in some moments, by her. (The white phantasm functions almost talismanically.) In the white mother/wife's absence, "her" black bodies realize that only she can shield them, son and husband, against the everyday machinations of (Quebecois) racism.

Once more, rendered formulaically: 1 > 2. One white body > two black bodies. Unfailingly, Ezra grasps a truth. However, as in Hegel's horticultural analogy, there is more work to be done. In politics, there is always more work to be done. In this regard there is Hegel's analogy:

> The bud disappears in the bursting-forth of the blossom, and one might say that the former is refuted by the latter; similarly, when the fruit appears, the blossom is shown up in its turn as a false manifestation of the plant, and the fruit now emerges as the truth of it instead. These forms are not just distinguished from one another, they also supplant one another as mutually incompatible.[4]

Hegel's "fruit," which manifests as a greater truth, is what Ezra must reach for, if not quite every day, then often enough. In Hegel's terms, according to the metric that is the "tree of truth," Ezra has progressed quickly from "bud" to "blossom." However, it is a historical certainty that there will always be days when even the most mundane form of racism will return him to the "bud" stage. Sometimes racism will assume a more egregious form; sometimes it will assume a less malignant guise. Increasingly, the older he gets, neither Jane nor I will be able to intercede on his behalf. He will have become his own "plant." It is, for now, up to us, his parents, to ensure that what he reaps is the training in discrimination—and love—that we have sown. We must hope, fervently, against all odds, that he will be able to reap, to repeat the biblical metaphor, what we have sowed, sowed as assiduously as possible.

Nip and I find Jane, and the three of us walk toward the lake. Boats bob gently on the water, and the scene is a study in peace and tranquility. Joggers run along the waterfront, some people take their meals, and others wander through the flea market.

Against this serene backdrop, Nip's and my encounter with casual Quebecois racism seems surreal, a political hallucination, so far is it removed from the summer pleasures before us.

On Sunday morning, Jane drops Nip and me at the Montreal Metro station and goes in search of a coffee shop where she can read. Nip and I will join her after the race for the drive back to Ithaca. The Metro bustles with activity, streams of fans sporting their team colors. Mercedes and Ferrari gear dominates. We get our tickets and board the train. We're a little lost. A white woman, who is with her husband and her two children (the family kitted out in Lewis Hamilton Mercedes garb), hears our uncertainty. She approaches and kindly offers to guide us to the track. She makes sure that she keeps us in sight, points us to the ticket booth, and wishes us a fun race.

Hamilton wins, in style, beating his Ferrari opponent Sebastian Vettel by some measure, allowing Hamilton to close the points gap on the German driver. Hamilton will go on to win his fourth F1 championship later that season.

On our way back to the Metro we pass the ticket booth, and I say to Ezra, "Do you remember that woman who helped us?"

"Yes," he says, "she was very nice."

"Right," I concur, but I know that it is time for a lesson in political discrimination, and I add, "not like that woman yesterday."

"No," he agrees, before mocking the store clerk's attentiveness to us once more.

"Where did she think we were going to put the furniture?" he asks once more.

I smile. Nip can be like this. He is like a dog with a bone, refusing to let go of something once he gets agitated about it. In fact, even now, more than three years later, unexpectedly, from time to time, and as recently as Halloween 2020, he still talks about our experience in the Sainte-Anne-de-Bellevue shop. He and I are strolling through downtown Ithaca, lamenting that there will no trick-or-treating this year, and Nip breaks out into that by now familiar refrain: "Do you remember that white woman in Montreal?" This is the black child's psyche scarred. It is five years later, and we still have not left that store in Sainte-Anne-de-Bellevue.

All of which takes us back to that moment when, within less than twenty-four hours, a lesson, first one and then the other. In less than twenty-four hours, the pendulum swings wildly. Subjection to pathologization (living as the essentialized black body; that is, the black body as a priori criminal)

> *In the cryptic, sardonic, bitingly accurate terms offered by Chappelle: a black man is a "suspect for everything except white-collar crime."*[5] *Word. To that list, add the impossible capacity that black folks have to hide furniture in the pockets of their pants.*
>
> *In every black person, a little bit of that David Copperfield magic.*

is followed hard by an object lesson in the unexceptional (the vaguely "lost" black bodies being guided by the white body). On this Sunday on the Montreal Metro all these bodies are bonded, Nip and I speculate, by their shared Lewis Hamilton–Mercedes affiliation. An almost uncomfortable symmetry: black bodies standing in unexceptional relation to white bodies because of their shared regard for the mixed-race body. Or, maybe . . . two mixed-race bodies, Nip's and mine (diasporic coloured from South Africa that I am), in relation to another mixed-race body.

Or Lewis Hamilton, the (English) elixir who dissolves racial animus, on a very small scale, for a brief moment, entirely unknown to him, through his skill as an F1 driver—the only black driver in F1, past and present.

In truth, Nip and I have no way of knowing how our white F1 "guide" understands us racially. However, we have too much experience—just twenty-four hours ago—not to think race, first, foremost, last, always.

Yet Lewis Hamilton remains, as such, dialectical. The *Darstellung* of Lewis Hamilton as Adorno's rejection of thought that finds its "only shelter" in the "dogmatic tradition."

Thought, we would be right to insist, we should always insist, must never seek "shelter."

And should it do so, the only appropriate "shelter" would be in the eye of the storm.

Thought must revel, as Chappelle says, in the "joys of speaking recklessly."[6] Word.

Adorno, as we know, is not wont to speak "recklessly," but he might be, in this instance, as Jameson suggests, a "better guide" for our thinking of the dialectic.[7] Adorno offers, for Jameson, one of the most useful ways to understand the contradiction in history. (For Jameson it is Brecht who takes pride of place in thinking the dialectic as contradiction.) For Adorno, "historical progression is not the movement from one victory to another, greater one: it is the movement of contradictions, which as they are worked on, dissolved, or even forgotten or left to fester, themselves produce new contradictions and radically new situations (which may of course be not for the better but for the worse). History as the temporality of these new situations and new contradictions."[8]

Nip and I in Sainte-Anne-de-Bellevue and at Circuit Gilles Villeneuve: caught in the "movement of contradictions." First a turn "for the worse," and then a turn "for the better." Unable to forget our experience in the store, compelled to "work on" the contradiction that is racism when solicitousness follows hard on the heels of suspicion. Not enough time to forget. As the black subject, we are, it seems, never allowed to forget. Do we want to forget? What is the cost of remembering? (Remembering, like Toni Morrison's house on Bluestone Road: "spiteful. Full of a baby's venom.")[9] Of always feeling historically compelled to always remember? Or is it that we are condemned to remember? Is remembering, bearing the burden of memory, being an apostle to memory (that is, repeatedly speaking what has to be remembered), at the core of the salvific? One way or the other, as Jameson points out, the reality is that every contradiction sets up the conditions for the next one. And so on.

Always with the proviso, as Jameson cautions, that every "new contradiction and radically new situation" may prove to be a "historical movement" "for the worse."

As such, are Nip and I now left to wonder about such a caution, such a bracing anticipation, to remember, lest we forget, that "we'll always have the Montreal Metro"? As though we were the father and son counterparts to Bogie and Bacall in the Francophone capital of Canada? Five years later, the experience remains with Ezra.

Our Bodies

This is the moment of the dialectic. Nothing can disguise the stark contrast between white surveillance and white kindness. Or maybe just kindness, the kindness one F1 Hamilton fan offers to another. In short order, first one, then the other. My head is spinning just a little. In the Montreal Metro encounter, it would seem that Nip's and my bodies are of little or no consequence: we are seen—responded to—as ourselves, as though we were not other at all. Just lost fans. Of course, this is purely suppositional (who can know another's thoughts?), but we have no reason for bad faith. In the Montreal Metro we can trust our bodies as bodies, obviating any need to be on guard for our bodies as other bodies. Here, in this moment, we are able to allow our bodies to be (as bodies, simply as bodies); we have no reason to mistrust our bodies. That is, temporarily, our bodies lie beyond the (routine) politics of suspicion, and, as such, for a moment, our bodies have no raced standing.

However, I do not know if Nip and I ever achieve that kind of ease in that Hamiltonian moment. Then again, in all fairness, how could we, given how our bodies were, just yesterday, literally, treated as raced objects subject to perpetual scrutiny? How are we to trust our bodies in public? Indeed, how are we to trust our bodies at all? What must we do in order to learn how to distinguish one mode of *Being* (the black body as unexceptional and, therefore, not black? Is that really possible?) from another (the black body as a priori disposed to criminality; always, before itself and because of itself, pathological)? We can chafe all we want, Nip and I, against the ways in which the world demands of us a "double consciousness," but we have just learned how important our powers of discrimination are to our capacity to operate as (thinking black) beings in the world.

The problem confronting Ezra and me, Du Bois might have said, derives from the condition of being/*Being* black. "How does it feel to be a problem?"[10] And what this problem demands is that we always have at our disposal a critical skill. That skill is the ability to discriminate. The ability to know what response is needed in a particular moment. The ability to know how to distinguish one encounter or situation, and, as such, one mode of address, from another. The ability to know when a situation requires, without forewarning or advance notice, a completely different mode of address.

And, what is more, in making these distinctions, we have to be able to do so with absolute uncertainty. That is, to operate on Heidegger's principle that to "judge is to form correct ideas," and then to pause there and absorb it, after which Heidegger immediately proceeds to undo that pronouncement with his qualification that in "forming ideas" we produce not only "correct" but "incorrect" ones too.[11] The work of judging, then, is neither infallible nor (ever) complete. In this sense, we can say that the work of judgment is political in that our (first) decision about an object/situation/person might very well be our last, it may very well be binding, but there is no guarantee of that. Even if our decision turns out be valid, that by no means assures that we will not have to attend to it again in the future. Every decision belongs exclusively to time itself—that is, to its own particular temporal "locale." Revisiting our decision-making process, revising our judgment(s), explicating our "incorrect ideas" ("ideas," as such, we can say emerge out of our judgments), and "correcting" them makes at least two demands on us. First, it requires that we understand our decisions; and second, it requires that we be able to enumerate the effects of our judgments and decisions, as Foucault enjoins us to do. That is, we must come to terms with the effects of our judgments. We must recognize what happens in the world because of both our good judgments and our "incorrect" ones.

Ezra will have to learn that, without a doubt more often than he will want to. He will have to learn that sometimes very little distinguishes his "correct" from his "incorrect" judgments and "ideas." This requires, in Heidegger's phrasing, "becoming first of all questionable to ourselves."[12] To live, then, both as a Du Boisian "problem" and as the Heideggerian interrogative that asks us to be "questionable to ourselves." To begin with the self as a question—the self as, to coin a phrase, a "questionability." In Nip's case his "questionability" amounts to a racialized self that is never allowed respite from the demand to question itself, from the recognition that the self is a question, that the (black) self is almost always in question.

Discriminationem

In order to learn how the body must respond to such an unpredictable array of possible encounters, to train the body to be ready for all that racism might throw at it, as it were, the black body must learn discrimination. (The verb in such an instance would be *discernere,* "to discern"—to be able to divide or separate one thing from another.) That is, discrimination in the Late Latin sense, that sense that obtained in the mid-seventeenth century. That is, when discrimination—*discriminationem*—meant the "making of distinctions," the making of judgments, political judgments (for our purposes), differentiating between one thing or person and another, rather than, as became more etymologically prevalent in the nineteenth century, the act of behaving in a prejudiced manner. In our moment we invoke "discrimination," all too easily, only in the latter sense, making of it exclusively a pejorative, as a consequence of which we lose the practice of discrimination as understood in the terms of its (circa) 1640 definition—"something that serves to differentiate."[13] "Discrimination," then, is proposed here as faithful to the (seventeenth-century) etymology of the term while being infused with the pejorative inflections that came to prominence in the mid-nineteenth century. The function of "discriminate" in the pejorative is to retain fidelity to the term without ceding its political contemporaneity.

It is recognized that "distinguishing between" demands the work of making a decision, of thinking our way toward deciding what is, say, good, or who is, say, bad. But judgment, as we have established through Heidegger, is not preordained, it is not—much as many would like it to be—overdetermined; it is political work that must be undertaken again and again. We must decide; discernment is what is required. We are never done with making decisions; there will always be a need to make judgments because our decisions, committed as they are in the moment of their coming to life, refuse absolutely to be done with us. We are held to making decisions by time.

The body confronting us is not already a political question that decides, in advance, itself—as it were. The body before us asks—nay, demands—that we decide on it. That we decide on it on the condition we have already, "first," made "ourselves" "questionable to ourselves."

In order to do the work of distinguishing, we might heed Hegel from that most famous of sections in *Phenomenology of Spirit,* "Lordship and Bondage." We would be well-advised to follow the line of thinking that derives from what Hegel names the "play of Forces," the "process" that

> splits into the extremes; and each extreme is this exchanging
> of its own determinateness and an absolute transition into
> the opposite. Although, as consciousness, it does indeed come
> *out of itself,* yet, though out of itself, it is at the same time kept
> back within itself, is *for itself,* and the self outside it, is for *it.* It
> is aware that it at once is, and is not, another consciousness,
> and equally that this other is *for itself* only when it supersedes
> itself as being for itself, and is for itself only in the being-for-
> self of the other. Each is for the other the middle term . . . each
> is for itself, and for the other, an immediate being on its own
> account, which at the same time is such only through this
> mediation. They *recognize* themselves as *mutually recognizing*
> one another.[14]

Hegel raises the question, the possibility that our constituent political categories, "self" and "other," are in need of reevaluation, of further—or is it a first?—thinking. The self is only itself when it operates in the mode of "being-for-self of the other." We cannot posit, at least not with any philosophical conviction if we work on Hegel's terms, an absolute rupture between "self" and "other," we cannot claim that such a dyad, or the "extremes"—the very fundament of, most notably, anti- and postcolonial thought—either exists or, for that matter, can be sustained. (In Lacan's terms, the other is constitutively present within the self; self is constituted by other so that there is no "escaping" the other within—or the securing of a self that obviates or can negate the other. We cannot, as Jameson argues, "cure" ourselves of the other.[15] No wonder, then, that all desire begins with the other; the other is, to phrase the matter crudely, the self's very *joussaince*—that is, "life force," as Lacan prefers, or death drive.)

The self can achieve or access itself only if it "recognizes" the supersession through which the self "overcomes" "being for itself." Or it is to think the—precise—moment that such a "recognition" and/or "overcoming" takes place. When is it that a/the "self" can be conceived of as possible? Or is it impossible for the self, and the other, to *not* be at risk in the encounter between self and other? (It is often in thinking the encounter between self and other, and the risk endemic to that event, that Judith Butler's work has the most to offer as regards contemporary politics, especially as it pertains to questions of gender and sexuality.[16] Following Lacan, we already know that the self is, a priori, at risk in any such self–other, self–other/self, encounter.)

This is a crucial moment, the kind of moment that can—according to Heidegger—"make man an object worthy of his thought."[17] In Hegel's terms it is in this moment that the self recognizes that it enjoys only the most precarious distinction from the other.[18] It is in this moment that it becomes possible for the self to come most fully into its own selfhood. Further, and no less important, it is in this moment that the self's commitment to "being for itself" is precisely what allows it to accomplish the following political ends. First, it enables the self to grasp, to come to terms with, the other; and second, it is in this moment that the self understands that it lives always under the sign of the evisceration by (or of) the other. An evisceration of the other, I hasten to add, achieved not through violence (although we can never eliminate the violence inherent to such a transactional exchange) as such but through a singular "awareness." This "awareness," which recognizes, in trepidation as much as in excitement at the possibilities *Being* opens up, that the other is already with-*in*, constitutive of, that self and other are, in Hegel's logic, "mutually constitutive." (Again, we recognize this encounter as self–other/self.) At the very least, the other is unfailingly present in the constitution of the self (that is, we would "arrive at" Lacan). (The self, then, cannot but be haunted by the other. Which is to say, the haunting of the self by it-self is constitutive, from the very first moment, of the self.)

Reductively rendered, the-other-is-self, self-is-the-other, after that "mediation" I would designate "thinking." An ineradicable entanglement, if you will, that is elucidated by Adorno, one of Hegel's sternest critics—and, very possibly, among his most faithful philosophical heirs—at the very end of *Negative Dialectics*. Adorno writes of an entanglement that turns, conveniently, for our purposes, on thinking: "Represented in the inmost cell of thought is that which is unlike thought."[19] What resides in the "inmost cell" of the self is that (the other) which is most "unlike" it-self; following this line of thinking, we might say that the self is, as we know from at least Plato onward, only vaguely aware of what is most intimately lodged within it-self and, as such, "needs" thinking. (The "need in thinking" is what makes us think" so that it might be possible to γνῶθι σεαυτόν—*gnōthi seauton*.)[20]

Hegel casts this provocation in a different light when he raises the impossibility of an other (/another) in precisely that moment (the "Lordship and Bondage" section) when we would expect the "master–slave" (as it is often referred to) dialectic to be most emphatically articulated.[21]

In moving, at what sometimes seems like a frantic pace, between places, between political modes, among various political bodies, it might be worth pausing for a moment. And not only in order to catch our breath. Rather, reading Hegel in such a "negative" fashion (how else are we to read Hegel, since negation is his stock-in-trade critique? A critique, we might say, taken up in the most determined— and dogged—fashion by Adorno) offers the possibility of, to borrow from Jean-Luc Nancy's work on Hegel, interrupting our thinking and comprehending what is before us "otherwise." That is, to think what is before us as other than what we have always thought it and as we now continue to think it. (Such a thinking is what amounts to, for Levinas in *Otherwise Than Being*, something on the order of "transcendence.")[22]

We arrive at this through Nancy's consideration of *Aufhebung*, a contradictory German word that can be rendered as anything from "lifting up" to "abolishing" to "preserving," from "suspending" to "sublation" (the last of which being the "definition" that Nancy is, appropriately, faithful to given that this is how Hegel thought it). Nancy calls for an approach to "reading Hegel otherwise," not in order to go counter to Hegel (although that is always possible) but so that we might "finally . . . come (back) to our 'object,' reading or writing *otherwise* the *Aufhebung*."[23] The "object," as such, retains a stubborn immanence, and it is precisely the "object's" refusal to recede from view that both commands our attention and provides the possibility that it can "finally" be apprehended as that which it is not (and, in all probability, never was). The "object," then, can be thought as if we are making its acquaintance for the very first time, unfamiliar with it though we understand ourselves to be. Thinking "otherwise" yields to critique, then, as the "object" in its revealed truth. Out of the "suspension" (*Aufhebung*) of the "object," then, truth.

"Aggregation/Segregation"

The politics of difference is a precarious project because, as Adorno warns us, to "aggregate what is alike means to segregate it from what is different."[24] A dialectic, then, that upholds, with more or less intensity, with a greater or lesser amount of dogmatism, that the distinction between "aggregation" and "segregation" be resisted. What is renounced in the dialectic, so construed, implicitly as well as explicitly, is the art of "becoming first of all questionable to ourselves": it is to approach what is being "aggregated" as entirely self-contained. What is "aggregated" regards itself as completely distinct and utterly removed from that from which it "segregates" itself, all the while representing itself as being outside the dialectic of self and other while its very being/*Being* depends absolutely on the interplay, shall we say, of difference, of marking "self" against other.

As such, setting "aggregation" against "segregation" can produce nothing other than an unsustainable affirmation; unsustainable because while it can only emerge out of the dialectic, it will not admit to the contentious workings ("contradictions," if you will) of the dialectic; "aggregation" as the antidialectical dialectic, if you will. "Aggregation" upholds self against the other, and in doing so it reinforces its difference while denying its dialectical relation to that from which it so desperately seeks a complete sundering—

"aggregation" as the impossible struggle against the (its) relation to "segregation." Affirmation, so delineated, can justify itself only on the grounds that it stands as a (or the) body formed out of the "aggregate" of (its own, sovereign) "correct ideas." So conceived, "aggregation" posits itself as that body set against that other body, the one formed out of "incorrect ideas" ("segregation").

Affirmation, as such, represents the practice of political "aggregation," a practice that measures political strength in terms of numbers and shared attitudes, values, prejudices—simply phrased, ideology. Affirmation is that ideological practice that offers political comfort premised on the fallacious notion that "aggregation" in itself not only marks the achievement of absolute "segregation" from the other but also, in so doing, negates the political force that is the dialectic. "Aggregation" no longer "calls for an ability to discriminate" because to "discriminate" is to, perforce, demand an accounting for and of difference.[25] To "discriminate" is to explain the "why" (the grounds) of its ideology—why its values and attitudes are different from the other's; why its prejudices are justified. "Aggregation," finally, as that ideological mode of being/*Being* in the world that will not admit of its experience as having been "contaminated by existence"; that is, "aggregation" is what allows a constituency to claim for itself an ideological locale outside—or above—the usual tensions that mark political life, such as the conflict between "classes" and, no doubt, the "relationship" of self to other that is race. "Aggregation" as the desire for transcendence; and, as we know, at least from after Nietzsche, there can be no thinking of transcendence that is not girded by an inclining toward ideological superiority—the "will to power," as such, about which Zarathustra gives us every reason to be cautious.

"What Is Different"

An overdetermined "inability to discriminate" not only constitutes an aversion to thinking but also fails to understand the terms of, in Adorno's designation, "what is different." Presenting the relationship between the "qualitative" and the "quantitative" as procedural and hierarchized (the "lesser" one leads to the more significant one—the "quantitative is the means to the qualitative"), Adorno explains that "what is different is the qualitative; a thinking in which we do not think qualitatively is already emasculated and at odds with itself."[26] The "quantitative"—let us imagine it as the assembling of numbers in the cause of building, solidifying, and/or maintaining "aggregation"—is constitutionally deficient, "already emasculated and at odds with itself." To be "emasculated" in this figuring means nothing other than to be incapable of thought; a critical and, quite possibly, terminal intellectual and political condition.

However, if the "quantitative" is indeed "at odds with itself," then it remains—despite itself—dialectically open to the possibility of "transitioning" to the "qualitative." That is to say, the "quantitative" must, for all the reasons delineated, be resisted, but it must also be recognized as containing within itself what Adorno names "critical germs."[27] That is, the "quantitative" is entirely capable of undoing itself; it is, to repeat, within its (political) capacities to "transition" into a practice hospitable (made so by dialectics), all outward appearances (and antagonisms) notwithstanding, to thinking.[28]

On this issue Adorno is declarative. "Thought as such," he writes, "before all particular contents, is an act of negation, of resistance to that which is forced upon it."[29] What is necessary in order to transform the "quantitative" is rather simple. Through "negation" the "quantitative" can be freed from itself; through "negation" it becomes possible for the "quantitative" to "resist" that which it has imposed upon—"forced upon"—itself. No matter the "particularity" of the "contents," or its determination to remain "quantitative" for that matter, by positing thinking as akin to—if not indistinguishable from—negative dialectics, the contradictions within can be released into thinking. "Aggregation," we might argue, cannot exclude everything; it cannot "segregate" itself absolutely, and because "segregation" bears upon "aggregation" (an original contamination, as such), the "particular contents" can never be completely sealed off from the "segregated" object. Within the "very same" there is a "dialectical movement" (that which we named "transition") that "rebels against the system."[30] (That is, there is the possibility for "dialectical movement" within every "very same.") Negative dialectics, then, as that mode of thinking that reveals—shows, in often entirely unexpected ways—what is lost if we admit of (succumb to) the "system's" insularity and impenetrability (or impermeability). No such prophylaxis against what is constitutive of and proximate to, as we have seen, is at all possible.

Let us posit it as determinate negation. It is the specific contradictions between what thought claims (the thought of the "quantitative") and what it actually delivers.

From Foucault to Sublation

In a statement on the refusal of difference, Michel Foucault argues, in his critique of the "empty form of salvation" (an "empty form" to which we must give "thought"), for the other as a necessary engagement in learning care of the self.[31] (That is, this is a Foucauldian statement on the refusal of difference as a politics in and of itself.) According to Foucault, the other is "indispensable for the practice of the self to arrive at the self at which it aims."[32] For Foucault the self is attainable only through that "practice" that compels the self to encounter the other—directly and, we might speculate, repeatedly—as that "passage" or process of coming into *Being* (selfhood, if we allow, if only for a moment) that secures the self for itself. No self, we can say with Hegel whispering in our ear, without that "practice" of selfhood that turns on the other. (The other, then, as instrumental, but instrumental in an entirely dependent and yet noncynical sense. The other on the order offered by Butler in *Undoing Gender,* particularly the chapter "Longing for Recognition.") What Foucault establishes through his argument is that the path to selfhood is achievable only if the self is able—and willing too, no doubt—to exceed itself. The "goal" of selfhood demands exposing the self to the other (which Foucault also describes, without a pejorative inflection, as "object," as we will see in just a moment) in order to stake a claim to the "status of subject defined by the fullness of the self's relationship to the self."[33] Without the other, then, we might suggest, the self runs the risk of forfeiting the possibility of subjectivation (the making of the subject within—and against—extant structures). More than that, without the other, the self is liable to reduce itself to unknowing "object," a status of which the self might be entirely unaware—a sort of fully conscious false consciousness, or abject subjectivity, if you will.

Cryptically phrased, the self as subject is a matter of/for the other. Both Nancian and Foucauldian subjects, as such, refuse an absolute distinction between self and other. In one way or another, selfhood as solely the project of the self, selfhood as inexorably within the grasp and capacity of the self, is shown to be illusory. And not only that: it is, we might say, unachievable. Foucault, in taking up Socrates on the passage "from ignorance to knowledge (*savoir*)," insists—for himself as well as for Socrates—on the indispensability of the other: "This movement cannot take place without another person."[34]

In the Absence of Larger Structural Changes

Watching the final of the Women's World Cup in France in July 2019, I am reminded about the important role the other performs in our psyche—an amorphous, categorical "our," I hasten to add, a politically desirable plurality. Jane, Ezra, Alex, ATrane, and I are watching the game with friends in Minneapolis, rooting for the United States. Not a one of us has any antipathy for the Netherlands, the opposing team. In fact, I've been impressed by the "Oranje's" skill and grit. (Dutch teams wear orange, which explains their all-too-obvious nickname.) What is more, Jane is of Dutch descent (via northwest Iowa), and my beloved Liverpool F.C. includes two standout Dutch players: Virgil van Dijk and Gini Wijnaldum.

However, once Megan Rapinoe scores the opening goal for the U.S. team, I cheer, loudly.

In the sixty-ninth minute, the talented young midfielder Rose Lavelle goes on a mazy run. Fed the ball by fellow midfielder Samantha Mewis in the Dutch half, Lavelle is all balance and poise as she attacks the Dutch. Thrown in for good measure is a Lavelle fake stepover, which serves only to intensify her single-mindedness. Lavelle commands the center of park with her run, forcing the Dutch onto their heels. With the Dutch retreating, Lavelle makes her move at the edge of the eighteen-yard area. Cutting hard to her left, away from her stronger right foot, Lavelle unleashes a sweetly struck shot that whistles by the Oranje's keeper, Sari van Veenendal. With her left foot, no less. Lavelle is naturally right-footed so she was, as they say in football, shooting—and scoring—with her "wrong foot." Lavelle's shot seals the game for the United States.

I cheer. Even more loudly.

Megan Rapinoe, you see, has made her opposition to Trump explicit—explicit to the point of the expletive. Rapinoe, furthermore, has declared that she will not attend any White House ceremony to celebrate a U.S. victory in the World Cup. An embarrassment and a hugely public rebuke to Trump, who loves hogging the camera, no matter if it is appropriate or not, taking credit for feats that are not his.

My appreciation for the "Rapinoe political effect," if you will, is the source of a great deal of my enthusiasm for this World Cup–winning team.

In the absence of larger structural changes, petty justice will do. Hardly petty, I know, this U.S. Women's World Cup victory. I

*am of the Bill Shankly school of football, which lives by the former
Liverpool manager's truth: "Football is not a matter of life or
death," Shankly is reputed to have said, "it's much more important than that." So, as I said, hardly petty but . . . it's the petty
embarrassment that Trump will have to endure that gives me (the
greatest) pleasure. Public rejection, before the world, a politically
motivated rebuke, Rapinoe giving the proverbial finger to Trump.
"Petty justice" is, as I have acknowledged, hardly the correct term,
but any form of public humiliation to which Trump is subjected
provides, in the absence of larger structural changes, a small
taste—appropriately—of what petty justice must feel like.*

*That's the "petty" for which I am settling. In any case, Rapinoe's
so cool—très cool. In addition to her politics, there is her dyed
(pink), spiky hair, her studded black leather jacket, and her accomplished partner (her spouse), Sue Bird. A championship point guard
in women's basketball at the collegiate level, for the University of
Connecticut, and a WNBA championship winner with the Seattle
Storm, Bird is the reserved one in the relationship.*

*At thirty-four years of age, Rapinoe remains a dominant player.
It is a pleasure to root for her, Lavelle, and their teammates. And,
what is more, they play good football. What's not to like?*

*For my birthday, Jane buys me a T-shirt that reads: "Rapinoe
2020."*[35]

To privilege "sublation" is to reject, explicitly, the prospect of continuing to operate at a "base" level. It is to embrace instead the other
philosophico-political possibilities so that it becomes possible to
think "preserving" and "suspending" in the same political thought,
or gesture. (The stubborn persistence of this "base" level as a political modality signals the refusal to rise to the potentiality of *Aufhebung*.) I want Ezra to reject, categorically, any kind of approach that
asks him to put—and/or keep—thinking in abeyance. I want him
to refuse this "base" level so that he can, if not exactly revel in, at
least give himself over—more or less willingly—to the struggle that
is *Aufhebung*.[36]

That is, I want him to negotiate sublation in its transitive sense,
to know what it means to "negate or eliminate (something, such as
an element in a dialectic process) but preserve as a partial element
in a synthesis."[37] That is, to struggle with a (/his) desire to "eliminate" that which presents something on the order of an existential
difficulty—in his case, say, the complications of being mixed-race.

Such a struggle itself constitutes a recognition of the reality of the difficulty that persists. Poorly phrased, it is the struggle that persists as—insists on its address as—the "ontological inheritance" that is Nip's ambiguous relation to whiteness and blackness.

This difficulty reveals itself, in the course of his struggle, "as a partial element," an "element" that Nip will have to decide whether he can or cannot "synthesize" into his *Being*.

In this regard, there is the always-welcome ghost of Countee Cullen, who wonders later in the poem quoted above:

> If merely brute caprice dooms Sisyphus
> To struggle up a never-ending stair.

Indeed, it might be better if Nip were not able to "synthesize," at least not with anything resembling philosophical ease. Let me render sublation, as it relates to Nip, thus (which is to say, crudely and speculatively): sublation is the struggle against that which refuses to be kept down; it is that "element" that will not be silenced. As such, it is that constitutive "element" that will not be submerged (cannot be kept under, as it were, from the prefix "sub"), but neither can it be allowed to rise fully to the surface. What emerges as sublation is therefore that struggle—provisionally located within the self—that must be accommodated, thought, because of the very force it exerts as an "element" of the subject's *aleitha*.

Sublation, then, as the struggle for political judgment, a task for which Ezra, the youngest child of a white midwestern American mother and a black southern African father, might be more predisposed than I want him to be.

Sublation, in this articulation, as that force of thinking that leads to the path already identified as discrimination. In setting out on this path Nip must "abolish" all forms of judgment that derive from and are restricted to that visage that is the body. Nip's thinking, as such, must incline toward, it must "marvel at," in Adorno's sense, the "transcendent": "Where the thought transcends the bonds it tied in resistance—there is its freedom. Freedom follows the subject's urge to express itself."[38] Important and, in fact, life-sustaining as the politics of "resistance" is, one of its more deleterious (because it is so unavoidable) effects, as Adorno warns, is the constitutive circumscription of "thought." Such circumscription, as Adorno reminds us, which stands opposed to "transcendence" because it is dedicated to maintaining those "ties" upon which "resistance" is founded, exacts a heavy price. To wit, "freedom," a "freedom" thwarted because the "subject" concedes its "urge to express" itself.

By "suspending" all a priori decisions about the body, Ezra will instead have to (after having "become first of all questionable to himself") do something very different, and infinitely more demanding. (Something, one imagines, that will, after a lifetime of ongoing difficulty, allow him to struggle—or, more likely, lurch—toward a metaphysical "freedom," which is distinct from "freedom" as a set of material relations.) In every instance, he will have to do the work of judgment. That is, he will have to find grounds (ethical or otherwise) for determining his relation to the white (as well as the black) body. He must learn to distinguish between—and, because of that, produce different responses to—the stereotypically racist white assistant in the upscale store and the courteous, thoughtful white mother who helps us find our way to Circuit Gilles Villeneuve. (Nip might or might not want to factor into his deliberations the fact that the white family favors Hamilton over the German Vettel and the Dutchman Max Verstappen—both white drivers.) In its most reductive instantiation, Nip will have to decide: Is that body good, or not? He will have to make, as it were, a "qualitative" decision. In the course of his lifetime, he will be called upon to make this decision a great many times. The exhausting, life-affirming, sometimes gut-wrenching political demand that is the living of a political life. Such a figuring proposes Cullen's "Sisyphus" as an idealized political actor, forged out of that terrible combination that is an indomitable political reason and an infinite capacity to work within—against— the force that is historical contingency:

> Inscrutable His ways are, and immune
> To catechism by a mind too strewn
> With petty cares to slightly understand
> What awful brain compels His awful hand.

Ratio, after all, "calls for an ability to discriminate."[39] Nip will have to produce, out of his "contaminated existence" (as all ours are), a ratio that can stand up to any and all (self-)scrutiny. A (self-)scrutiny, if we follow Adorno, that makes of Ezra a "discriminating man" who understands that "discrimination alone gets down to the infinitesimal."[40] The devil, as they say, is in the details, or, in Adorno's rendering, it is to be found in the "infinitesimal"—in the granular moments and acts that constitute, mostly without reflection (or thought), everyday life, acts that may very well seem, on the face of it, "inscrutable" or even capricious. Such is the condition of being.

Lest we forget or overlook it, herein lies the political courage of Sisyphus.

The "infinitesimal" matters, as Adorno correctly insists, because the very granularity and ordinariness of the "infinitesimal" so often escapes us, as it takes its place (is made to take its place) beyond the purview of the concept—the concept, broadly understood, as a structure of knowledge, ideas, and truth. That is, the paradigm, the governing philosophico-political rubric, the "superstructure" or the "culture," as Jameson prefers to render it in his "Utopia" essay, within which we live our lives.

The work of "discrimination" can only begin, to borrow from Jameson's delineation of Adorno's "struggle of thought," by "undermin[ing] [in this instance 'abolishing' might be the preferred term] that logic of recurrence [as endured in the figure of the type that is the salesclerk] and of sameness in order to break through to everything sameness excludes."[41] (The work of "discrimination" is understood here as an ethical project.) There can be no doubt that Ezra will find himself subject to, in Nietzsche's terms, the "law of [eternal] recurrence."[42] The "contamination" (of his first F1 race day) Nip experienced in Montreal will very likely prove to be the norm, not the exception. Alas.

However, this is where the "infinitesimal" reveals its political use. Rather than retreating into the lair that is "aggregation," Nip would be better advised to think at the level of the "infinitesimal." That is, he must struggle against the temptation (an explicable but never justifiable political impulse) to overdetermine the politics of all bodies. Reductively phrased, the black body is neither inexorably good nor bad. And so with the white body. Sometimes with greater sophistication, often under the sign of prevarication, Nip will have to operate at the level of the granular. ("Abolition" as such is an absolute prerequisite.) A political rule of thumb: do not trust the body. Think it. Discrimination is all, especially as it pertains to keeping key distinctions in place.

On this score, Claire Colebrook warns about fusing the body, à la the new materialisms, and "thinking," my term, not hers. In an essay titled "Hypo-hyper-hapto-neuro-mysticism," an "awful portmanteau" for which she apologizes, Colebrook argues that "theory is *not theory* (and philosophy is not philosophy) if it is grounded in the tactility of the body."[43] Theory and philosophy have to be, by

Colebrook's account, marked by a "necessarily critical distance . . . , even if that distance is contaminated."[44] The body, we can say, is free to "contaminate" thinking—"theory, philosophy"—through its proximity to thinking, but the "tactility of the body" cannot be permitted to dominate and certainly not overwhelm the practice, the critical apparatus we know as thinking. Here Colebrook sets herself firmly against Karen Barad, who numbers among the new materialists. To render Colebrook's argument in its most base formulation, the "tactility of the body" can support, if necessary, "theory," but the body as such cannot rise to the status of thinking. In the relation between the body and thinking the two are not, no matter the new materialists' urging, equal to thinking (or "philosophy," Heidegger would insist). In the work of thinking, there can be no "delimit[ing] the questions and problems posed"; thinking does not permit of the "potential for disturbance to be lulled in advance."[45] It is, we might say, precisely in the "disturbance" that thinking might germinate or come fully into flower, or both. "Lulling," as such, figures as the anaesthetizing of thinking.

It is through the "disturbance" that the conflict (which depends not only on an imbalance in, say, power but also on the fecund irreconcilability between two opposing intellectual forces), which for Adorno is between the "quantitative" and the "qualitative," comes fully into its own, producing the "need" for thinking. Adorno's "need" for thinking, we can say, turns, before itself, upon Colebrook's "disturbance"—the disturbance that obtains, has been fomented, or threatens to emerge out of nowhere. (That is, as I have argued elsewhere, the event.) Dialectically speaking, the "need" of thinking, the "need" to think, thrives under the sign of "disturbance."

Hence the condition that Adorno enables by implicitly inviting us to think because of the constitutive deficiencies of the "quantitative." That is, to think against the prospect of "emasculation" in order to think thoughts "at odds with themselves." (Or, in Colebrook's terms, to insist, as an absolute nonnegotiable, that the "tactility of the body" is *not theory*. To assert thinking against, in a Heideggerian spirit, what it is not.) To think for the "qualitative" that resides in every "quantitative." To accede to what Adorno offers as the "need for thinking" because the "need is where we think from," the "need is what makes us think."[46] To think is to recognize, to cling to, desperately or willingly, the "need"; and, more often than not, the "need" begins in negation. Or out of the "need" to negate, as when, "(following a certain Heideggerian tradition) thinking is taken to

be a comportment to the world that is without home, solace, identity or body."[47] It is only through the cruel dislocation, through the
power of deracination, when we are "without home, solace, identity
or body," that it becomes possible to embark on the path to thinking. Disposing the self to thinking begins in negation.

Nothing to do then but think. Incessantly. Think from "bud"
to "blossom," think from "fruit" to "plant." Such a rendering is, of
course, consistent with Hegel's unique notion of what we might
name the "logic of development," where the entire history of philosophy is marked by its partiality rather than its lack of veracity.
As history develops, so the "partiality" is recognized and addressed.
The history of philosophy understood, so phrased, as an infinite
dialectic (a history of the dialectic that runs from Hegel to Marx,
from Adorno to Jameson's critique of Adorno), a dialectic relentlessly in search of a truth that stands resolutely against the absolute
(*negative dialektik*) because it understands itself as always subject to
philosophical revision. Philosophy unfolds, even if that sometimes
means folding back into—and as—itself.

This logic is borne out in Hegel's elaboration of his horticultural
analogy. He writes: "These forms are not just distinguished from
one another, they also supplant one another as mutually incompatible. Yet at the same time their fluid nature makes them moments of
an organic unity in which they not only do not conflict, but in which
each is as necessary as the other; and this mutual necessity alone
constitutes the life of the whole."[48]

Therein lies possibility for Ezra in his thinking toward judgment. Nip's ability to distinguish "bud" from "fruit" will, I have
no doubt, be tested, perhaps severely. However, it is in the very
contradictions—that moment when the "fluid nature" of the "organic unity" reveals itself as most troublesome—that the need to
think the "life of the whole" presents itself as most urgent. To coin
a phrase, *reflexiones kategorie*: contradiction as a category of and for
reflection, as a category that transcends contradiction as exclusively
negative. Contradiction, then, as that mode of critique that enables
the particular not to be taken up, willy-nilly, into the universal and
as a consequence to be transformed into something beyond all recognition. Instead, the contradiction makes it possible for the particular to flourish in its particularity—*negative dialektik* as restoring
integrity and sovereignty to the particular, allowing the particular
to, as it were, come into its own. In so doing, it is *negative dialektik*

that makes it possible for the particular to remain itself. Contradiction as a form of philosophical patience and stamina—letting the thing be in its *Being.* Yet one more *Darstellung* of the granular. In the granular we encounter *aleitha.*

Of course, it is not always possible—or, for that matter, politically desirable—to remain (at the level of the) particular. After all, the "movement of contradictions" "produces new contradictions and radically new situations," and this requires our attending to the effects of those "forms" that are in "conflict." This means that the effect of the "conflict" (the "mutually necessary conflict") is that no political struggle is ever settled. Ezra will thus have to negotiate, again and again, between that which is "fluid" and that which appears resolutely solid. As Marx and Engels phrase it in the *Communist Manifesto,* we cannot trust how things seem: "All that is solid melts into air, all that is holy is profaned, and man is at last compelled to face with sober senses his real conditions of life, and his relations with his kind."[49] As such, Ezra will have to decide between that which seems on the verge of being subsumed by what succeeds it (the fear that it will be gone forever, that he has no ballast in the midst of all this flux) and that which seems constant and unshakable (constant, for good or ill).

To decide to live his life in this way will be a significant commitment. It will constitute a crucial moment because to so decide is to know, to anticipate (without fully being able to know), the intense demands that life will make on him. These demands will obtain now. They will continue to obtain, and have (in all likelihood), unbeknownst or barely known to Jane and me, obtained for the entirety of his short life; what life has already demanded of him. He will be expected to, as the moment presents itself, announce himself willing to take apart the "organic unity," to submit to the "profane," to "compel himself to face with sober senses his real conditions of life," and to avail himself of the liberty to rearrange the structure of things in such a way as to make his life livable. The "need to think" will make itself immanent. Nip has to think his life, he has to think for the "organic unity" in which the truth (*aleitha*) he seeks is most sustainable—and he has to do so in the hope that this truth will sustain him. In Montreal, Ithaca, the United States more generally, wherever he finds himself, this will be the condition of his life. This is what will be demanded of him when—it is never "if"—he finds himself confronted by antagonistic modes of *Being,* by those modes of *Being* always at work in the world, modes of being toward *Being* (Trump, his acolytes, the white Canadian store clerk) that constitute an attack on his *Being.*

Nip's entire *Being* would be, under these circumstances, well-advised to remember Hegel, to remember the conflict that he experienced in the course of less than twenty-four hours in a foreign country, but one not so different as to be indistinguishable from the one in which we live.

Nip's *Being* would also do well to remember Heidegger's injunction about us "becoming first of all questionable to ourselves." In this interrogative spirit, Nip will "need to think" how it is that his *Being* questions, and whom his *Being* questions, and on what grounds his *Being* questions. To understand the Heideggerian "questionable," then, as that mode of inquiry that is indelibly marked by and grounded in thinking. To think the question in such a way as to render his *Being* entirely vulnerable to what the thinking pursues, "truth" (*aleitha*), and, as such, to make his *Being*—body, mind, spirit, if you wish—its own first subject of thinking.

This will require Ezra to think the body, then, as the site of thinking, and also, in order to remain faithful to Hegel's injunction, to understand thinking as that mode of *Being* in the world that can produce, for a moment or for an extended duration, a being—a body—capable of love. Or, more, of thoughtful love, of a love—for the self that will not admit of the other—committed to making the body the first articulation of thinking that can sustain (and must sustain) the difficulty of conflict and judgment as well as the pain or joy of decision. That is, his body, and perhaps it is only the body (holding in abeyance, for a moment, the Cartesian mind–body split, and parenthesizing Colebrook's critique), which can hold thinking. Following Derrida, we might say that it requires a Levinasian body to do this work. Quoting Levinas, Derrida writes, "The word *I* means *here I am*, answering for everything and everyone."[50] To understand the body, a body, as utterly responsible, beyond itself, the body extending, provisionally, to include "everything and everyone."

All the while making of his body a question.

5 Haunting

It Takes You Where You Don't Want to Go

As the 2016 presidential campaign unfolded, Ezra became increasingly agitated. He grew ever more anxious. He was worried that Trump would win. In light of this, Ezra's questions about the effects of a Trump victory assumed an ever more pointed tone. Ezra's inquiries had an unsettling effect on the household, especially, as we will see shortly, for me. The unintended effects of Ezra's queries were, as well they should be, beyond Ezra's political imaginary. These were effects over which Ezra had neither control nor command, effects on which he could not hope to impose himself. With rhetoric about the "wall" swirling, given its racist inflection and the threat of deracination it evoked, Ezra asked Jane and me whether we would be able to continue living in our house in Ithaca if Trump won. A startling concern, one with historical reverberations for both Ezra and me, if with distinct resonances.

Nip's anxious, historically grounded, line of questioning was taking me back to a place I thought I had left behind. Even though, as I well know, one never truly leaves anything behind.

Passing

"Will we have to move?" This question that Nip asked was not so much about our ability to stay in our home, although it was that too, as it was for me an inquiry that derived from my experience in apartheid South Africa. It was a question that seemed more obviously applicable to the political locale in which I had been born.

Nip's inquiry turned on the matter of rights. Specifically, because of who we are, a mixed-race family (white mother, black father, mixed-race son) in a predominantly white American college town, it raised the issue of our right to stay in our home. In a word, Ezra wanted to know what rights his mixed-race body, our bodies, black and white, this racially blended family of his, would have in the event of an electoral victory he feared.

Ezra, I should note, is adopted. He became our son when he was eight days old. His biological mother is white, and, as far as can be determined, his biological father is African-American.

With his long, tousled hair (like Jane's) and his rich cream complexion (like mine), Nip looks for all the world (and to all the world) like a perfect blend of Jane and me. In truth, Nip could easily "pass," in two senses.[1] First, because he looks so much like us, Nip could "pass" himself—off—as our biological son. (The problematic, offensive, and trauma-inducing effects of the term "passing" come fully, that is to say, painfully, to life in this application.) Second, and here I hesitate to use the problematic and offensive discourse of miscegenation, but it obtains with a certain usefulness in Nip's case—a usefulness that demands caution, historical awareness, and interrogation, but a usefulness nonetheless—Nip could "pass" as white.

Nip determinedly proclaims himself "black"; "I am African-American," he says to Jane and me. For our part we try, gently, to draw his (unreflective, understandable, but not always sustainable) certainty into question. I wonder about proffering some milder form of the Cynics' advice, *Virtutes discere vitia dediscere est*—Learning virtue is unlearning vice. Nip's racial certainty does not rise to the level of a "vice," but it could do with just a little levity, a little more uncertainty, the smallest dollop of doubt. Learning the complexity of his racial self would, for Ezra, unquestionably constitute something on the order of a political virtue.

Even now, as I write at the tail end of 2020, more than a full election cycle removed from November 2016, Jane and I continue to try, but not too hard, to explain to Nip that he could easily be racially mis-taken. To all "visual" intents and purposes, Nip could be just another white kid. When I see him, from a distance, at public events in Ithaca (basketball games, concerts), walking in the hallways with his Montessori classmates, he strikes me as indistinct from the majority of (the other) white kids. (This is an Ithaca Montessori school, with the concomitant price tag, so most of Nip's classmates are the children of Cornell University and Ithaca College faculty.) Ezra's body seems to me more of a physical—racial—piece with those of the white kids than with those of the (very) few African-American children, the fair sprinkling of kids from all over the Asian diaspora, and the couple of Latino kids. Except to Jane and me, of course, because we are privy to the luculent confidence, the absolute clarity of thought and expression, with which Nip locates his racial self.

At some point, and this intervention (that virtue just touted) will surely be called for in the not-too-distant future, we will have to trouble—complicate, unsettle, through confrontation—Ezra's confidence in his racial self. It might be necessary to propose a more meditative contemplation of how he understands his body. Ezra will have to think carefully, perhaps more carefully than he wants to, about the way(s) in which his body is perceived publicly.

It is in moments that turn on, shall we say, racial misperception (misrecognition to his racial "advantage") that Nip will have to take up the difficulty that is Derrida's "extradition of sovereignty." Ezra will have to decide, when he is in the company of black friends (or, black and white friends, for that matter), what he is going to do when his "recognizably," "unambiguously" black friends find themselves under threat.

Nip is twelve now, almost a teenager, tall, at five foot ten and a half and gaining, a lot taller than his peers, and gangly. He loves to ride his bike and his scooter with his friend, L., at the skateboard park at the south end of Ithaca. Like Nip, L. is mixed-race. Unlike Nip, L. is "identifiably" black.

Lots of young kids, teenagers, and a variety of adults hang out at the skateboard park. A racially diverse crowd, where skateboarders coexist (for the most part happily) with kids on scooters and bikes. For Nip the moment of difficulty will present itself when he will have to decide what he will do if L. is, say, harassed for being black. Such a moment, for parents, seems inevitable. When, never if.

How will Nip enact the "extradition" of his (racial; racially misrecognized) "sovereignty"?

Will he interpose his body between L. and, say, the police or a group of white kids who are giving L. a hard time?

Will such an encounter become a *reflexiones kategorie*?

How will Nip's sense of his racial self—that is, his heretofore self-confident blackness—adjust itself to the "contaminations," nay, the privilege, "of experience"?

This, we might say, is what it means to live a racialized life at the (ontic) level—on the very political ground—of the "infinitesimal."

Will Nip become "questionable to himself"?

Will he understand how thin yet powerful the line is that distinguishes "aggregation" from "segregation"?

How will Nip come to terms with the recognition that "virtually all thoughts," as Adorno says, "cause a negative motion"?[2]

How will a black soon-to-be teenager who is publicly "refused" his blackness think negative dialectics?

In that encounter, in that moment of (racial, political) truth, Nip will have to pay careful attention to how he speaks. He will, in that moment, more than in others, confront the "need for thinking" because he must articulate precisely what it means to "extradite" his "sovereignty." He must speak to what is at stake: the safety of his friend, the integrity of their friendship, the truth of his thinking (*aleitha*). (The essence of his *Being* will depend on what it is he says and how he says it. Nip's truth is what will be in question.) His need for thinking truth must manifest itself in, and because of, that moment.

Nip's language, "words," the "raw material" of his thinking (as Jameson puts it), must take into account that, as Adorno phrases it, "what is vaguely put is poorly thought. Expression compels stringency in what it expresses."[3] His words, every single one of them, must not be "poorly thought." "Expression compels stringency" in order that it might "express" exactly what needs to be said. Neither Nip's words nor his thoughts can venture into "vagueness"; above all else he must eschew all that is "poorly thought." He will have to declare, "Here I am": "Here I am, answering for L. and for myself." He will have to stand alone, enfranchised by a "sovereignty" that he has, for mostly good reasons, long sought to disavow.

Such an encounter, we can assuredly say, constitutes a moment of truth.

"Here I am," he will have to say before a world that "misrecognizes" him, a world that perceives him as self (white) and not as the (black) other he understands himself to be. He will have to be responsible to that perverse privilege that is (racial) misrecognition.

"Here I am," he will have to say, "I speak in defense of the other as an other. I am the other whom you will not countenance as other."

He will have to, at once, embrace and refuse his "misrecognition."

This is how "contradictions move" in a black body that is not perceived as black.

This is how "radically new situations" produce "new situations and new contradictions."

I am asking a great deal of Ezra. There is nothing to do but ask everything of Nip.

A Library for Nip

By way of preparation for this moment, by way of introduction to the peculiar difficulties that racial "misrecognition" raises, Jane and I might be well-advised to read Nella Larsen's novellas, *Quicksand* and *Passing*, to Ezra. But then again, maybe not. Larsen's mixed-race protagonists are all doomed by virtue of their miscegenation, destined for inexorably fatal ends. There is gloom, and certainly doom, social destruction, and death, everywhere in Larsen's novellas. Or maybe we could turn to the poetry of James Weldon Johnson's collection *God's Trombones*, published in 1927, two years before Larsen's novellas. More contemporary choices might include Paul Beatty's novel *The White Boy Shuffle* and Danzy Senna's *Caucasia*. All are possible candidates for this project: the education of a mixed-race child. I have long since done my preparation for this parental task by teaching Larsen, Beatty, and Senna in my classes. Or so I tell myself.

Alternatively, I could tap into the prose and poetry of a generation of coloured South African writers whose work I know well: Richard Rive, James Matthews, Alex La Guma (short story writers, novelists); Jennifer Davids and Arthur Nortje (poets). For these writers, this issue, racial ambiguity and precarity under apartheid, constitutes the defining concern of their work. As Nortje so tragically phrases it, "And I, hybrid, after Mendel / caught between the wire and the wall, / being dogsbody, being me."[4] Nortje, a poet who died too young, a poet for whom I have a great deal of affection, is hardly a fount of optimism. Everywhere in evidence, it would seem, is the specter of the tragic mulatto. The inescapable trope of the tragic mulatto.

Another way will have to be found. It might involve another body or a different literary canon, or not. No matter, a way must be fashioned, a way that allows Nip to be in the world without his life, his future, appearing so gloomily overdetermined, always in struggle— in one way or another—with this deeply racialized language of the body and the violence it does to the mixed-race psyche.

Precisely because I lived agonistically, antagonistically, dialectically (like Nip, I declared myself "black," a self-designation and mode of *Being* I have never relinquished), as a disenfranchised (coloured) body in apartheid South Africa, this racialized discourse, with its gradations of color (which cannot then avoid the logic of a racial hierarchy), goes against every antiracist bone in my body. Rive's "miscegenation," Nortje's "hybridity" and his "dogsbody half-breed," Davids's "mixed-raced," La Guma's ill-fated coloured working-class rebels—all these terms, all these modes of representation, constitute a language that still, today, sits poorly with me. Much as I understand the politics that informs these authors' thinking, it makes me wince. It smacks of overdetermination. It unsettles me, this language, this *Darstellung,* and not only because of political familiarity or lived experience.

It is, after all, a language—the discursive and political force of miscegenation that Nortje, out of poetic necessity, analogizes through the scientific work of the Austrian Augustinian Abbott Gregor Mendel, a language that often evokes the old colonialist trope of mongrelization ("being dogsbody, being me / buffer you still")—in which I have had a long intellectual training.

First in a racially segregated South African university, then in more rarefied U.S. institutions, I acquired this literary-political training in graduate school. It is a body of apartheid-inflected knowledge that I have had to rethink. It is a political and intellectual necessity for which I am eternally grateful. This is the benefit of living in the diaspora. It is a knowledge now supplemented with some three decades of immersion in African-American/American letters and culture. It is a mode of *Being* refined in the course of teaching in the United States over the course of the past twenty-five years. It is a mode of *Being* that is, I would have to say, sometimes tempered, often inspired, and not infrequently marred by the experience of living race in the United States.

I do not need to belabor the facts. We are all familiar, intimately familiar in the case of those who look like me, with those all-too-typical experiences of being a black man, just a black man, not a diasporic black, living in America—living always the condition of being permanently suspect, perpetually vulnerable, often on the edge of conflict. A lot like being disenfranchised under apartheid, and yet not. Not because being black in America has proven, in some ways, more "universal" (apartheid's racial stratifications do not obtain here, at least not in the same way; however they do, they affect me less) and, because of this, I sometimes think it "easier" (it is never easy, of course) to just be recognizable as black. That is, to be "indistinct" from all other black bodies. An impossible desire, as I am well aware. I am made distinct by my accent (decidedly not American), my (primary, enduring) frame of cultural reference (which waxes and wanes, as with the tides), and my "imported" discomfiture with living in a declining hegemon, apart. This is what I have to offer my son. Out of this raw material I must help him forge his way in the world.

6 And So I Turn to James Baldwin

Born into an apartheid society, after more than three decades in the United States, I have experienced a coming to blackness, a blackness that is a distinct, partly diasporic, insistently exilic blackness. Mine is the inhabiting of a blackness increasingly untethered from nation of origin. (Never entirely severed, but with every passing season, the ties that bind are loosened ever more. But at the least expected moments they jerk me back to *that* place. There is always that Nortje phrase that haunts me, "Origins trouble the voyager much.")[1] In this way mine is, I remind myself when I make my offerings to Nip, an experience that is diametrically opposed to that of one of American letters' most prominent black "exiles."

James Baldwin's experience was always, of course, a painful push-and-pull relationship to his saturation in his Americanness, his desire to escape U.S. racism, and his constant to-ing and fro-ing between, metonymically figured, New York and Paris. (His travels in Europe, a remote Swiss village, Istanbul—everywhere his blackness marked him, as did his gayness.) In his essay collections *Nobody Knows My Name* and *No Name in the Street,* Baldwin reveals a process of discovery: the uncovering of a distinct national—and racial—identity. In his essay "Princes and Powers," among other works, Baldwin comes to terms with the fact that he is a black American before he is anything else. He acknowledges that this mode of blackness is distinct from the ways in which other black intellectuals—namely, the Senegalese Cheikh Anta Diop and the Martinican Aimé Césaire—inhabit and articulate their own modes of being black.[2]

Then there is the lesson Baldwin addresses in *No Name in the Street* about relations between diasporized Algerians and the French state. There can be no illusions about the power dynamic between the colonizer and the colonized for Baldwin when he witnesses the French police beat "an old, one-armed Arab peanut vendor senseless."[3] All the while, white French café patrons look on, unconcerned, to Baldwin's horror. Or, even more horrific, they do not take a moment from their drinks to so much as look at—observe, register, acknowledge—let alone act on what it is they should see happening but do not bother to cast a glance toward.

James Baldwin Knows Terror in a Conradian Register: "The terror, the terror"

What we have here, then, is a glimpse of the reasons Baldwin never took completely to life in France, much as he loved his home in Saint-Paul-de-Vence, much as he enjoyed being with friends and lovers in the Provence village on the French Riviera where he spent so many years. Perhaps I now understand my own relief at being able to dispense with, even if just for a moment, the condition that is Nortje's scientifically cast hybridity. Ah, to be able to *be* black. For his part, Ezra might already know this. There is reason to be grateful for that even though I have no idea how it is he has acquired or come into or come to inhabit this mode of *Being.*

The Unexpected Benefits of Miscegenation

As I have just made clear, maybe all too clear, miscegenation is a political trope that features prominently in my psychopolitical and literary inheritance. As such, in its many iterations (always indistinguishable from the ideology of racial purity, a language that obtained under apartheid and continues to have resonance, more so now in Trump's America) it is a language—as I will show—that offers pedagogical political possibilities for Nip. It is a language and a mode of *Being* in the world about which I, clearly and with an odd admixture of reluctance and commitment, have something to teach him.

I have a body that is racially marked in ways similar to his, even if there are distinct differences between the logic of apartheid and the ongoing history of racism in the United States. I have at my disposal a body of knowledge, a literary history on which I can draw, all of which will complicate things for Ezra. Complexity, aided by Baldwin's essays, the poetry of Nortje, and the teaching of the Cynics, might indeed be the best thing my body, my intellectual training, my racialized knowledge and literary inheritance, can offer him.

I must offer Nip this because, as I have tried to suggest, the extant vocabulary—"mulatto," "hybrid," "creole," "mestizo"—is wholly inadequate for thinking diasporic blackness and mixed-race identities in our historical conjuncture.[4] This essay, then, for all its invocation of this older vocabulary, is an attempt to forge another vocabulary altogether, for which the term most ready to hand might be "thinking the self" or the "thinking self." On the face of it, this term can be said to "overcome" race (an advantage, after a fashion) or may be critiqued for eliding race (a political drawback, to be sure). However, neither is the intended outcome. Rather, the "thinking self" simply registers—marks, highlights—what this essay seeks to do. To install thinking as the first, last, and, by extension, default response of the self in its relations to the world. Thinking is that response that will emerge, viscerally, if at all possible (the viscerality of that practice named "thinking"; practicing thinking in order to condition or discipline thinking into becoming the first, "unthinking," if you will, response on any and all occasions), from the self in the self's engagement with the world—with the other, with institutions, within the socius or in solitary contemplation. Thinking, as such, is how the self (Nip) marks itself as in struggle with the extant set of terms— thinking out of, thinking with, thinking in opposition to, "miscegenation," in this moment—so as to not rehabilitate these older terms with their fraught (generously phrased) histories but rather install the "thinking self" as *the* mode of *Being.*

The "thinking self" emerges out of having no name adequate to Nip's condition of *Being,* his *Dasein,* in the world. The lack of a "political self" is a point that Danzy Senna makes toward the end of her novel *Caucasia,* when the characters Cole and her sister Birdie (living incognito as "Jesse Goldman") recognize that there is no name for them. No name, bodies compelled underground, as it were, bodies and psyches facing the prospect of death. Birdie says:

> "Now Papa says I'm not black or white anymore. He's changed his tune completely. He's stuck on this canary thing. It's too much to keep up with."
> She [Cole] laughed through the crying. "I know. Canaries in the coal mine. Choking on all the fumes."[5]

Where there is no name, there has to be thinking for the name so that the "political self" can pronounce itself—"identify" itself, if you insist—as a "thinking self." Thinking proffered here in the sense of *poiesis*. That is, something—a name in this case—that has to be brought into being with and through thoughtfulness. Much like this essay, *Caucasia* addresses bodies in the world, bodies in motion, psyches moving, sometimes in slow motion, sometimes at warp speed. Often like the canaries in search of light and air, air and light, trying to escape the claustrophobia—impending death—that surrounds them (*jouissance* as a deadly "life force"), that threatens to overwhelm them. After all, Cole has been to Brazil and back, and Birdie's mother ("Sheila Goldman") was on the run before taking up refuge in New Hampshire.

Ezra's body and the bodies that surround him speak of their dislocations and relocations. A mother transplanted from the Midwest, a diasporic father who has known deracination, and Nip, himself, taken up—adopted—into a new family when he was barely a week old. His body moved from one place to another; his body now, all shaggy hair and skinny legs, seemingly a blur as he is consumed by his love of basketball, making cuts, calling for the ball, setting screens, dribbling, playing defense—and lowering the hoop in the driveway so he can dunk.

So, if we know anything about bodies in motion, it is this quasi-Newtonian truth: all bodies seek to be at rest. Whether that be for an extended period or a fleeting moment, or, for that matter, whether the body in motion desperately wants to secure regular respite. The body in motion that is also the body that will seek rest (momentary/extensive/regular rest) can safely move (at whatever speed) or rest only if it is able to think itself. The body on the move must think its motion, the body at rest must explicate to itself (let us say, "understand" in the sense of *Ver-stehen*) why it withdraws from motion into rest.

For Our Adopted Son: The Teachings of the Adopted Son

In order to care for our son, to take on the impossible task of preparing him for what lies ahead (and maybe not too far ahead), Jane and I could start with Baldwin's essay "My Dungeon Shook: Letter to My Nephew on the One Hundredth Anniversary of the Emancipation." Ezra, our adopted son, instructed in, initiated (literarily) into, the vagaries, pleasures, and complexities of blackness by another adopted black son. In addressing his nephew, James ("my dear namesake," in Baldwin's tender prose), Baldwin begins with a reminder of how he cared for James's father, David (so named after Baldwin's adoptive father, David's biological father), from infancy to adulthood.[6] Baldwin remarks that through such a long relationship, "you gain a strange perspective on time and human pain and effort."[7]

In this regard, mine is hardly a "strange perspective" on the question of miscegenation. After all, decades of immersion in the works of Rive, Nortje, Davids, and Larsen have given me an insight into the "effort"—the immeasurable human cost of living in the interstices, the political responsibility—it requires to articulate the "human pain" that is innate to the condition of being a "child of Mendel." So that I care for my son, it is incumbent upon me to trace the wending pathways—literary and otherwise—that map this particular form of "human pain."

Part of the reason that Baldwin's "Letter" has endured is simple. Baldwin recognizes that to speak the condition that is "human pain" can never be a straightforward undertaking. Part of the reason that the "Letter" remains salient to this day is Baldwin's ethicopolitical advocacy, for want of a better term. It is no small thing that Baldwin asks of his nephew: James the uncle, James the elder, calls on the Negro to love those who hate him. White Americans, in Baldwin's telling, are in desperate need of Negro love. Only Negro love can save young James Baldwin's white compatriots.

Ohio: "The Land of Poor White People"

Dave Chappelle is in sparkling form in dealing with the opioid epidemic currently sweeping white America:

> Poor white people . . . love heroin. . . .
> This opioid crisis is a crisis. . . . It's as bad as they say. . . .
> You know what it reminds me of, seeing it? It reminds me of us.
> These white folks look exactly like us during the crack epidemic.
> You know it's really crazy to see.
> And all this shit they talk about on the news about how divided the nation is. I don't believe it.
> I feel like nowadays we're getting a real good look at each other.

Because why . . . because I even have insight into how the white community must have felt watching the black community go through the scourge of crack.

A pregnant pause, and then Chappelle delivers the hammer blow:

Because I don't care either.
Hang in there, whites.[8]

Resorting to an avuncular strategy, Baldwin counsels his nephew, "The really terrible thing, old buddy, is that *you* must accept *them*. And I mean that very seriously. You must accept them and accept them with love. For these innocent people have no other hope."[9] Baldwin, true to the Gospel of Matthew (5:44): "But I tell you, love your enemies, bless those who curse you, do good to those who hate you, and pray for those who mistreat you and persecute you." Love in the face of hate. Only love that rises to this level can begin to approximate God's love. In Matthew's Gospel we encounter Jesus-the-Christ at his most Christological: love one another as I have loved you. Baldwin, fully immersed in the teachings bequeathed to him by his stepfather the preacher.[10] Baldwin, evincing the insights he achieved as a teenage preacher (from the ages of fourteen to sixteen) at Fireside Pentecostal Church in Harlem, testifying in the spirit of the apostle Matthew. Baldwin in the company of Martin Luther King, who argues for agape as "an overpowering love which seeks nothing in return"—"when you come to love on this level you begin to love men not because they are likeable, not because they do things that attract us, but because God loves them."[11] To love those who are "unlikeable."

The brutality of Dave Chappelle, "Because I don't care either," stands in the sharpest contradistinction to Baldwin's and King's apostolic imploring, to Baldwin's explaining to his nephew that he needs to love those who cannot love themselves.

The black avuncularity, the revivalist credo of "Love thy enemy," of James Baldwin is dead. Sacrificed on the alter of "poor white people."

"Poor white people": "poor" in spirit, "poor" in worldly riches (plain broke).

Chappelle too is "poor" in spirit, so no surprise that he refuses to pick up Baldwin's mantle. Who will go and tell it on the mountain now? Who will give meaning now to the Gospel of Matthew?

The spirit of Baldwin's Fireside Church has died on the Atlanta stage that Chappelle commands.

Its death was instigated a long time ago, but its certificate of passing is signed in Atlanta in the name of Dave Chappelle. Dave Chappelle: the pathologist of white American death.

The Epistle of St. James promises something very different, a Lord who is "very compassionate and merciful" (Gospel of James 5:11).

Atlanta, where Baldwin wrote of the murders of black children.

In place of James Baldwin's call for "compassion and mercy" is the unmistakable utterance that is racial revenge. This is revenge delivered with a kind of bravado, insouciance, and, yes, indifference to the suffering of white families and communities. A damning on this order, can it be rendered only by the farceur? Is it only the farceur who can render a succinct condemnation masquerading as mock support?

"Hang in there, whites."

The echoes of historic atrocities against the black body rever-berate in the "suspension" that is "hang."

You, "whites," are condemned to destroy yourselves. You might as well be "hanging" yourselves. You are, in truth, "hanging" yourselves.

Opioids: rope, noose, and tree.

Well and truly hanged.

In contradistinction to the Epistle of St. James: "Mercy triumphs over judgment" (Gospel of James 2:12). Was James Baldwin ever properly named, anointed with the spirit of his apostolic name-sake? Baldwin should properly be known to us as "James," "Biblical James," "James of the Bible." Of the New Testament, birthed to a single black mother, educated and trained on the streets of Harlem, rebelling against his stepfather the preacher whom the stepson out-shone as a man who could preach God's Word.

Chappelle's message to whites is clear. In this crisis, they are on their own. Just like blacks were, remember, when crack ravaged the black community?

When crack hit and black communities were torn asunder, white America pathologized its black compatriots, urging—no, damning—blacks to draw on personal reserves, to access structural resources that were nowhere to be found because white America denied them to black America.

"Just say 'No,'" white America intoned in the voice of a superior (patrician) New England matron, bedecked in upmarket pearls, married to power, perched securely in stately quarters at 1600 Pennsylvania Avenue.

The state, as always, abandoned black America, had long since abandoned black America. Come to think of it, it could not have abandoned black America because it never, ever embraced its black populace.

In telling black America to say no, the state was, once more, doing what it does best in relation to black America. Withholding desperately needed resources, saying no to ravaged communities. The effects of black disenfranchisement writ large, for all to see.

Black America has long lived a life of abject negation, of "quiet desperation," to borrow a line from Billy Joel, who borrowed it from Henry David Thoreau. Only black America has experienced worse. Much worse.

So do not pretend surprise, white America, do not dare to express outrage and condemnation. Stand and face the harshness of Chappelle's metonymic "judgment." Seek to know its origins, try to understand its vituperation as emanating from history. The history in which white America exercises power.

Black America has learned at least this much from history: what goes around (crack, devastated black families, destroyed black communities) comes around (opioids, devastated white families, destroyed white communities).

Langston Hughes famously says that blacks "laugh to keep from crying."

Now, now, you see, its black America that, for once, is laughing; just laughing, not crying.

Could there be a better time for every crack-addicted "poor" white to channel their inner Barbara Bush? Surely, don't you think crackheads of, crackheads for, the new millennium need a little help? From the state.

Let's revisit that advice: "Just say 'No.' What's so hard about that?"

The Epistle of St. James is not without its harder, sharper, edges. In the spirit of those cutting edges, the question must be asked: "Who are you to judge another?" (Gospel of James 4:12).

"Remember when y'all said that to us?"

Now white America says, in solemn and somber tones, "These people are sick, they're not criminals."

How come these crackheads are not "criminals"? Black America was. What's the difference between white America's addictions and black America's?

Simple, really: black drug users were "criminals," and, as such, black America was criminalized. White America gets to have an "epidemic"—and, as we know, being laid low by an epidemic is not a criminal offense.

All those white opioid addicts, in their unkemptness, their depravity, their aptitude for petty theft ("Gotta feed the habit," Chappelle would say) and violence, are immunized by the state against the charge so casually, ruthlessly, mercilessly, brought against black America. White America is suffering from an illness. Black America was committing a criminal act.

Black America urges you, opioid junkies, "Just say 'No.'"

Try that as a drug addiction treatment plan.

The deep, entrenched racism of American political logic always reveals what is obvious. That it is never the chemical dependency itself. It is always the race of the person who is dependent that determines who is a criminal and who is "sick."

"Who are you to judge another?"

This, Chappelle implies, is no time to pretend white "innocence."

Instead, the suggestion is post-Conradian in its disposition. In place of "the horror, the horror" is unfeeling condemnation. Blacks have decided, Chappelle informs white America, "I don't care either." "We don't care either."

Therein the pronouncement of its own brand of horror: utter indifference to the plight of the white other.

The farceur, Chappelle above all others, is going to stand by and watch whites die. And laugh while doing so.

The bitter edge of a sense of historical justice. Hear this, white America, hear this clearly: this your time for suffering.

> *Welcome to the experience.*
>
> *Baldwin, as is often the case, may be spectrally present, haunting America, an apparition that Chappelle cannot dispel, but the brutal, unapologetic judgment of the farceur is what happens when "we get a good look at each other."*
>
> *Now that we've looked at each other, it is time once more to "aggregate" and "segregate."*
>
> *"Segregation today, segregation tomorrow . . ." Segregate the sick from the criminals.*
>
> *America is a divided country, once more. As always.*

On the face of it, there is no Christian argument that can counter Baldwin's appeal, his clarion call for a Christlike sacrificial love. What Baldwin, that teenage preacher possessed of a rare Pentecostal fire, advises is consistent with the most fundamental tenet of Christianity. He is simply following biblical injunction. Specifically, Baldwin shows himself true to the teachings of the Gospel of Mark (12:31), "Love your neighbor as yourself," and, even more powerfully, he recalls the Gospel of John (13:34) in its magnificent grace: "A new commandment I give you: Love one another. As I have loved you, so you must also love one another." And, of course, there is the Epistle of his namesake: "You shall love your neighbor as yourself" (Gospel of James 2:8).

> *The joke about saving whites from themselves, from their own child-inflicted gun violence, that was—or maybe it wasn't—just a setup for that most damning, racially divisive of punch lines: "I don't care either."*
>
> *Dave Chappelle evokes James Baldwin—"Fuck yeah, we should do it. . . . It is incumbent upon us to save our country."*
>
> *However, in "expletivizing" into our moment, Chappelle rejects Baldwin, with a ruthless finality.*
>
> *The farceur is, if not quite the incarnation of "the fire next time," then assuredly an oracular blowtorch. The farceur cuts fiercely through the history of white hypocrisy. The farceur weaponizes the pathologization of black pain; the farceur is the harsh flame that eviscerates white moralizing. The farceur turns the tables on those who judged so easily, those who dispensed with context, those who had no time for historical understanding (structural abandonment of all kinds, from an inadequate edu-*

cation system to decrepit housing to a lack of medical resources), those whose dismissal coalesced in cheap sermonizing.

"Just say 'No.'"

Now that it is your turn, white America, let's see you try a spoonful of your own bitter medicine.

Let's cut the crap, shall we? Why don't you try just saying no? Come on, try it, won't you? See if it works for you.

The farceur would be recognizable to Baldwin only as a cynical Old Testament prophet of yore. Cynical, with a decidedly acrid edge. In this guise the farceur represents an anathema to Baldwin, who inclined toward the promise of the New Testament. Jesus-the-Christ, as we know, refuted the notion of "an eye for an eye" (Gospel of Matthew 5:38–42), but his very negation revealed, inter alia, that revenge on this order was well known to him as a form of justice.

"An eye for an eye," in Chappelle's logic, translates as "an epidemic for an epidemic." History as equal-opportunity, indiscriminate actor—in the service of Big Pharma, but, no matter, savage in the violence it exacts upon addicted bodies, psyches, and souls.

In our moment we can understand the opioid epidemic as "petty justice" of the most excruciating order.

Chappelle's farceur will have no truck with tolerance, no sympathy for the other. And, because of that, the farceur knows exactly how to say no, as dogmatic negation, in the most acerbic way.

However, still the farceur begins with or in a Baldwinian tone. And in so doing, he recalls the cadences, imprecations, and sense of unbreakable belonging to a racially unjust nation.

"No matter what they say or how they make you feel, remember, this [pause] is [pause] your [pause] country [pause] too . . ."

Can we say, in the spirit of Baldwin, that there is always an inkling of "mercy triumphing over judgment"?

The Eleventh Commandment

The Gospels of Mark and Matthew, the Epistle of St. James, read in conjunction with Baldwin, individually and collectively, have a singular political force. Salient among these writings, however, is the verse from the Gospel of John (13:34): "A new commandment I give you: Love one another. As I have loved you." John writes, for us, the eleventh commandment. This commandment, the one that is unwritten and as such does not have the status of "commandment," is nothing less than the *only* commandment. It is the commandment, the only one, that does not require Mosaic inscription. It stands by itself, above all the others, as, quite simply, *the* commandment.

"Love one another. As I have loved you" is the commandment that is not a commandment but should be the only commandment. It is the commandment in which Jesus-the-Christ's radical call for unconditional love is clearly audible. "Love one another. As I have loved you." The eleventh commandment is that love which surpasses all human understanding. The eleventh commandment should be apprehended as a mode of *Being* in the world that inclines toward grace—and grace, as we have established, is nothing less than the incomprehensibility of love. Grace: love beyond love. As such, because only God can dispense grace (granting grace, agape, is beyond the capacity of human beings), the eleventh commandment brings us as close as we can possibly be to God. God alone knows love beyond love because unlike, say, Abraham, God sacrificed his Son in our name. (God spared Abraham's son, Isaac, once Abraham proved his absolute fidelity to God by being willing to sacrifice Isaac. In his fidelity to God, Abraham was not only willing to sacrifice Isaac, but he also showed himself prepared to put God above his wife, his family, and his community. Abraham apart, this is an act of fidelity that none of us could equal.[12] That is why God alone is capable of grace.)

"Love one another. As I have loved you." The eleventh commandment not only encompasses but also eclipses all the other commandments. More trenchantly phrased, this unwritten commandment is the one that superannuates all the others. "Love one another. As I have loved you." It can include, with philosophical ease, the commandments to love and honor; it can accommodate all the Mosaic proscriptions—not to kill, not to covet . . .

"Love one another. As I have loved you."

The Eleventh Commandment: How Could It Possibly Apply to African-Americans?

However, surely not. Surely Baldwin is not enjoining African-Americans to aspire to love on the order of grace. Surely that is not what can be asked of African-Americans. Is this not too much to ask, even by God's standards of grace? No, this is by far too much to ask of those who have been subjected to a history of violent deracination, exploitation of all kinds, and ongoing brutality and disenfranchisement. How are the black body and psyche supposed to forgive those who raped and pillaged? How is the black collective memory to forget those who denigrated and humiliated, those who continue to impose their authority on the black body with unjust force? How much can be asked for in the name of love? Has Baldwin forced us to the limits of love?

> *The terror of love. The terror of what Baldwin asks of black love. Is this what Kojève prepares us for when he insists on the necessity of "living in terms of terror"? Are Kojève's the "terms" on which "terror" overwhelms sovereignty, leaving the self rudely exposed to Baldwinian love?*

Upon reflection, Baldwin's call for love may be an object lesson in why God should have a monopoly on grace. After all, how much can one people forgive? Not how much *should* an oppressed people forgive, but *why* should they respond with love to those who have a history of violence toward them? No matter the conundrum that Baldwin poses, no matter his positing of (a) love that extends far beyond any notion of (historic) justice, he has hit upon what is crucial and, indeed, constitutes *the* element—the elemental, that which is foundational—in Christianity. It is a faith that inclines always in the direction of grace—an understanding of grace that includes clemency, pardon, mercy, forgiveness, and reintegration into the community but cannot be contained within any of these acts individually or even collectively.

> *Some form of relation to the other, limning the bitterness of the farceur, is a mode of* Being *that Chappelle can neither escape nor fail to address.*
> *Some form of relation to the other is what Chappelle struggles toward, if only through a series of halting, ungainly, reluctant lurches.*
> *Ohio: the land of poor white people, poor white people subjected to philosophical contemplation by the farceur son of a Kenyon College professor.*
> *The black farceur, son of a college professor, who dropped out of public life, gave up fifty million dollars, and fled to Durban, South Africa, only to return to live in this "land of poor white people."*
> *Historical needs must? What, who, haunts Dave Chappelle? Is it his search for love of the Baldwinian variety?*

In his essay "Christianity and the Survival of Creation," writer, Kentucky farmer, and lifelong environmental activist Wendell Berry offers a potential explanation for why it is impossible for Chappelle to free himself from the specter of Baldwinian Christianity. Indeed, why it is impossible for any American to free her- or himself from the ethos of Christianity. Berry writes of this inheritance: "There are an enormous number of people—and I am one of them—whose native religion, for better or worse, is Christianity. We were born to it; we began to learn about it before we became conscious; it is, whatever we think of it, an intimate belonging of our being; it informs our consciousness, our language, and our dreams."[13] Dave Chappelle, the blunt-smoking Muslim convert, the convert who probably downs a forty now and then, who is married to a Christian woman of Filipino descent, can no more distance himself from the Christian inheritance that Berry delineates than can James Baldwin, the Christian who struggles with the faith of his father, David. This faith, Christianity, that Baldwin has, in one way or another, made his own. This faith, to phrase the matter awkwardly, has a *Being* that makes Baldwin its own.

> About Chappelle we can say that he has not yet fully understood or come to terms with his philosophico-religious inheritance as an American. Until he does, Chappelle can only speculate as to what haunts him, what informs, shapes, and indelibly marks the "language" that is "intimate to his being."
>
> About Baldwin, however, we can say this, and we can pronounce it with certainty: James Baldwin is explicit about the struggle involved in what it means to "love one another. As I have loved you." Baldwin has, for "better or worse," embraced his "native religion."
>
> Wendell Berry, a thinker who acknowledges his debt to Buddhism, came to understand what James Baldwin always knew. What James Baldwin always knew as his inescapable, for good and ill, birthright.
>
> It is for this reason that Baldwin casts such a long shadow over Chappelle. After all, what is the decision to live in the "land of poor white people," "poor white people" afflicted by the opioid epidemic, if not an inclining in the direction of the struggle James Baldwin inherited from his father, David Baldwin? A struggle bequeathed to his nephew James Baldwin, the struggle now taken up in a Chappellian register unfamiliar to "our" James Baldwin, but a struggle true to its Christological, Baldwinian core.

What does it take to live among those who hate you, Dave?
How does one live in the midst of "poor white people's" hate,
Mr. Chappelle?
    The very "language" you have to hand, the only "language"
you can command, that "informs your consciousness," comes from
what is at once inside you and comes to you from outside you.
"For better and worse."

Baldwinian love—can we rise to it? Can we arise, like the Son, in it? How much of Jesus-the-Christ resides or is hidden within us? That is the acid test of Christianity to which Baldwin subjects his nephew. Such is Baldwinian love. Fairly or no. Baldwin has made his wager with humanity, beginning with the Negro (his designation) and America. And it is a stark proposition that he presents to us: we love or we perish. In its absoluteness, Baldwin's love is the spirit of Christianity distilled to its core: "Love one another. As I have loved you."

As St. James would understand it, love is the work of faith. That is why the road that is the Way of St. James is long—as the pilgrims who undertake El Camino de Santiago, or, in its native Galician, O Camiño de Santiago, well know. As Jesus-the-Christ would render it, love is the only work that is of consequence. "As I have loved you." So, in the terms of this terrible love, you must love. This commandment James Baldwin understood, all too well. That is why, diasporized to Europe (France, Turkey), he never sought to free himself, fully, completely, of either America or Christianity. That is why James Baldwin had no option but to always take the long way home. The long way home always runs through the way of (St.) James—or "Santiago," the transcription of "St. James" into Spanish.

Baldwin, Philosopher of Love

We should be clear. James Baldwin is no patsy for Christianity. In "Down at the Cross: Letter from a Region in My Mind," the second essay in *The Fire Next Time*, Baldwin offers a stinging critique of Christianity while simultaneously making a strong circumstantial case for the historical necessity of God:

> It is not too much to say that whoever wishes to become a
> truly moral human being (and let us not ask whether or not
> this is possible; I think we must *believe* that it is possible) must

first divorce himself from all the prohibitions, crimes, and hypocrisies of the Christian church. If the concept of God has any validity or any use, it can only be to make us larger, freer, and more loving. If God cannot do this, then it is time we got rid of Him.[14]

Baldwin establishes a hierarchy of Being: "larger, freer, and more loving." There can be no raison d'être—for God, for believing in God, no reason at all for Being—if our Being does not, as Baldwin says, enable us to expand our sense of the world, our sense of responsibility toward ourselves, and, perhaps more important, if it does not increase our responsibility toward others. As Martin Luther King puts it: "When Jesus said 'Love your enemy,' he was not unmindful of its stringent qualities. . . . Our responsibility as Christians is to discover the meaning of this command and seek passionately to live it out in our daily lives."[15] There can be no raison d'être if it does not liberate us from ourselves, if it does not make "stringent" demands on us, if it does not require us to think Christianity ("to discover the meaning of this command"), if it does not seek to "alienate" us from our past into a different mode of "daily living," if it does not free us from our sense of who it is we understand ourselves to be into a "passion" of righteous living. We can be free only if we liberate ourselves from ourselves, if we take up the heavy burden that is Jesus-the-Christ's cross. If we are willing, that is, to no longer be held captive by who it is we are in the world, by how it is we are in the world. Vladimir Jankélévitch renders this responsibility deterministically, almost tautologically: "Good is something that everyone can do on the condition of willing it. . . . In order to will it, it suffices to will."[16] Jankélévitch shifts responsibility to us, entirely—all we need do is "will it." It is possible to be in the world in a way other than how we are in the world now. In this way, enacting the will becomes not merely an "attitude" or even a decision. Instead, enacting the will marks a "break" in temporality—enacting the will as event.

   With Jankélévitch's tautology of the will in mind, let us extend the thinking of the Cynics. We must be willing—we must "will it"—to unlearn both our virtue and our vice. Or, we must be open to thinking our virtue as potential vice. Whether we can identify a virtue in our vice, well, that is an entirely different matter.

   It is always, as we well know, a matter for philosophy. And so we turn to Gilles Deleuze and Félix Guattari's What Is Philosophy?, in which the authors argue that philosophy can be truly comprehended only in the latter stages of life, reminding us how this applies to Kant's *Critique of Judgment*. According to Deleuze and Guattari, *Critique of Judgment* is "an unrestrained work of old age," a work in which "all the mind's faculties overcome their limits, the very limits that Kant had so carefully laid down in the works of his prime."[17] For Deleuze and Guattari, the accomplishment of *Critique of Judgment* is that it liberates Kant. He is free, achieving what they label "sovereign freedom" (that moment "in which all the parts of the machine come together") to ignore, disregard, and overwrite "all the limits" that he had previously imposed on himself.[18] Freedom as the negation of "limits," as the philosopher wandering, unsupervised, into the forbidden realm where the logic of "limits" does not obtain.

It would certainly not be accurate to claim that Baldwin's tripartite structure of *Dasein* coincides with Deleuze and Guattari's concept. However, because "sovereignty" cannot be conceived without a measure of (self-)mastery and the possibility of a self that understands the "limits" and possibilities of "freedom," Baldwin's demands for what God and humans must do (or "will") makes of all subjects—terrestrial and otherwise—fellow travelers in search of a "sovereign freedom."[19] A freedom that knows itself as free, a freedom that is free to liberate itself from, à la Kant, all its self-imposed "limits." Baldwin's structure of *Dasein* as the "sovereign" imperative to be free in the world and to love out of love and toward freedom; toward and because of the love of freedom.

In explicating for us the work of God, then, Baldwin is also—in the spirit of Deleuze and Guattari—revealing to us the work of philosophy. Indeed, read, or rendered, through Deleuze and Guattari, among the other paths we might take, we find ourselves confronting Baldwin's philosophy. In delineating his structure of *Dasein,* we can see how Baldwin shades into Deleuze and Guattari—philosophy becomes possible only at that moment when we no longer lend any credence to the notion of "limits."

To say nothing, of course, of how Baldwin's thinking aligns with that of King, Derrida, and Jankélévitch; again, inter alia. Philosophy, so conceived, is always an excessive force—if thinking has any standing in philosophy, it is only insofar as it begins with the intention of destroying, with all the requisite intellectual violence, the limit. Thinking (for) the limit in order to dutifully overcome (triumph over) and surpass the limit; that is, philosophy as the straining against what-is. Derrida straining in the direction of that which is-not:

> What I dream of, what I try to think as the "purity" of a forgive-
> ness worthy of its name, would be a forgiveness without power:
> *unconditional but without sovereignty.* The most difficult task, at
> once necessary and apparently impossible, would be to dissoci-
> ate *unconditionality and sovereignty.* Will that be one day?[20]

That which is-not: "pure forgiveness," a forgiveness "unconditional but without sovereignty." That is, a forgiveness that neither
makes demands—it begins from the condition of not stipulating
conditions—nor has the "power" to do so. To be "without sovereignty" is to have no authority over the other and yet to extend the
self unconditionally in the direction of the other. Such a forgiveness
is, for Derrida, both a matter of urgency ("necessary") and unattain-
able ("apparently impossible"). It may all, then, be understood as a
temporal matter. That day when "unconditionality and sovereignty"
can be "disassociated." Derrida can apprehend such a moment only
interrogatively: "Will that be one day?" The arrival of such a day
seems to lie beyond Derrida's purview. The time is out of joint.
  The time is out of joint for both Derrida and Baldwin. In addressing his nephew and marking the prematurity of the celebration of
one hundred years of emancipation, Baldwin presents a new reality:
"sovereign freedom" is that mode of *Dasein* (being in America) that
will take a lifetime (of experience) to learn.

Sein ist Liebe

However, at the very least, Baldwin, in the spirit of St. James, has
given us an idea of God's work. God's work is designed to help us
enlarge ourselves. It is a project that demands that we enlarge our
sense of the world, and doing God's work opens us to that force
of *Dasein* (*Being* in the world) that makes us free from and of ourselves. In this way Baldwin brings to mind Jankélévitch's concept of
"megalopsychia": greatness of soul, exceptional in that it is "solitary
in its magnanimity."[21] It is impossible to conceive of a "greatness of
soul" without imagining as part of that process the expansion of self.
As well as, of course, an opening of the self to the world as it is in
order to make of the world what it is not-yet. (As such, Baldwin's
thinking toward/for God contrasts sharply with Heidegger's famous
pronouncement on "god." Baldwin holds out the possibility of salvation without the conditional upon which Heidegger's plea rests.
Heidegger, speaking out of his well-known technophobia, is almost

apocalyptic—"Only a god can save us now." This phrase, no matter that it is evoked parenthetically here, will be returned to shortly.)

In Deleuze and Guattari's thinking of philosophy, a question emerges for Baldwin. How are blacks to achieve a "sovereign freedom"? How is a historically oppressed community, one that has never known "sovereignty" in any form, one for which "freedom" has often seemed a cruel promise, to be encouraged to struggle for "sovereign freedom"? As King so memorably phrases it in his "I Have a Dream" address, "America has defaulted on [its] promissory note insofar as her citizens of color are concerned."[22] Or is it only through love, through the difficult, demanding, inequitable practice of "loving," that a "sovereign freedom" can be secured? (Is it only love that is beyond the capacity of the "sovereign" self? Is it only, in the spirit of Hegel and Lacan, the other who can give the self love? Is it only the other who can instruct the self into love?) Or might it be that love liquidates "sovereign freedom" because it is so much more than (simply) "sovereign freedom"? Is it in the "concept" and "utility" that is God, in imagining what God can do and speculating as to what God can make us do, that the distinction between "sovereign freedom" and Baldwin's structure of *Dasein/Being* in the world can be found?

After all, Baldwin's "moral" arc ascends toward love. (Baldwin reaches upward, reaches higher, if you wish, in the direction of love.) The expansion of self and the freedom of (and from) self forms the base of this pyramid. At the apex of Baldwin's structure is the increased capacity for love: for "loving." God must teach us to love, or there can be no earthly use for God. In E. M. Forster's colonialist terms, "God si love." Regardless of Forster's inverted *i* and *s*, the intent—as read through Baldwin—is unambiguous: "God is love." "Love is God." "God = Love." (Each in her and his own way, Forster's Adela Quested and Dr. Aziz would surely concur: it is "loving" to which Forster's protagonists in *A Passage to India* incline; it is love, lost, Dr. Aziz's dead wife or no, for which they search.) James Baldwin has put God on notice. *Sein ist Liebe.* Aspiring toward love in this way is "megalopsychia"—a condition that, if shared, promises to make all those who reach for greatness of soul to become less "solitary" in their quest.

In this letter to his nephew, what we have is a (little) addendum to God. Baldwin is addressing God directly, assigning to God the work of God. In Baldwin's thinking, God's work is to facilitate human self-expansion and self-liberation. In concert with an equal amount of human effort, God must open within humans the possibility of approaching, of approximating, grace. Following this, God must then show us humans how to love more: to love beyond our all-too-confined "limits." God's existence—or, more trenchantly phrased, God's utility—in our world is contingent on "His" ability to achieve this. Our ability to achieve "His" ends rests, in the first and last instance, with God.

The intent of this is to always live inclined toward the impossible. That is, the emulation of that love which is willing to sacrifice its own flesh and blood, no matter the Son's innocence. As such, love is that mode of *Dasein* that imposes, from the very first moment, from birth, as it were, an unjust burden on those who would aspire to (Baldwinian) love.

Once more, succinctly rendered, *Sein ist Liebe.*

Dramatized so magnificently by Barack Obama, accessing, among other spirits, James Baldwin, as the president broke into the opening strains of "Amazing Grace" during his eulogy for the Reverend Clementa Pinckney at the Emanuel AME Church in Charleston, South Carolina. (This is the hymn that Baldwin sang, from the grave, as it were, during his funeral at the Cathedral of St. John the Divine in 1987. The funeral service featured a recording of Baldwin singing "Amazing Grace.") Pinckney was one of nine African-Americans shot by the then twenty-one-year-old Dylann Roof, a white supremacist who had sat in the company of these self-same people for an hour. Sat with them, had been invited to sit with them as the Bible instructs Christians to welcome the stranger, during their Bible study. Sat with them and listened to their meditations on scripture. The families of the victims forgave Roof, prompting Obama—after borrowing the writer Marilyn Robinson's phrase "reservoir of goodness"—to find his inner gospel voice: "Amazing Grace, how sweet the sound . . ." This act by the grieving families constitutes what Jankélévitch names "true forgiveness," a "*gracious gift* from the offended to the offender."[23] In Obama's taking up of this spirit into song, we see "amazing grace" at work. This is the "magnanimity of the many," the highest peak that "megalopsychia" can reach. At the Emanuel AME Church in Charleston, we encounter *Lumens Christi*: this is how the light of Christ shines on the faithful.

A moment of sheer terror. However, not terror in the sense of what might be done to us, what injury the self might have to endure.

Although, in truth, that too. But that terror does not rise to the level of this terror. No, this is terror of an entirely different order. This is that terror that resides deep within our Being. This is (the) terror that terrorizes the self because it is capable of knowing the Being of the self.

Heidegger knows this terror: "If, in spite of our neediness, the oppressiveness of our Dasein still remains absent today and the mystery still lacking, then we must principally concern ourselves with preparing for man the very basis and dimension upon which and within which something like the mystery of his Dasein could once again be encountered. . . . We must first call for someone capable of instilling terror into our Dasein again."[24] *A daunting prospect: to plunge deep into our* Dasein, *to confront the terror of knowing our* Being. *In so doing, we might come to know what it is that knowing our* Being *makes us capable of.*

Obama, in remarking on the sheer incomprehensibility of the offended forgiving, without condition, the offender, did not linger on this terror.

Heidegger, for his part, does not merely pause and consider this terror, he calls out to it. Heidegger urges all of us to reach out to that "someone" *(and in so doing to dispense with* "idols") "capable of instilling terror into our Dasein again."[25] *It might very well be that it is not the* "terror" *that we fear, but rather that we had this* "terror" *within our grasp, within our* Being, *and we lost it.*

To live in "terror," *as Heidegger insists we must, is to live in and with the full array of possibility that is our* Dasein. *To live in and toward, to live for,* Being.

The families of Dylann Roof's victims, in their forgiveness, provide a glimpse—but only for a moment—into what the "terror" *that is our* Being *makes possible for us, what* "terror" *of that magnitude opens us up to.*

To be sure, "the terror, the terror," *is not* "the horror, the horror," *but neither is it entirely discontinuous with the Conradian specter.*

To look into Being *and to know* Being *is not to reveal unimaginable vistas (though there are certainly elements of that) as much as it is to reveal a self laden with portent and prospect. Anwesen, that is Heidegger's term for the bringing forth of that in which we live in terror.*

Heidegger's "terror" *is not without the possibility of a terrible good.*

*Obama was able to circumnavigate it only through—and in—
song: "Amazing Grace." Baldwin, one suspects, knows this "terror"
up close. He has his own name for it, "love," but he knows it just
the same. Baldwin is afraid, terrified, of it; he cannot live without
seeking, again, going in search of He who "instills terror." Baldwin
wants a second bite of the cherry that is Heidegger's "terror." Baldwin wants to go "there," "again."*

*A foreboding prospect for the (black) self already living with/in
the terror of Trump. To have to live now with Heidegger's trumping
of Trump: Dasein poses a more signal challenge to the (black) self
because it derives from within the very Being of the being itself.*

*The work of philosophy, Heidegger argues in his lectures on
metaphysics, is to "terrorize" Dasein in-to life.*

*(Black) Being, the terrifying and, it must be said, necessary
determination to live a life "instilled" with "terror."*

*No, to live for, in the hope of, "terror," because terror is vital to
Dasein, constitutive of Being.*

*To live in "terror," as more important than, as Baldwin, King,
Foucault, Levinas, and Jankélévitch would argue, to establish a
relation to the other, because to live in "terror" is to live toward
Dasein—the being-there of Being.*

The congregation rose at hearing the president's first halting notes, waiting a moment before joining Obama as he transitioned from the oratorical, an evidently deeply felt eulogy, to a singing voice that offered itself as a balm, Obama seeking to soothe the congregation (and the nation's) bloodied, wounded soul. And perhaps breaking into heartfelt song served as a balm for Obama himself, considering—as he surely had—on the occasion of death and forgiveness, the path that had led him to the presidency. A path almost as old as this nation, a path that wended its way through slavery, the failed promise of Emancipation, Jim Crow legislation (the first default on the "promissory note"), the Civil Rights struggle (the second default, if you will, on that self-same "promissory note"), and the racist dog whistles of Reagan and both George H. W. and George W. Bush.

In the hymnal of black America, there was no other choice for Obama. "Amazing Grace" is that hymn that bears within it the promise of redemption, of God reaching out to offer a helping hand. Of God, in those dark moments when humans are deep in pain, providing succor to these, deemed by some to be the "children of Ham":

Amazing Grace! How sweet the sound
That saved a wretch like me!
I once was lost, but now am found
Was blind, but now I see.

'Twas Grace that taught my heart to fear,
And Grace my fears relieved.
How precious did that Grace appear
The hour I first believed.

Through many dangers, toils, and snares
I have already come.
'Tis Grace hath brought me safe thus far
And Grace will lead me home.

Above all, "Amazing Grace" provides a glimpse of what God's grace might look like—grace will "relieve" human "fears." Grace is a place called "Respite," a place where the faithful can, finally, dwell in peace: "Grace will lead me home." In the African-American experience, the possibility—however far-off the prospect, or precisely because it is such a far-off prospect—of such an "amazing" act of "grace" could be said to assume an otherworldly aspect; utopian, at worst.

In the moment of an unfathomable act of violence, white rage, hatred, and the multiple black deaths that emanate from it, solace can be derived from that rarest of phenomena: grace made immanent. The Word (of) grace, melodic, moving, humbling, spiritual, spiritually uplifting, a tonic for the historic black soul and its oft-pummeled psyche. Nevertheless, Trump's capacity to stoke the fires of a race war (and the eager response that his supporters, and they are not few, evince) makes critical the difficulty of black forbearance: How deep is the "reservoir of goodness"? How often can black Americans draw on it without replenishment? Surely this is not an infinite "reservoir"? Can grace be granted, can another mode of life be made possible, before the reservoir of black goodness runs dry?

We stand on the precipice. Only if we can find someone—"idol," or Heidegger, maybe?—or something "capable of instilling terror into our Dasein again" will we be able to draw back. But for now, we stand on the brink. And few among us are brave enough to look into the void that is this strange amalgam of terror(s). What terrors lurk in the abyss?

"Only a God can save us" / Nur ein Gott kann uns retten

Let us abrogate Pascal's wager and agree that God's existence might be a conditional affair. What is not in question is that the *"concept* of God" is a strictly human matter. On this matter Deleuze and Guattari are decided, even as they try to find a new way to ask their titular question, "What is philosophy?" Philosophy remains for them the "art of forming, inventing, and fabricating concepts."[26] To construct a "concept" is, at the very least, to attempt to structure human thinking. This is no doubt why Deleuze and Guattari understand the "philosopher [as] expert in concepts and in the lack of them."[27] As such, Baldwin's "concept of God" is, to state the obvious, a structure of human making. This proposition could as easily be inverted. The "concept of God" derives from the "lack" of sufficient understanding of what God is. After all, Baldwin punctuates this particular reflection with a nuclear possibility: "If God cannot do this, then it is time we got rid of Him." Either "God" is a viable possibility or we must take our leave of "God," posthaste. Baldwin's "concept of God" is, as such, dialectical—"God" as Baldwin's philosophical "concept," a "concept" as such that can both and by turns affirm and negate God. Baldwin presents us with a stark choice: "God" is useful or we give God up, abandon God entirely. Regardless, it is only possible for Baldwin to posit (or understand, even condemn to irrelevance) "God" as a "concept," where the "concept" itself is what provides the structure for thinking—imagining, believing in, submitting to (the will of), praising—"God." And "God" as such is nothing other than a determination to achieve the essence of *Being. Aleitha,* the essence of our truth, that toward which it is we want to be.

It is precisely within the aporia between affirmation and negation that Baldwin's structure creates that we can locate Heidegger's famous pronouncement, "Only a god can save us now" (Nur ein Gott kann uns jetzt retten). If the Baldwinian "concept" is in struggle with itself, if Baldwin's is that "concept" that is unsure of its own ground, then another "concept" can take its place. If the "concept of God" is a constitutively insecure one, then what Baldwin's affirmation/negation conditionality brings to light is more than the precarity of "God." The conditionality of affirmation/negation foregrounds the existential need upon which Baldwin's "concept" is founded. What matters is not "God" as such, but the notion of the "concept." If it is the "concept of God" that is constitutive, then Heidegger's "god" (lowercase, to restate the obvious, *ein Gott*) can do the job as well. It is in this ruthlessly conditional logic that the primacy of the "concept" is revealed.

No wonder, then, that Deleuze and Guattari argue that in turning so committedly to philosophy, "the Greeks might seem to have confirmed the death of the sage and to have replaced him with philosophers."[28] The "sage" differs from the "philosopher" in that the "old oriental sage thinks, perhaps, in Figures, whereas the philosopher invents and thinks the Concept."[29]

For all intents and purposes, Heidegger's salvific "god" and Deleuze and Guattari's "philosopher with a Concept" perform the same intellectual function. Both make it possible to think the world, to think the place of the human in the world, and, as such, both are first and last preoccupied with *Being*. (The question, in a word, always emanates from *Dasein—*our being toward *Being*.) However, Heidegger's "god" and Baldwin's "concept of God" differ from Deleuze and Guattari's "Concept" in that the former seem to have, if for reasons that have little in common, a more urgent sense of humanity's existential crisis. Heidegger, as he has for so long, warns against the dangers of technology, which have led to our wanton and willful neglect of *Dasein,* our stubborn refusal to go in search of "terror." For his part, Baldwin fears for the well-being of the black subject in America; as much, that is, as he fears for the future of America itself. Under such circumstances, of course, any "god" will do, "God" not least of all.

Baldwin's "truly moral human being" is, no doubt, American in profile, character, spirit, tone, and disposition (even if we are left to argue about this figure's race, or, more precisely, the responsibility of one race for another), and that is why Baldwin so desperately "must *believe*" that such a being, such a *Being,* made and looked at from above by "God," is "possible." As with William Carlos Williams's red wheelbarrow, "so much depends upon" the bringing to life of this "moral," salvific, "human being"—*Dasein* (the being-there of god/God). It is only the love of this "moral human being" that can save America, that can indemnify America against itself, against its worst predilections, against its most self-destructive inclinations.

In this way, Baldwin, not always convincingly, deftly, or in (or with) full command of the distinction between his metaphysical and spiritual registers, is able to posit "God" on the one hand while reinforcing human responsibility on the other.

Baldwin demands of the Negro an unconditional, historically unprecedented capacity for, in at least one regard, forgiveness. Not passivity, as in the Gospels of Matthew (5:38–39) and Luke (6:29), but love as an active extending, the act of extending to the other that which aspires to grace but can never be grace. In Jankélévitch's rendering, an "apophatic or negative philosophy of forgiveness."[30] A creative negation on the order of terror in that forgiveness is that knowledge of God obtained through negation. The confrontation with *Dasein* determines that forgiveness, in its full complication, is the only way into secure *Being*—and out of this *Being* emerges *Mitsein.* The path to the other runs through terror. In this regard, not even King's most stringent formulation of Christianity rises to the level of terror: "We are gravely mistaken to think that Christianity protects us from the pain and agony of mortal existence. To be a Christian one must take up his cross, with all of its difficulties and agonizing and tragedy-packed content, and carry it until that very cross leaves its mark upon us and redeems us to that more excellent way which comes only through suffering."[31] What might be "instilled" in *Dasein* appears a much more terrifying encounter. As it should. *Being* is at stake. In Heideggerian terms (on condition that we take account of Heidegger's lifelong struggle with Catholicism), to be a Christian is not to *Be.*

Given its druthers, the test of forgiveness that forms the core of Baldwinian love is an examination that most human beings would fail, happily. It is a test that few, if any, of James Baldwin's contemporaries would have agreed to take. (On this question *The Fire Next Time* is clear: the Nation of Islam's leader Elijah Muhammad cannot even contemplate such an encounter. It is well beyond Elijah Muhammad's ken. It is on this ground that Baldwin takes his leave of Elijah Muhammad and the Nation.) It is a test that, in truth, James the nephew and his contemporaries would not have granted any legitimacy in the turbulence that was American politics in the 1960s—marked as the decade was with struggles around race, gender, sexuality, warmongering, and colonialist imperialism.

What kind of ethics is this? What use this Christian ethics of love? What use this Christianity for a (black) people descended from slaves, survivors in a nation that emancipated them without truly freeing them (Jim Crow laws testify to that) or granting them economic recompense? What good can forgiveness and love do in the face of this bloody history? In any case, whom does it benefit (materially, at any rate) except those responsible for the atrocities? (How might we, given Jameson's injunction about the material relations that condition freedom, think the material relations of forgiveness?) First, white America commits the brutalities, and then it is not asked to bear its actions? Again, the question presents itself, each time more assertively: What kind of ethics is this? If, that is, we understand in this articulation, to distinguish "ethics" here from how Barthes renders it, reductively; that is, stripped of philosophical complexity and nuance and distilled as the self's capacity to know—intellectually as well viscerally, in what we might name a "commonsense" way—what is right from what is wrong.

This is an ethical difficulty that resonates with the one Nietzsche presents in the "Tarantula" section of *Thus Spake Zarathustra.*

7 Do Not a Tarantula Be

A Nietzschean Interlude

> But thus do I counsel you, my friends: distrust all in whom
> the impulse to punish is powerful.
>
> —Friedrich Nietzsche, *Thus Spake Zarathustra*

In strictly political terms, the questions listed at the end of the previous chapter all stipulate to an irrefutable logic. However, for all that, I remain haunted by the challenge that Baldwin's ethics poses. I find myself unable, and unwilling, to dismiss it out of hand. I am reluctant, not to mention incapable, of dispensing with Baldwin's delineation of what the work of a Christian ethics entails. All the while, I cannot shake the sense that Baldwin is calling on us—all of us—to think more deeply about how it is we are in the world. In order to do so, we, and assuredly whites above all, must do away with the racial/racist/white supremacist suppositions that ballast our sense of who we are. For too long, Baldwin argues, the belief that "black men are inferior to white men" has been the ruling ideology in America.[1] This despite the fact that, as he writes to James,

> many of them, indeed, know better, but, as you will discover,
> people find it very difficult to act on what they know. To act is
> to be committed, and to be committed is to be in danger. In
> this case, the danger, in the minds of most white Americans,
> is the loss of their identity.[2]

Baldwin's is an unarguable logic. There can be no politics without action. (St. James, as always, asks us to *do* the work of Christianity.) That is, as long as we keep Heidegger's provision, that we do not act "too much" and think "too little," firmly in mind.[3] (As far as possible, all political action must take the form of thinking.) Following this logic, it would be fair to assume—again, these are Baldwin's terms—that "commitment" to a politics that overturns (or at least challenges) the American racial order will have a commensurate political effect. The greater the "commitment," the more transformative—and maybe even radical, if not revolutionary— the effect. Indeed, such a logic is entirely of a piece with Baldwin's delineation of politics, especially because it raises the (always very real) specter of "loss." There can be no politics worthy of the name "politics" that does not risk something, possibly even everything (or, its at best, politics is only that which risks everything), and in so doing threatens the very self—the very constitution of the self.

> *Here, in this articulation, we—because of Baldwin—are one with Heidegger, recognizing how he had already anticipated Kojève's injunction in his thinking on metaphysics: we live in the "terms of terror" in order to "instill terror into Dasein again." Above all, for Heidegger, it is "terror" that reminds us to return to thinking Dasein, which is what we should have been attending to all along, anyway.*
> *Thinking Dasein is where we encounter the good of "terror."*

That is, the "loss of (white) identity" is at risk because without submission to the possibility—inevitability?—of this "danger," there will have been no white risk. That is, there will have been no white politics, no white taking up of arms, à la John Brown, against an oppressive regime in which every white American, no matter their political intent, is directly implicated, if not directly complicit with, and is the beneficiary of, in either material or psychic terms or, as is more likely the case, both.[4] To "know" is for whites to be called to action—to act, against "their" world, to do something to their world, to undo their world as it is. To *be* in the world differently. (That is, to establish an entirely new mode of being with the other—a *Mitsein*— new in that it is universal too.) To "know," to have knowledge, is to be confronted with an ethical choice. Indeed, knowledge as such may impose the only ethical choice of historical record: to answer Baldwin's call, a call that speaks for—in this specific instance— black America, it is the call to act against what-is, how it is (*Dasein*), and, quite simply, because it is as it is. The white self is required, and not only by *Dasein* but by Baldwin too, to "instill terror into" itself in order that through the dual achievement—*Dasein und Mitsein*—it will begin to *Ver-stehen* the (white supremacist) terror it has inflicted upon the other. It is in the cause of such a project that Jankélévitch's "will" can be put to work.

Dasein, Mitsein, stands in sharp contradistinction, as we are well aware, to the ways in which white identity has been mobilized by Trump. Acting for all the world like a racial majority terrified of the inevitability of the "browning of America," which will result in white America becoming a majority minority, Trump has deployed the language of white supremacism to rally whites to act aggressively to defend their racial/racist interests. "Make America White Again." Consequently, this mobilization has found its rhetorical voice in events such as the vigilante white supremacist rally in Charlottesville, and in Trump's attack on the predominantly black city of Baltimore as a "disgusting, rat and rodent infested mess." The geopolitics of Richard Wright's *Native Son* lives on; Bigger Thomas, progeny of black postwar northern migration struggling to survive in a derelict South Side Chicago apartment would surely, in the terms of Trump's racial dystopia, be right at home in the late Elijah Cummings's twenty-first-century Baltimore. Wright's "rats" have migrated east, from the Great Plains toward the Atlantic coast. Decades have passed, but the time of black life has remained steadfastly, contrary to Prince Hamlet's protestation, "in joint." Of a piece with the history of degradation that African-Americans have for too long endured.

Wright's radical protestations against the racist American order, Cummings's vocal opposition to Republican policies, like Baldwin's ethical call, are entirely inaudible to Trump. As well they should be. After all, Baldwin's is an ethical call, to be sure, and a signal one at that. Signal because Baldwin locates responsibility for what is within the framework of an inarguable truth; Baldwin assigns responsibility for what America is, for how America is in relation to its black subjects, in a logic that is explicable to all except those who do not want to comprehend it. (Again, the path from *Verstand* to *Vernunft* is the road not taken by white America.) That is, Baldwin places responsibility for the violence of history with those who have perpetrated it and those who, refusing to understand themselves as "beneficiaries," in Bruce Robbins's terms, refuse to "act on what they know."

Ezra, Baldwin—and I do not think that I ascribe too much to him—is asking a great deal of us. The work he is undertaking requires that we negotiate between responsibility—holding whites accountable for their transgressions, historic and ongoing—and forgiveness, in its full philosophical complexity. He is asking for white accountability and, almost in the same gesture, making no demands on whites. Baldwin is following his Nietzschean "impulse"—asking James to love whites because they cannot love themselves and, in so doing, cautioning against all "powerful impulses to punish."

And then there is the work of "instilling terror" in the self. In order to be.

An irreconcilable conundrum: to demand accountability while giving up any right to "punish." How is accountability to be enforced?

Impossible, except if we put ourselves in the "territory" ("terms") of where "terror is instilled." Dasein is to be close to and familiar with "terror."

The question that Baldwin poses, again, to white (supremacist) America, is a pointed one: How is it you want to be in the world?

On this, there is no ambiguity for Baldwin. As he explains to his nephew, trying to present to young James a picture of his father as his uncle knew him:

> I know what the world has done to my brother and how narrowly he has survived it. And I know, which is much worse, and this is the crime of which I accuse my countrymen, and for which neither I nor time nor history will ever forgive them, that they have destroyed and are destroying hundreds of thousands of lives and do not know it and do not want to know it.[5]

The violence itself is bad enough, a violence that has "destroyed thousands of lives." It is, however, in the simplest and most common of conjunctions, "and," that the wrath of Baldwin's anger resides. In what reads like a run-on line, a breathless "and" obliterates the difference between ignorance—"do not know it"—and willful irresponsibility (denial of the highest order)—"*and* do not want to know it." At the end of this sentence, white "not-knowing" has been absorbed into/as historic disregard—as if "knowing" how things came to be were not even worth the white self's time or trouble.

In the face of white historical indifference, Baldwin resorts to philosophy. "Knowing" (to do the work/s of St. James, that is, to think about what the self "knows"), "knowledge" of (the acquisition, retention, institutionalization of valued information), the violence—that is, accepting, acknowledging, recognizing the self's implication in the violence—is, finally, submitted by Baldwin to time itself. The self's willful ignorance is a crime against time, a failure to act against what has been and what is will not be forgiven by time. (Again, Jankélévitch: it is in our power to "will good.") The self, all selves, will stand forever in the dock of time, accused of not acting on what it knew. To know is, in Baldwin's moral calculus, to be called upon. To be called upon to bear witness, to repeat what is known in order to secure the sanctity of that which is known. To know is to be called upon by no less a force than time immemorial. Time, even more than Baldwin, will never forget. The self can never escape time. Because time is sovereign, what the self does will always be held within and subject to, ultimately, the dictates of time. The judgment of time. This Heidegger knows: *Sein und Zeit*. Being and Time.

Time, understood as a sovereign ethical force, makes demands on both white and black Americans. It holds, over infinitude, one presumes, white Americans to account—it haunts them, in the terms of Toni Morrison's *Beloved* and *Paradise* ("They shoot the white girl first," goes this novel's opening line), among her other writings—and it conscripts Baldwin and James into its Simonian work. Or Cyrenian, if you prefer.) The task set before black Americans repeatedly, generation after generation (extending over more than two centuries), is accountability to time as the archive of historical record. And so Baldwin holds his nephew accountable:

> You know, and I know, that the country is celebrating one hundred years of freedom one hundred years too soon. We cannot be free until they are free.[6]

To which King adds:

> One hundred years later the Negro is still not free; one hundred years later, the life of the Negro is still sadly crippled by the manacles of segregation and the chains of discrimination.[7]

Despite King's lament, for Baldwin black America's task remains clear. Whites must be loved into freedom. Above all else, whites must be freed from themselves, from their lack of courage, from their fear of knowledge, from their aversion to truth. To know, to know truth, is to be capable of love—*Wahrheit ist Liebe.* Or, better still, *Wahrheit und Liebe.* In Baldwin's moral calculus, to know, to be capable of acknowledging who the self is, what that self has inherited and what that self has done (its crimes against history; its crimes that rise to historical proportions), and then processing knowledge, I would name it "thinking," is impossible without love.

Specifically, again in Baldwin's terms, without the love of the other. The self can come into itself and, finally, overcome itself only if it is loved by the other, because of the love of the other.

> *This is the "terror" that (white)* Dasein *must instill in its* Being.
>   *And then it must face this "terror": to love the other after having been loved by the other.*
>   *After the "terror" it has visited on the other; still visits on the other.*
>   *Is that not the most terrifying "terror" of all?*

If, that is, the self is shown how to love, is confronted by what love is, is exposed to the work of love. Love from below, as it were— subaltern love, if such a Gramscian turn of phrase might be permitted, but a love in no way proscribed. And, let there be no doubt, the pun is intended, in all its salaciousness, with its overtones of physical and psychological subjugation, and in all its ugly historical truth.

8 "Bagger Vance"

The inextricable relationship between self and other. Baldwin, always flirting with the "Bagger Vance" complex by assigning blacks the work of saving whites from themselves, rehabilitating whites, and then tending whites back into social well-being. "Bagger Vance," of course, refers to the title character in the movie *The Legend of Bagger Vance* (2000), which is set in the early 1930s. Vance, a mysterious black caddie played by Will Smith, serves as a golf whisperer of sorts for a broken-down World War I veteran from Savannah, Georgia, Rannulph Junuh (Matt Damon). Vance appears out of nowhere, into which he later dissolves. The enigmatic, reticent Vance's mission is apparently to help Junuh recover his swing in a high-stakes contest—love and money are on the line—that pits the Savannah native against the Depression-era American golfing greats Bobby Jones and Walter Hagen.

Bagger Vance represents a familiar trope in American culture. That is, the character is well known to both white and black Americans, if in discrete but intersecting articulations, to mix metaphors. It is possible to trace "Bagger Vance," if we begin with antebellum America, to Harriet Beecher Stowe's pillar of self-sacrifice and moral rectitude, Uncle Tom; Charles W. Chesnutt's loyal and dutiful Sandy in *The Marrow of Tradition* (1901) might well be seen as a fin de siècle complication on Stowe's character. Introduced in 1889 (meeting her end in 2020), the brand character Aunt Jemima trades on the "Mammy" trope, giving a face and a name to dutiful black female help. "Mammy," of course, functions as a source of domestic labor that always carries within it the possibility of sexual vulnerability; that is to say, the black female domestic worker is understood to be sexually available, often without her consent.

The dominant vehicle of black beneficence of our moment (or at least the recent past), as evidenced by *Bagger Vance,* is the "buddy movie." In this regard, there is Danny Glover's black police force veteran Roger Murtaugh in the *Lethal Weapon* franchise. Glover plays the straight, married, stable (black) cop to his white partner, Martin Riggs (Mel Gibson), a suicidal, manic, former Green Beret. An unorthodox cop, Riggs creates chaos and mayhem wherever he goes; it falls to Murtaugh to try to head off the oncoming disorder or to clean up the mess created by his effectively unhinged white partner. There are also the sage roles that Morgan Freeman is particularly good at, including those of Hoke Colburn in *Driving Miss Daisy,* in which he serves as an elderly white woman's driver-cum-confidante, and "Red" Redding in *The Shawshank Redemption,* who helps his fellow inmate Andy Dufresne (Tim Robbins), a white banker wrongly accused of murder, survive in prison. As therapist-caddie or in any of the several other iterations just named, "Bagger Vance" is eminently recognizable as a (negative, because self-sacrificial) type that is especially problematic as a mode of black cultural representation.

"Bagger Vance" is a (continuous) form of black servitude, whether cast as the benign or the oracular. As a form of servitude, it extends a history of black subservience (imposed, learned, survivalist), self-denigration, disenfranchisement (the right to speak, the right to speak in a register of choice rather than one dictated by "custom," and so on), and political vulnerability (from lynching through Jim Crow to our moment's racist police brutality). As such, "Bagger Vance" is, to say the least, an objectionable subject position for blacks. Objectionable not only because it assigns blacks the role, into an infinitely extended future, of attending (of tending), first and as a matter of historic inexorability, to the needs of their white counterparts. Such a representation also presumes, without reflection, that "Bagger Vance," in any black incarnation, himself has no life. To be "Bagger Vance" is to deny the black self its own desires. As such, "Bagger Vance" marks the refusal to acknowledge the black need for love; it ignores black domesticity outside of subservience to whites; it obliterates the black subject's own difficulties, trials, traumas, heartbreaks, disappointments, appetite for pleasure, and right to respite. (It is precisely this lack that August Wilson's plays so powerfully address—and redress.) In short, "Bagger Vance" negates the black need for need. It does not afford the black self the right to care for that self.

After Dave Chappelle's "Because I don't care either," we can confidently say that the black farceur has happily taken leave of Bagger Vance and his ilk.

Miss Daisy is just going to have to drive herself, isn't she?

And Yet Not . . .

Again, on the face of it, "Bagger Vance" is precisely the responsibility that Baldwin assigns his nephew. No wonder, then, that Baldwin charges his countrymen with historical accountability. The history of white violence and the effect it has had on blacks is what white America must know—although we can say, of course, that white America has long known it. It is this knowledge on which white America must act; this is the knowledge that must be acknowledged through works. Baldwin recognizes that it is in the process of taking this action that who, and what, white America understands itself to be, its "identity," is likely, very likely, to be "lost." The wages of historical sin, as it were, is the (potential) death of the self.

Nietzsche, as one would expect given Zarathustra's travails with the "all-too-human" he situates himself among, grasps what such a death would entail. "What knoweth he of love," Nietzsche ponders, "who had not been obliged to despise just what he loved!"[1] Understood in terms of Baldwin's demand of white America, such a conception of "love" achieves a rare—but historically necessary—intensity. In recognizing itself as historical actor, in its many valences and in view of the several consequences attached to its hegemony, white America is called on to consider an extreme response. In order to learn to "love" itself, an undertaking Baldwin views as beyond it, white America is (first?) "obliged" to "despise" itself. White America must learn how to regard itself properly in relation to itself and the other, a self-examination that will, of necessity, require a series of self-confrontations that must not turn from disgust with the self or from disdain and contempt for the self. However, such self-loathing must not be raised to the level of what Nietzsche would name, with derision, a "virtue." To indulge in such a Nietzschean "virtue" would be to obviate any meaningful self-reflection, thereby releasing the self from any accountability to itself, to the other, and, as important, to its ongoing historic inheritance. Nietzschean "virtue," understood in terms of the strident critique to which Nietzsche subjects it in his chapter "The Bestowing Virtue" (a critique sustained throughout the work), works to do nothing but immunize the self from itself, demonstrating a complete ignorance of and aversion to "knowing love."[2]

Of course, it is not only the white self that finds itself presented with a difficulty. For the black self, "loving" the other is a priori conditional on black self-abnegation. To "love" the other who has done unspeakable violence to the black self, the black self must refuse itself the right to "despise"—to restrict ourselves to the Nietzschean—the perpetrators of historic violence against the black self. In so doing, the black self opens itself to a cruel knowing. In ceding the right to "despise" the other, a right to which it has an inarguable claim, and to extend its Baldwinian "love" to that other, the black self must *Ver-stehen* that it has now, almost certainly, set itself upon a path that will end in the black self despising itself, whether it wants to or not. A dual mode of self-"despising": "despising" the black self for its self-abnegation (not "despising," hating, or resenting the white other); "despising" itself for "loving" that which history implores it to "despise." In dispensing its "love" to the other, the black self is made to count the enormous cost of Baldwinian—which is to say, Christian—"love."

The black self is made to face itself as a terrible specter. A terrible specter entirely of its own making.

Chappelle's salvific impulse returns. "Will we save them?" To which Baldwin replies in the affirmative.

Once more, into the breach steps the black self. The guise that the black self assumes is ever more familiar. Names that echo: Bagger Vance, Uncle Tom, Sandy. Each time the cost seems just a little more inordinate. Once more, drafted into duty.

How easily Simon of Cyrene, as we will see shortly, morphs into the Good Samaritan. Not only rescuing the stranger, but, as is often overlooked, assuring the keeper of the inn where the Samaritan deposits the stranger that he will return at week's end to settle the stranger's account.

> *"The terror, the terror." The way to* Being *runs, directly, through* "terror."
>> *The other alone is "capable of instilling terror" into the self.*
>> *To be "terrorized" into* Dasein.

In "loving" those it should "despise," the black self becomes the "creator" of its own terror. With a proviso: that we know, "all creators . . . are hard."[3] How difficult is it to "create" a singular terror produced at that conjuncture where Baldwin and Nietzsche make each other's acquaintance.

> *Through such a "loving" it seems possible that we come to understand how it is that "man is something to be surpassed."*[4]
>
> *Does such a "loving" enable us to exceed, even if only ever so slightly, that "Last Man" whom Heidegger urges us to go beyond?*
>
> *Is such a "loving" constitutive of the "leap" we must take so that we might come closer to glimpsing the Overman?*
>
> *Nietzsche holds out such a possibility, if only we will endeavor to know love: "Beyond yourselves shall ye love some day! Then learn first of all to love."*[5]
>
> *What know we of love?*
>
> *Why know we not of love?*
>
> *Why do we not set out to know love? To know how to love?*

To act politically is, then, always (and certainly in this instance), nothing other than an autoimmune project.

Life through Death

In order for white America to confront what it knows, white America must risk its own death. By dialectical implication, if white America does not act on what it knows, it enmeshes itself more deeply in what it knows to be unethical.

To be unethical, in this sense, is to turn from "terror."

White America makes itself unethical before itself, in the face of what it knows. It is into this maelstrom of the obvious (and deliberately ignored) truth, self-deception, and continued inaction, to say nothing of a blatant lack of historical commitment, that white America thrusts itself.

The white self turns from "terror." The white self will not "despise" itself. Is it even capable of self-"despising"?

Whatever, and however terrible, the wages of sin might be, surely it is nothing compared to the wages of self-imposed self-ignorance. To make the self, willfully, ignorant of what it knows, what it knows to be true. To commit the self to not knowing what it knows. That seems a fate of tragic proportions—να επιλέξεις να μην μάθεις τι ξέρει ο εαυτός σου για να είναι αληθινός: to choose to not know what the self knows to be true.

We could name it, without hesitation, self-delusion, or self-deception. (We dare not name it "false consciousness.") Regardless, it is tantamount to denial of the highest historico-philosophical order because it turns from *Dasein*.

There might, however, be a more apt name for it: a tragedy of Delphic proportions, if the oracle bears the name Baldwin. To choose not to know what it is there to be known. To choose not to know what calls for knowing. Could there be a more violent act against the self than this? What use the Delphic oracle? All this preoccupation with the self, critical as it is for Baldwin, should not obscure the question of effect—the effect that the self's refusal to act on its knowledge has on the other. The (white) self's violence against itself will have, as it always has, disastrous consequences for the other. (And, as Baldwin, King, and Heidegger know, each in his own register, for the self too. Nietzsche, as we know, makes a demand that begins with the self subjecting itself to self-interrogation.) We know those consequences as the ongoing politics of racism in America.

It is, in this regard, worth reflecting, again, on what is entailed when Baldwin touts the importance of commitment. It takes courage to commit oneself to politics. It takes courage to act on the basis of what it is the (white) self knows. It takes courage because the effects of those actions can never be known—neither in advance nor in the kinds of effects that will result from the self's actions. Following the logic of autoimmunity, Baldwin already knows what at least one of those consequences will be. In fact, he knows what the most important consequence will be. In confronting itself with what it knows—and by this Baldwin means that the self knows what is, unarguably, true (the truth *is*)—the self must have the courage to set in motion, through its actions, its own dissolution.

In any case, how do you run from your own *Dasein*? Can you even hope to outrun your being-there?

To act itself to death. In Derrida's terms, it is precisely by answering the call to act that the white self not only risks itself but also stands to possibly gain—or save—itself.

Autoimmunity is nothing less than a fatal possibility, and as such it is absolutely necessary to bring such actions to life. Baldwin's search for the redemption of all Americans depends on this action, these acts, individual and collective. That is, a new, entirely new, American can be born out of the ashes of the destruction of the white self. The courage to act while risking the possibility of death is ameliorated by a much grander promise: the coming into

Being of an American self liberated, through its own courage, into a new, nonracist selfhood. The prospect being held out here is nothing less than the being of *Being* itself. (Autoimmunity, as rendered by Derrida, provides its glimpse—and maybe even more than a glimpse—into the Conradian-Heideggerian heart of terror. The key for Heidegger, of course, is the refusal to look into the abyss that constitutes the real "terror." Hence his insistence that our being reacquaint itself with "terror." *Dasein* as the being-there, the willingness to be in "terror." For Conrad it is almost the opposite. It is not that Kurtz will not look into the heart of terror. It is, rather, that he is unable to know the "terror" that he looks upon as "terror" and as such is unable to extricate himself from it once he finds himself immersed in it. Kurtz submits to the "terror," notwithstanding the colonialist-inspired xenotropic promise of this "terror." Marlow, after all, is under no illusion. The "terror" to which Kurtz gives himself over is a sure sign of Kurtz's having "gone native.") A self, we can assert, freed from itself. Freed from itself into the truth of *Dasein*. To know the self as the self has never known itself before. To know the self as it had never imagined it could know itself. To know the self in, and as, truth. To be for the essence—truth—of *Being*.

(A Parenthesis: Freedom)

To know freedom on such an order of *Dasein* is, for Adorno, entirely possible if "thought transcends the bonds it tied in resistance—there is its freedom."[6] The work of freedom, then, begins with the negation of the self's history. Adorno's is a signal insight, a sobering and unsettling one, because of its point of critique—or point of attack, if you prefer. What "tied" the self in (and, therefore, to) "resistance" must be sloughed off, rejected, given up. In a word, what constituted (the self in) "resistance" is now the very stuff that must be resisted. (Autoimmunity of the perversely affirmative variety. What must be resisted is *Dasein*'s aversion to "terror.") A self that speaks itself, that can and wants to speak itself, is possible only if the self is "untied" from itself (if its "tongue" is "untied," as Marlon Riggs might have it); a self, we should be clear, that is not abandoned to the past—to history, as such; a being intent on reacquainting its *Dasein* with "terror"—but recuperated against itself into something more, something it, as suggested before, could not have imagined itself to be. This is the "terrifying" promise of Adorno's death and Heidegger's "terror."

Out of this resistance to "resistance," as difficult an undertaking as it might be, emerges the possibility of freedom. In Adorno's terms, "Freedom follows the subject's urge to express itself."[7] What mode of "expression" "follows," can "follow," "resistance"? All such "expression" will, out of historical necessity, be tentative, speculative, preordained to reveal shortcomings as much as it might yield a mode of "expression" freed from—freed through—"resistance." No matter, it is precisely—expressly—such "expression" that must be risked, much as Baldwin asks his fellow Americans to risk death.

Simon of Cyrene

This particular mode of knowing constitutes a call, on Baldwin's part, for a recognizably Christian course of action. In biblical terms, one might suggest that it is appropriate that Baldwin calls on black love—you must love them, James, because they do not know how to love themselves—to facilitate the pathway to a new self, no matter the history and practice of (white) violence. Like Simon of Cyrene, a New Testament figure conscripted, on the spot, by the Roman soldiers to carry Christ's cross to Calvary (King's the "cross we bear"), black Americans must bear an undue, unjust, and unasked-for burden in their attempt to secure this new political (American) self. After all, the labor that Simon performed was nothing if not an act commanded by an imperial force, an act commanded by those who had the power to extract labor from the populace without the possibility of refusal. The empire, in almost any instantiation, does not fear reprisal. (And it assuredly offers no recompense. That, it turns out, is work best left to biblical adherents.)

What distinguishes the Roman soldiers from the white American self is, paradoxically, their "ignorance." Unlike white Americans, the imperial soldiers had no foreknowledge as to what act they were setting in motion by crucifying Jesus-the-Christ. For those soldiers, Simon was nothing more than a subject they could draft, regardless of his wishes, into labor. In doing so, those Roman soldiers, of whom we know nothing, made Simon the Cyrene into a historic (biblical) figure. The unknown imperial soldiers inducted a subject into history. At their own expense, we might say, because his story far outlived theirs—like most foot soldiers, they are condemned to anonymity (after having been conscripted into ignominy). Their victim survives, enshrined in a great historical narrative.

Biblical scholars are in agreement about Simon's origins, if not his faith. They concur that he was in all likelihood from Cyrene, the capital of the Roman district Cyrenaica (modern-day Libya) at the time of Jesus-the-Christ's crucifixion. Scholars are undecided as to his faith, although many suspect that there is good reason to believe that he was Jewish, given the large number of Jews in Cyrenaica; there is nothing like unanimity on this question, however.

Scholars do seem to agree in describing Simon as a man possessed of a "swarthy" complexion. On these grounds, an argument has taken root that he was a "black" man. Such a depiction of Simon accords analogically (and anatomically, we might add) with the role that Baldwin assigns James. (Also bringing to mind, of course, one Bagger Vance.) In this adjudication, because, we should be clear, it is a judgment of Baldwin, "Letter to My Nephew" can be heard only in a recalibrated Yeatsian register, that one in "The Second Coming" that calls on the "best" to act with "intensity." Recall the memorable lines, "The best lack all conviction, while the worst / Are full of passionate intensity."

Fidelity to Thinking

Nip, this Cyrenian spirit, the hesitations and trepidations (resentment, anger, exhaustion with the difficulties that attend to the history of my subject position) may very well be the best and most intellectually honest template I can offer you for how to be in the world.[8] To be wary of the easy answers as it applies to race and racism. To reject the simplistically conceived notion that black is universally good and white is its exact opposite.

Instead, I urge you, having shown yourself to be instinctively drawn to the dialectic, to align yourself with the negative dialectics located at the very core of thinking. "Thought as such," Adorno writes, "before all particular contents, is an act of negation, of resistance to that which is forced upon it."[9] Thinking, "thought," as first of all an "act of resistance," if by "resistance" we understand thinking that which is absolutely set against all imposition—thinking will not abide that "which is forced upon it." An engagement with what is to hand begins from the impossibility of easy resolution. Indeed, what is to hand might even refuse resolution entirely, and that is a good thing.

Nip, I hesitate to ask, but is that which is not dialectical a priori a thing of terror?

Thinking, then, as "negation," but never "negation" for its own sake, "negation" not simply to nullify that which has been "forced upon it." Rather, "negation" intent on "resistance" so that it becomes possible to think free/d from imposition. Thinking, we might say, as freedom itself—and, as we know, for Adorno "freedom" can be attained only once thinking has gone beyond the contradiction, once it has exceeded the dialectic. Once more, Nip, I implore you to think "resistance" to what-is (to not know "black" or "white" in advance)—the pressure that is brought to bear on thinking, "being importuned to bow to every immediate thing"—because "resistance" as such constitutes the backbone, the stubborn, unbreakable will, if you prefer, of thinking.[10] Without this refusal to succumb to what-is, "every immediate thing," thinking would, and of this we can be sure, run the very real risk of negating itself. That is, clearly, a negation of the negation to which Adorno is militantly opposed.

Embrace the terror of the dialectic, my son. It is the stuff of life-affirming thought.

Once More, against Affirmation

Without such an unruly interface (it could not be any other way) and its political effects, what we run the risk of producing is unthinking affirmation. Affirmation is *Darstellung* planted, and carefully nurtured, in the soil of "aggregation" and "segregation." In order to think, it becomes necessary not only to refuse acquiescence—to "revolt," without apology, against "every immediate thing"—but also to pronounce that every cause is not a just cause, that every cause is not worthy of support simply because it has the political capacity to compel obeisance, to compel deference because "revolting" against it would result in public disrepute. Or silencing. Or professional ostracism. In order to encourage us to "resist," to gird ourselves against co-optation or to steel ourselves against the effects of any form of censorship, Adorno provides us with what amounts to a slogan in his oeuvre: "Rage is the mark of Idealism."[11] (A position to which Nietzsche might not be unsympathetic.) "Resistance," under almost any circumstances, is an angry, and possibly even a violent, business; at the very least, it is a fury-inducing undertaking. "Maladjustment" is, I would venture, King's more tempered way of "raging," not with a Dylan Thomas-esque futility, but rather a "raging" against what-is, what-was, and what threatens to be. Ever more. "Maladjustment" is King's "call" to terminate what-is in order that it might never-be, again.

Thinking does not meet the threshold of "thinking"—ever—if it inscribes risk aversion as its first condition and limit. Or the presumption that the other is incapable of transgression. That is, the other's politics are always, by simple virtue of being the other's politics, above reproach. That the other's politics is, in strategic moments (which is to say, politically critical junctures), incapable of expedient mobilization. Or, simply, expedience.

Certainly not, if Hegel and Lacan whisper their critiques in our ears. Certainly not if we want to "rage" against an institutional ethos of infinite accommodation for the other on the sole basis that the other is other. Certainly not if we incline in any way, however slight, toward "Idealism." Adorno's "Idealism" is demanding and disruptive, conditioned on thinking, so that it never submits to the Agambenian logic of feeling good about feeling bad. Feeling good about feeling bad, raised to the status of political virtue, is a liberal indulgence. (Against this has Nietzsche cautioned us.) It is not even remotely related to what constitutes politics. Feeling good about feeling bad is a noxious logic in that it, in its Agambenian articulation, apprehends everything before it as the "camp." Agamben's is that logic that constitutively refuses to distinguish, to render the matter reductively, and to that end I take sardonic liberties with it, between shopping at, say, Walmart and penal incarceration.

In what historical epoch has thinking ever been a safe enterprise? And, again, why should it ever be safe, in any space, to think? A reorientation along the lines of King's argument in favor of "maladjustment" is in order here:

> There are some things within our social order to which I am proud to be maladjusted and to which I call upon you to be maladjusted. I never intend to adjust myself to segregation and discrimination. I never intend to adjust myself to mob rule. I never intend to adjust myself to the tragic effects of the methods of physical violence and to tragic militarism. I call upon you to be maladjusted to such things.[12]

In this spirit, let us "maladjust" ourselves always, so that we, before ourselves, are always already inclined to thinking. Let us always err on the side of "maladjustment" rather than underwrite that which does not trouble us. Let us "maladjust" so that we stand with that which rankles, that which, above all else, demands to be thought. Let us feel good about thinking.

We have come to a pretty pass when we would even contemplate turning away from thinking. Thinking constitutes, above all else, the state—the mode, the very *Dasein,* if you will—of intellectual risk. Any adjustment in any other direction is, in whatever guise it assumes, under whichever umbrella it seeks cover, a dereliction of intellectual duty. It amounts to the abdication of intellectual responsibility. Adorno is, it must be said of *Negative Dialectics,* brilliantly prescient in this regard: "Criticizing privilege becomes a privilege."[13] Touché. In the process of disenfranchising those who are subject to critique, "privilege" transforms itself into a political monopoly. It reserves for certain constituencies, and those constituencies only, the right to "criticize." The terms are such that only those who belong to a particular constituency (we might understand them as majoritarian or marginalized, as you wish, with allowances made for discrepancies in power, of course, as Foucault would urge us) have the right to "criticize" it. Criticism as a (conveniently, viscerally) closed shop. A closed shop to which admission is (granted) by special permission only. Criticism with not only a prescribed set of objects that are to be engaged but also that mode of apprehension that establishes a predetermined outcome.

This is the terrifying price that is paid if we abandon the "terms of terror." We remove ourselves to that place where *Dasein* has fled, proclaiming itself in mortal fear of the absolute absence of "terror."

"Dialectical thinking," Adorno is emphatic, is opposed to the exclusionary because it "defies reification also in the sense, that it refuses to confirm the individual as singled-out and in separateness; it ascertains precisely this isolation as the product of the general."[14] The power of "privilege," the (political) status of the ("reified" and) "singled-out" "individual" is absolute insulation against and outright aversion to any *reflexiones kategorie.*

Marx's mockery of bourgeois frippery and mimeticism (the grandeur of the Roman Republic and Empire is what is longed for) would find a sympathetic and receptive ear in the farceur writ large (Chappelle, no less than any other):

> In the classically austere traditions of the Roman Republic its gladiators found the ideals and the art forms, the self-deceptions that they needed in order to conceal from themselves the bourgeois limitations of the content of their struggles and to keep their passion at the height of the great historical tragedy.[15]

We must not abandon thinking. It is at our peril that we ignore Marx's warning that every politics that seeks to inoculate itself against criticism by silencing those outside it can only lead to "self-deception." The desire for that privilege that privileges privilege is what, if left uncritiqued, extends privilege so understood into an inviolate right. We should feel bad about what is bad. Out of that extension, questions abound. Questions such as: What constitutes a "historical tragedy"? How "thin" is the "line" between "historical tragedy" and perfunctory offense? Shouldn't that "line" be clearer, firmer, and more effectively defined so that our understanding of what constitutes a "historical tragedy" does not descend into perfunctory offense?

If not the "proletarian revolution," then at the very least, the dialectic—as delineated in Marx's second preface to the first volume of *Capital,* thinking dialectically—is called for "because it regards every historically developed social form as in fluid movement, and therefore takes into account its transient nature not less than its momentary existence; it lets nothing impose upon it, and is in its essence critical and revolutionary."[16]

The dialectic is a singular form of political work. It asks that the object's "transient nature not less than its momentary existence" be held together, coconstituents of a single political thought, united, divided, now one, now the other, now neither one nor the other; stubbornly independent, "it lets nothing impose upon it," containing with it that germ of critique capable of producing "revolution." Fertile ground for thought, fertile ground from which to think, all because it urges us toward the "affirmative recognition of the existing state of things."[17]

Fidelity to thinking is a commitment to living with "terror," and living in "terror" of "no-terror." (To "love" that which you should "despise," to learn to "despise" the self in order to "love" the other.) "Terror," so conceived, is a mode of being toward *Being* utterly alien to Trump. The "terror" that Heidegger and Kojève bequeath us is a suit of armor against Trumpian "no-terror." Nip, best to live for "terror," then, my son.

To Be in the World

In order to retrieve or preserve for Ezra the power of thinking who and how he is in the world—Ezra's body, Ezra's thoughtfulness, his understanding of how to be in the world, as a being/*Being* constitutive of and constituted by and in the world—out of love for my son, I find it absolutely necessary to insist upon the primacy of thinking. It is for this reason this essay confronts its conflicted relationship to—its being held within—the logic of who he is. And it is also for precisely this reason that who Ezra understands himself to be is subjected, as rigorously and relentlessly as possible, to thinking. On these grounds, this essay privileges thinking (the body as constituted by, or out of, thinking, first and last) unapologetically in no small measure because it is stridently opposed to any tendency that will make Ezra subject to the politics of affirmation, to the "soft bigotry of low expectations" and the new materialism's allergy to the "linguistic turn," "social constructionism," "culture," "representation," and "discourse" (in short, no matter the protestations, to the "abstraction" that is thinking).

It is out of this contradiction, and arguably only out of this contradiction, that it will be possible to craft a politics that can do more than simply withstand both the base and the superstructural force that is the "eternal recurrence of the same." (Itself, of course, no mean or insignificant project, precisely because "the same" does not "recur.") However, because the white mode of *Dasein* structures everything, there is only one way overcome it. That is, to *Ver-stehen* Trump not as singular—for all his peculiar capacities, for all the dangerous conjunctures he enables—but rather as historic. That is, Trump as symptomatic so that there will always be, until it is finally undone, the need to think the self's (as other) intimacy (exposure to violence, vulnerability, unequal relation to, moments of shared interest, desire for, empathy with, if you insist) to white structures of *Dasein*. The contradiction, then, as the theoretical tool of choice in the undoing of that mode of (white) *Dasein* that has shown itself to be not only resilient (its longevity) but also constitutively violent. The contradiction, as interrogative mechanism, is that force for thinking that will not permit of the self as declarative. As in, "I am . . ." The contradiction as, a priori, drawing any claim to self-knowledge, any prioritizing of somatic and material realities (for its own sake, at the expense of, say, "representation" or "culture"), and *Dasein* itself into question; into that which must, before all else, be thought.

Such, I am happy to report, Nip, is the upshot of Heidegger's "terror."

Adorno's Critique of Identity

In this regard Adorno is especially useful because he will not relent on the demand to think. Adorno is wise to the autoimmunity of "identity"—understood for our purposes as the politics of self

(-affirmation), or insistent, insufficiently reflective self-naming, if you prefer. He recognizes that identity cannot sustain itself because the contradiction it so stridently seeks to negate—or outfox, overcome, avoid—is precisely what it is so wholly indebted to: the contradiction. Adorno writes:

> Contradiction is nonidentity under the aspect of identity; the dialectical primary of the principle of contradiction makes the thought of unity the measure of heterogeneity. As the heterogeneous collides with its limit it exceeds itself.
>
> Dialectics is the consistent sense of nonidentity. It does not begin by taking a standpoint. My thought is driven to it by its own inevitable insufficiency, by my guilt of what I am thinking.[18]

Adorno makes two critical claims here, and, independent as they appear, they are nevertheless linked, perhaps inveterately, by a shared, constitutive or "inevitable insufficiency." The first is that contradiction reveals both the (unfulfillable) desire of "identity" for "autonomy," the capacity of "identity" as such to stand alone in the world, to be sufficient unto itself, and its desire to "exceed its limit." That is, "identity" wants to stand by and as itself while at the same time it wants to be something that is more than itself, something that can stand beyond itself. Adorno's second claim is that dialectics "begins" in the recognition of its "own inevitable insufficiency" and is inherently productive. This Adorno states clearly: "My thought is driven by its own inevitable insufficiency."

The gift of Adorno's "dialectic," so to speak, is that it is able to convert (what in other political actors would be white liberal) "guilt" into a condition for thinking. The only way to overcome "guilt" is by thinking for that "thought" (dare one say?) that makes it possible to address—overcoming is surely impossible—the "inevitable insufficiency" from which the "guilt" derives. "Guilt," then, not as a state of consciousness that debilitates, but rather as instilling the awareness to, as it were, "think" something else, "think" in some other way, or "think" from a different place, one where "guilt" as such does not have a stranglehold on "thinking." "Guilt," so conceived, as the bedrock of Agambenian politics. Again, white liberal guilt is what allows the white self and its allies, of every hue and identity, to feel good about feeling bad. We should know this as the perversity of privilege.[19]

In every register that Adorno offers it here, "identity" is informed by the understanding that "identity" as we know it is unsustainable. As such, the force of "contradiction" is already, in advance of itself, gnawing away at "identity," steadily, if unspectacularly (even unknowingly), undoing "identity" in its quest to "exceed" itself. That is, "identity" is constitutively dissatisfied, unfulfilled, with itself as it is, as it finds, articulates, understands itself in the world. (In part, one might speculate, because "identity" lacks the capacity for *Verstehen*, unable to command the necessary Reason or to "see" what-is clearly.) "Identity" reveals itself as, in Jean-François Lyotard's term, the *économie libidinale* (libidinal investment), seeking to appropriate what-is-not to it. The desire for such appropriation (desire, as we well know, is always girded by an eros of one stripe or another) is precisely the "space" as such into which "nonidentity" inserts itself, or, better still, the "space," created by the "more" (+; as in, "identity+," that is, where the "+" signifies what is not-yet identity; that is, "identity+" marks the time more than the "space" that "identity" currently occupies) in which "identity" wishes to assert itself. Adorno names this "identity's" "demand for totality . . . for whatever is not identical with it."[20] Whatever, that is, it would like to make "identical with it" presenting "identity+" as the triangulation constituted out of "identity," "nonidentity," and the infinity that X marks. As such, X points to everything still outside "identity" that "identity+" has in its sights. What could be more "libidinal" than such limitless, irrepressible, desire? Desire unchained, *désire sans frontières*.[21]

"Identity," at its most appropriative, located both within (its inner core) and at its outermost extremity, wants to make everything (let us name it, with the requisite fidelity to Adorno's thinking, "nonidentity") "identical" with it. That is, nothing less than "totality." It is this utterly disruptive struggle that begins within "identity" and mutates its way to the very "limits" that "dialectics holds up to our consciousness as a contradiction."[22] Adorno, with good reason, "thinks" the contradiction, seeks to remind us of its historical necessity, because, as he says, "total contradiction is nothing but the manifested untruth of total identification."[23]

Audible in the repetition of "total," in its diametrically opposed meanings, is Adorno's caution, his concern about what "total identification" might yield. The (poisoned) fruits of "total identification" can be revealed, naturally (although this is by no means an easy undertaking), only through vigilance and a strict adherence to the interrogative capacity contained within "total contradiction." It is, of course, a meeting of extremes deriving from the antagonism between extremes, both of which give cause for pause.

At its sharpest edge, the contradiction performs a geopolitical function, or spatiopolitical, metaphorically rendered. It serves to mark that juncture where "libidinal investment" in the self is called upon to account for itself in relation to both itself and what is around it. That is, the world as the time and space of unending conflict, a world that will, sooner rather than later, tire of the "performance of libidinal investment." At that moment, in establishing itself as the juncture of record, the self's "libidinal investment" becomes that "unbearable burden" that the political realities of the world refuse to bear.[24] This juncture, it is possible to hope, is where the desire that is "identity+" encounters its political reckoning. Every desire to "go beyond," to accrue more to itself, to add innumerable +s, cannot be undertaken without some "idea" (as it were) as to the rationale, the "why," if you will, for and of the project of, to vernacularize Marx, infinite accumulation.

Dialectics as an irrepressible force, responsive and alive to both the difficulties of the moment and the challenges presented by those realities it has inherited; the dialectic as unstoppable in its ability to undo even the most recalcitrant, reactionary, and recidivist of counterforces. Dialectics, always struggling against what-is, against the imposition of circumscription. Dialectics, in its myriad articulations (which we are enlisted to think philosophically, each theory in its turn, in one rendering after the other, all the postulates, together), whether or not we submit to the opacity that is the history of the present, strain as we might against all manner of claims that insist on their own "transparency."[25] This is what Marx's thinking on the dialectic makes available to us.

I "need" Ezra to think. I do not want him, in matters of the intellect as they concern who he is in the world, to be condemned to or by affirmation. If Nip responds to the "need" for thinking, then I am more confident that he will not succumb to the temptation—the hue and cry of "identity" that is all around us, the cacophonous voices that raise themselves so confidently in their self-assertions—of being affirmed tautologically. That is, being affirmed as a mixed-race kid simply because he is a mixed-race kid. Affirmation as such is never enough. I want Nip to know that affirmation of self is not a political good. Neither is it a good place to begin or to end, for that matter, the work of thinking the self. (Nietzsche's might be an extreme demand, but it remains a provocative place from which to interrogate the kind of self-interrogation the self is willing to subject itself.)

Instead, I want him to know (to *Ver-stehen*) that knowing himself is always an intellectual project; an intellectual project to which there can be no end. I want my son to think because the failure to think is the most catastrophic failure of self. In these terms, self-affirming affirmation (Adorno's "identity") is where minds go to die. What is more, it would amount to an act of violence against him-self.

When moments of affirmation arise, as they surely will, I would ask that Ezra first recall the role of the "need"—"The need in thinking is what makes us think"—and that he then heed Adorno's "need" as a form of and a responsibility to the self. "The motor of the need," Adorno argues (in such a way as to remind us of St. James, with undertones of Heidegger), "is the effort that involves thought as action."[26] The first "need" is always to think the self, followed by the "need" to care for how it is the self thinks its "contaminated existence." No self without work, without works—works on the order of (St.) James.

Nip

Nip, James Baldwin wrote a letter to his nephew, a letter intended to reach America writ large. (Letters always reach their—proper—destination, so say the Lacanians. No matter, that is, the circuitous path a missive may take and regardless of the delays between dispatch and receipt.) As is clear by now, despite what follows, the only way I could find to address you, Ezra, is through my search for what Jameson names the "possibility of another kind of writing."[27] And, yes, as Jameson goes on to remark, "another kind of thinking," for our purposes "another kind of thinking" about race and racism, about how much I value thinking, about how I understand thinking to be the only way to be in the world as a human being.[28] Thinking as second only to *Being, Denken* as, in truth, indistinguishable for me from *Dasein*.

I am, then, writing to you in order to think toward "another kind of writing and thinking." And, in calling on Jameson's "another kind of writing and thinking," Nip, I am doing no more than acknowledging that every "writing" is nothing other than one more articulation of a struggle—about thinking—that I am conducting with-in myself. Any other form of address than the one I present you, informed as it is by these various intellectuals (Socrates, Baldwin, Adorno, Jameson, and so on), with those Dave Chappelle interludes, would have amounted to a failure to address you. A "letter," as such, or an "essay" in any conventional sense, seemed to me constitutively insufficient when I set out to write to you. Out of the "need" to address you, I have sought to forge this, "another kind of writing."

I submit to you, my son: expect more of yourself, my son, always more. If you submit to the logic of affirmation (confirmation of self that may or may not be warranted or justified), I strongly expect that it will do damage to you. I have no doubt that it damages those whom it indulges. It is the logic of feeling good that does the self no good. It damages those whom it indulges because it affirms the self for its own sake. It almost never raises the difficulties that are integral to the interrogative.

It affirms when it should instead challenge the very students it is ostensibly teaching. It affirms rather than making thinking central to the project of learning. Affirmation stands in the place of the figure who should be a disciplined teacher, instructing the students into thinking—understanding the privilege that is standing at the front of the classroom. Affirmation, whatever guise it assumes, inhibits thinking; that is, when it does not outright negate the work of learning.

Teaching, learning, is an occasion for thinking. Affirmation as such blunts critique when it should sharpen a line of argument. When it should demand that every student seek to make their thoughts more cogent, more durable, more able to withstand critique.

Affirmation does this damage, without ever acknowledging it, finding—or seeking, as the case might be—political and pedagogical cover under the name of "identity."

It is the deleterious pedagogical consequence of feeling good about feeling bad.

It is a pedagogy-politics that creates an intellectual environment where teachers of all ideological stripes, be they white liberals or black radicals, white reactionaries or black nationalists, give themselves license to expect less from you. They do so in the name of "racial solidarity" or white liberal guilt (an unctuous political mode, to be sure) or white supremacist disregard for your intellectual well-being.

It will, here, suffice to metonymize this predisposition as follows: white liberals, however much they may disdain to acknowledge it, expect less from the other than they would from their own. Black nationalists will offer "solidarity," succor, and solace in place of the intellectual demands they should be making on you.

There is, it must be acknowledged, a time and a place for racial solidarity. There are moments when a kind word can make a difference. But neither solidarity nor support should detract from intellectual demand. The latter follows the former. The order of things must never be reversed.

No teacher should, a priori, excuse people like you and me when he or she should hold us accountable. I can tell you too that, to our shame, there are people like you and me who are only too willing to—expediently, cynically—exploit and harness this indulgence, and who perpetrate this act—this violent act—against learning.

However, as you must know, this pedagogical-political modality does no one any good. Least of all us. It diminishes us because we accept it, in the name of political tendencies I would rather not be associated with; it diminishes those who practice this pedagogy (or politics) because they are insufficiently self-reflexive as to the harm it does. To us. It is nothing other than the failure of thinking because thinking opens us to the effects, or potential effects, of our actions.

That is why, as you know only too well, I insist on "proper grammar" and "proper pronunciation." "Propriety of thought, and propriety of diction, are commonly found together," writes Thomas Babington Macaulay in his reflections on Machiavelli.[29] The fidelity of your thinking—to thinking, "propriety of thought"—can be borne only by a precise use of language—"propriety of diction." Only a felicitous use of language, careful, attentive use, can bear the responsibility of thinking. Here I follow Heidegger's etymological fidelity.

As such, Nip, mastering language (your own, first of all— grammar, pronunciation, in its narrow sense) is more than a primary form of self-discipline. To behave "properly" in relation to language speaks of the respect we have for language, for how it is we ask language to do the work of thinking.

"Commendable" and "excellent" are, and this hardly seems co- incidental, two of the meanings that date back to the fourteenth- century etymology of "pronunciation." To be "commendable" and to achieve "excellence" requires, one could fairly argue, self-discipline of the kind that "proper grammar" demands. What "proper grammar" demands is that which is "appropriate" to it, as such consistent with the Old French etymology of propre. What is not, then, "appropriate" must rise, surely, to something on the order of an "offense," a transgression that must, at the least, be explained

and not, as it were, permitted. Permission is indulgence writ large. What is propre *is nothing but that which is true to itself.*

By being true to language we command language. We find in our vocabulary the precise word or words that can bear truth. "Propriety of diction" produces "propriety of thought." It is for this reason that being able to construct a complex sentence as readily as a simple one resonates in the world. Knowing the correct tense to use, how to command grammatical construction, that is what matters. It signals a fundamental mastery of how it is you are able to address the world, even if the world does not respond in kind.

It is for this reason that every time you mispronounce a word and the white teacher or black instructor does not correct your usage, then you should understand something: that is an act of intellectual violence against you. At best, it is an act of grammatical negligence and pedagogical delinquency.

Formulaically rendered: "Diction" ↔ "Pronunciation" ↔ "Thought."

Every time your mispronunciation or grammatical inaccuracy goes unremarked upon, you are being intellectually shortchanged. More than that, however, you are being marked—silently, loudly—as other, by teachers black and white. These teachers might or might not know it, but either way, they are holding you, publicly, to a lower standard. Simply because you are black.

These teachers feeling good about feeling bad is bad for you.

Let me retract that. Those teachers, black and white, know exactly what it is they are doing. They would rather indulge you than correct you. The white teachers do so because they fear being labeled "racist"; black teachers who eschew the demand for correct grammar do not want to be considered race traitors of the grammatical variety—that is, they do not want to stand accused of "speaking white."

Nip, I know this difficulty. I grew up around my peers an English speaker in a community where "township" (the equivalent of the "projects" in the United States) Afrikaans was—and remains—the lingua franca. I understand the need to adopt a discursive register appropriate to the context. I recommend it. However, I knew then, as I know now, exactly what register was required in an institution of higher learning. I know the costs of both contexts, and I am willing to pay the piper. But I will never do so at the cost of my commanding language in the classroom—or any such equivalent context.

> How is it that both groups of teachers cannot see that it is the reverse that is true? That it is they who demonstrate their racism when they will not hold you to account.
>
> How is that black teachers cannot see that what they do is at least as grammatically offensive, as deleterious to your learning, and as intellectually destructive as white liberal "forbearance"? The effect is the same, is it not?
>
> The effect is the same when those who look like us transgress in the same way. That, my son, whatever permissively "race argument" is mounted, is not racial solidarity. It is pedagogical violence.
>
> It amounts to a dereliction of pedagogical duty. It shows a disregard for the black mind. Like many others, I have struggled too hard to inhabit institutions of higher learning as an other to accept indulgence or forbearance.
>
> One should, as other, always be on guard against anything that hints at pedagogical compromise; that is, that expects less of the other on the basis of the other's being other.
>
> The word, my son, is "ask"—phonetically rendered, "äsk." It is not a blunt tool (or sharp one, for that matter; but the utility or preparedness of the implement is not our concern here). It is decidedly not to be pronounced "axe"—"ak-siz," "æks." You, my son, as I know from the hours we spend cutting and splitting wood, are good with an "aks." (Too good, in your sister's opinion. But that is another matter.) In fact, you are so good that I have bought you your own collection of "ak-siz."
>
> To pose a question or to request something from someone is one thing (it is to "äsk"), to split a piece of oak with a sharp metal object is an entirely different matter ("aks"). English, because it is not phonetic, provides us with enough challenges when it comes to pronunciation. Do not create any more in the name of "race" or "culture."
>
> Do not have any truck with those who look like us who imagine that flouting the rules of linguistic discipline is a radical act.[30] Which it is, I regret to say. Radically negligent, of an inverse but equal piece with white liberal guilt.
>
> Give both sets of undemanding teachers a wide berth.
>
> Or, better still, relate the following story about a Black man. I rephrase: relate this story about a man named Black.

His name, Nip, is Joe Black. That is the authority on whom I rely. Joe Black, the first Negro (to deploy the term in its historical context) pitcher to win a World Series game. Black, signed to a minor league contract by the Dodgers in 1950, joined the Jackie Robinson Brooklyn Dodgers after teaching at Plainfield Junior High in his hometown of Plainfield, New Jersey. Black was a graduate of Morgan State University, a liberal arts college for African-Americans located just outside Baltimore. "Gigantic Joe Black," the legendary Dodger scribe Roger Kahn dubbed him, a pitcher who intimidated, a pitcher not afraid to go, as they say in baseball, "headhunting." "In 1952," Kahn writes, "the [then New York] Giants were afraid of Black. They could not beat him when they had to. Black stopped Stan Musial in St. Louis and Del Ennis in Philadelphia and Ted Kluszewski in Cincinnati. He stopped all the best hitters by throwing to spots and keeping them loose, and his relief pitching won the pennant."[31] "Keeping them loose" is Kahn's euphemism for Black's ability to keep hitters off balance by throwing really close to their bodies (with their heads especially vulnerable), thereby making them afraid of being hit.

Much as I warm to Joe Black the relief pitcher, however, it is the resolute, canonical teacher in Joe Black that I wish to invoke here. Specifically, Joe Black the phonetician, Joe Black the philologist, I am almost tempted to say, because of the ways in which he is sensitive to the history of language. More to the point, how Black is sensitive to the relationship of his people to language. It is for this reason that I find solace in Joe Black the teacher, the teacher who insists, almost solemnly, on correct pronunciation—a fellow philologist from another place, a fellow grammarian from a different time, but one whose politico-linguistic sentiment I am all too eager to endorse. As Kahn writes:

> He [Black] makes one point to everyone. It is bigotry to exalt the so-called special language of the blacks. "What is our language?" he asked. "'Foteen' for 'fourteen.' 'Pohleeze' for 'police.' 'Raht back' for 'right back.' 'We is going.' To me any man, white or black, who says whites must learn our language is insulting. What he's saying is that every other ethnic group can migrate to America and master English, but we, who were born here and whose families have lived here for more than a century, don't have the ability to speak proper English. Wear a dashiki or an African hairdo, but in the name of common sense, learn the English language. It is your own."[32]

For Black, diction and disciplining the other's relationship to her or his native tongue is of consequence because, as Heidegger writes, "it is language that tells us about the nature of a thing, provided we respect language's own nature."[33] (In support of this demand, of course, we have Macaulay from the nineteenth century.) In a word, each in his own way, Heidegger and Black evince a reverence for language; each strives to "respect language's own nature"; each is a guardian of "propriety" and "thought." Each, in his own distinct register (the politics of race; philosophy; political theory), is attentive to the precision (pronunciation; diction; "respect" for each and every word) and specificity ("nature"; "propriety") of language because it is through and because of language that we are able to "dwell" (*Wohnen*) in this world. It is only in language that we can be: *Dasein*. Inscribed in the possibility of *Wohnen* is, for Heidegger, a sacred (sanctified by the "fourfold"—earth, sky, mortals, and divinities) relationship to language. The inscription of a responsibility that requires us to understand that to dwell means to "spare and preserve . . . to take under our care. . . . What we take under our care must be kept safe."[34] "What we take under our care" can "be kept safe" only if we dedicate ourselves to "mastering" it.

Language has been entrusted to "our care," and it falls to us to "spare" it, insofar as possible, from all manner of violence. Mispronunciation, and then the raising of that mispronunciation to the level of (racial) pride, amounts to, in Black's pedagogical estimation, wanton violence—deliberate, premeditated, rationalized only in its aftermath. In other words, it is a failure to keep language "safe," to "safeguard" it from phonetic harm. This is tantamount to willful historical neglect, a determination not to heed the charge of "keeping safe."

What follows wanton violence, and the aspect of taking pride in phonetic violence, is nothing other than, as current "common sense" (offensively articulated, itself taking a liberty with Black's usage; but Black is nevertheless audible here, across the generations, despite the more than half century that separates his time from ours) holds, the "soft bigotry of low expectations." That is, the decision not to dwell in language is what produces "ak-siz" and "pohleeze," to say nothing of claiming the right to play fast and loose with "was" and "were." The "soft bigotry of low expectations" violates the "relationship between man and space," a critical recognition in this instance because for Black "space" signifies as blacks' birthright (the right to be in America); at the core of the "relationship between man and space . . . is none other than dwelling, strictly thought and spoken."[35] There can be no disputing the importance that Heidegger assigns to how it is we speak, because in speaking we give voice to "dwelling"; at the very least, we attempt to do so. Heidegger locates "dwelling" in the strictest—that is, most faithful, binding—relationship to thinking ("thought") and speaking ("spoken"). The failure to follow Black's proscriptions produces, to coin a phrase (itself a risky and potentially violent proposition) "commonsense dwelling," the proclivity to "exalt the so-called special language of the blacks," a proclivity venerated by the other itself, sometimes with less self-aggrandizement than others, as well by the self.

Derrida's Idiom and "Chin Music"

"A language," Derrida cautions, "is no idiom."[36] The "idiomatic" can be borne within a language, it can occasionally carry the weight (the burden, if you will) of a language, but it will never rise to the status of a "language." One (Derrida's "idiom") must never be mistaken for the other ("a language"). We do so at our own peril because our *Dasein* can be borne only by "a language." The "idiom" is insufficient, as Heidegger would be sure to remind us, to *Dasein*.

None of this means that because of its "limitations" the "idiom" should be dismissed. *Au contraire.* In fact, as baseball fans know, the idiomatic "keeping them loose" also goes by another, and in this case convenient and apt, moniker. Throwing close to the hitters is also known as "chin music."[37] The pitcher's principal intent when inducing some "chin music" (making the batter bob and weave, preferably nervously) is, as always, to keep the batter honest, as they say. That is, keep the batter from leaning too far over the plate, keep the hitter guessing instead of trying to gain an advantage on the pitcher. Giving the "chin" something to think about, as it were; precisely, making sure that the "chin" thinks about not being hit by the baseball.

Little wonder, then, that when Joe Black implores other African-Americans to "speak proper English" it is music to the ears of grammarians and phoneticians everywhere, to say nothing of run-of-the-mill English teachers waging the battle that is instructing their charges in the art of "speaking proper English." The temptation here is to follow the lead of Shakespeare's Duke Orsino and ask that in his lamentations, or because of them, Joe Black be allowed to "play on," to "give me excess of it."[38] May this appetite never die.

Out of, constitutive of, Black's "insatiable appetite" is the prospect of African-Americans acquiring the skills necessary to "master English." There can be no mistaking that through the demonstration of such "mastery" what emerges is an irrefutable claim to the language into which African-Americans are born. A language, like every other, largely devoid of innocence. That is, a language redolent with beauty, poetry, and the gift of surprise; a language, like every other, burdened by its history of violence, degradation, and inadequacy.

Wohnen, *for a Further, Brief, Moment*

The determination to make a *Wohnen* of the English language, as given to us by Joe Black, refracted through Heidegger's thinking; recognizing the right of the other to live in the only language it knows. To that end, there is nothing to do but *gebaut* (build) an English in which (African-American) *Wohnen* is possible. Or, *Durch, in und wegen der englischen Sprache zu leben,* to phrase Black's project in Heideggerian terms: the desire to, as it were, live through, in, and because of the English language. Or, to return, by way of a Joe Black inflection, once more to that most memorable of Heideggerian political reflections, *Nur die Sprache, unsere Sprache, kann uns jetzt retten.* What this Heideggerian political statement reveals is the absolute claim that Joe Black makes on the English language. Joe Black's claim on the English language *is,* in its fullest sense, nothing short of his locating himself at the very heart—the speaking, beating heart—of the English language itself. Through linguistic discipline, fidelity to phonetics, and conservation of grammar, the English language has, whether it wants to or not, been made fully Joe Black's. Let us announce it as Black's crowning glory, his coup de grâce in that now long-ago exchange with Kahn, his directive that African-Americans establish nothing less than a proprietary relationship to English. After all, as Black declares, with good historical reason, "It is your own." This language, "It is your own."

"Yes, I only have one language, yet it is not mine."

For his part, on the right to "ownership" of his native tongue, the Algerian-born French philosopher Derrida demurs. In fact, Derrida is not only hesitant about his right to make such a claim, about his right to claim the French language as his own, he throws the question of rights directly into question. As we know from his work in *Monolingualism of the Other*, Derrida is well acquainted with the condition of living the complications of language, of living complications in language, of living through this language with which you are in struggle, in such a struggle that your very life depends upon it. Derrida knows this condition intimately. All of the political difficulty of living language that possesses the speaker but cannot be possessed (owned, claimed as a birthright that seems always on the verge of being annulled) is compacted into Derrida's memorable statement "I only have one language; it is not mine."[39] We could propose Derrida's monolingualism in a Heideggerian register so that it is understood as the condition of being owned by the language that is yours while not being able to, as it were, dwell in that language. So that, in fact, the language is, at once, yours and not yours; not yours and then, again, yours. (Language as the "building"—*Bauen*—rather than the "dwelling"—*Wohnen*—"in" which humans inhabit their "native tongue.")

However, Derrida will not permit such a proposition. Having spoken monolingualism, he immediately invokes Heidegger and, in so doing, puts paid to the notion that monolingualism is incompatible with dwelling. "I am monolingual," Derrida declares. "My monolingualism dwells, and I call it my dwelling; it feels like one to me, and I remain in it and inhabit it. It inhabits me. The monolingualism in which I draw my very breath is, for me, my element. Not a natural element . . . but an absolute habitat. . . . I cannot challenge it except by testifying to its omnipresence in me. It would always have preceded me. It is me. For me, this monolingualism is me."[40] Heidegger's philosophy ought, for all intents and purposes, to suffice in this instance.

After all, if "dwelling" (*Wohnen*) has been achieved, then *Being* (*Dasein*—being-there, being in the world) is, at the very least, made imminently possible. Clearly, however, for Derrida this supposition—or Heideggerian logic, if you will, dwelling is *Being, Wohnen est Denken*—does not obtain. Monolingualism as the negation, at the very least, the undoing, of *Wohnen est Denken*; as such, monolingualism uncouples *Wohnen* from *Denken*, raising the speaking of a language to the status of an altogether different order of political problem—perhaps, we should allow, to the status of an irresolvable one that must nevertheless be lived with, or, monolingualism must be lived as the irresolvability of living with-in (a) language. That is, language that possesses but is at once endemically in-hospitable and hostile. (This relationship is borne out etymologically as there is a close link between "hospitality," *hospitalite,* Old French—*hospitalis,* Latin—and "hostility," *hostis.*) The condition of the (colonialized) speaker, as Derrida testifies, reveals the im-possibility of "owning" a language, of language's in-hospitality/hostility to the prospect of being possessed. Language is, as such, constitutively, at least in relationship to the colonized speaker, hostile to the speaker.

Instead of securing *Being,* monolingualism reveals language in its colonialist guise (Derrida's *Monolingualism* iterates the condition of growing up a dis-/enfranchised Jew in Vichy Algiers; in the Jewish neighborhood of El Biar, perched just above the Algerian capital, where Jacques went by "Jackie").[41] Or, differently phrased, as an ambivalent colonialist inheritance. French, as such, is the only language that the Algerian-born Jew can lay claim to as his own; French, as such, is the (first) language, the very language, to deny him possession. If the speaker's first language, "I only have one language," denies him the right to possession, then the speaker—and, by extension, all speakers—can, at best, lay claim to a language. As such, what language does, through obdurate, uncompromising self-possession, is grant the speaker just enough access to give voice to the language. That is, language—this is, we might say, the gift of language, the gift that language makes available to its speakers, holding us always in the thrall of language. Monolingualism "grants" (the gift of language) competency, familiarity, fluency, proficiency, and, at the "higher" or optimal end, a persistent (inexorable) dis-comfiture in relation to the language.

The speaker, we can say, is able to "dwell" (in its "reduced," Derridean sense; that is, not in Heidegger's sense) in the language by demonstrating competency, fluency, and the like but can never fully "own" (the) language. That is, the speaker is, no matter the level of proficiency achieved, always discomfited in, through, and by the language. The language, as such, always withholds itself from the speaker; the language always keeps the speaker at a distance of its choosing from the very language in which the speaker articulates her- or himself, the very language, that is, in which the speaker thinks her or his relationship to language. The language, in its sovereignty, more than anything, holds stubbornly to its "mastery" over the speaker. The language, as it were, trusts only itself with its deepest secrets. The work of the speaker, in seeking to come to terms with this relationship of dis-comfiture, is always Sisyphean. The work of the speaker, then, is not to achieve "mastery" as such, but to labor toward reducing the level of dis-comfiture—to achieve a working level of comfiture that is always informed by the unerasable presence of dis-comfiture. In Heideggerian terms that do not follow Heideggerian logic, it is to build—*Bauen*—a working relationship to language that can never achieve the standing of a dwelling—*Wohnen*.

Joe and "Jackie"

In truth, what both Derrida and Heidegger mark is limit. The limit of the relationship between speaker and language. What Derrida for his part reveals is the way in which language is able to hold itself from—at a distance from—the speaker even as the speaker imagines her- or himself as anything along the spectrum from fundamentally literate to highly proficient (let us say, for the sake of argument, highly "literary") in the language that the speaker speaks.

On the face of it, then, it would seem that Derrida (diasporized, Vichy-disenfranchised Jew) and Joe Black (effectively disenfranchised African-American) are advocating very different relationships to language. However, it is also possible to recognize in monolingualism the establishment of a democratic relationship between all speakers and language, or between all speakers and all languages. To do the work of speaking is always, without exception, to operate under the condition of dis-comfiture. At best, fluency in (a) language is superficial or illusory because it can only mask, momentarily, the intensity that derives from dis-comfiture. In other words, all speakers are in the business of reducing dis-comfiture.

As such, it is the shared dis-comfiture that is monolingualism that allows Black's proprietary relationship to grammar to come fully into its own. The only way to live in language is to submit to the formal structures and demands—grammar, primarily, in this case—in order to reduce (never overcome, of course) the aporia that separates speaker from language. Language, as it were, is the common adversary that is also the only sustainable bond between the speaker and her- or himself.

However, language represents no common (garden-variety) adversary to Joe and "Jackie." Rather, it is that shared adversary that is formidable because it is upon this common adversary that all speakers are equally dependent, in which all speakers are equally (let us pretend, for a second) saturated; the common adversary is the common facilitator. It is the common adversary that mediates the relationship among all speakers, even as every speaker strives, Sisyphus-like, to overcome the unbridgeable aporia. Finally, we might say, it is the specter (that is, the desire for) that is Heidegger's *Wohnen* that haunts not only monolingualism but all other speech as well. Both Black and Derrida, in their own ways, struggle to make language more hospitable, or, phrased as a negation, strive to make language less in-hospitable.

Sisyphus

Language, as such, is the promised land at the top of Sisyphus's hill that retains the most privileged vistas for itself, and itself only. Language, then, lords its "supremacy" over us, making it all the more important that all speakers pool their (formal) resources so as to maximize the possibility of gaining even a glimpse of the vista denied Sisyphus, were his boulder signed "language."

Monolingualism, then, marks that place where our two strangers, others both (each, of course, in his own way), *les autres autres,* Joe Black and Jacques Derrida, encounter one another, a meeting place named, for one, "proper grammar," and for the other, "it is not mine." A meeting place overdetermined by the other's struggle to make language bear the racialized aspirations, the difficulty of speaking a language that is/not yours. A struggle, moreover, to craft out of what is to hand a form of speaking that can bear the truth of all *les autres autres'* experience in and of the world.

In their turn, Black and Derrida offer Ezra the opportunity to think about what it is he can do with language. As much, that is, as he must ponder, seriously but never abjectly, what language can do with and to him; how he can be enthralled by language, which often means that he will be held in the thrall of language, and, as such, his relationship to language will always demand that he attend, above all, to how it is he uses language because of what language, as such, can do.

It is in this push and pull that Derrida's critique reveals a crucial insight. Monolingualism, it can be argued, speaks Derrida's attempt to move beyond the dialectic that is the to-and-fro between being captivated by language or being held captive by language, on the one hand, and, on the other, the always explicable but impossible determination to bring language to heel, to make it subject to our speaking, to demonstrate our "mastery" over it. Monolingualism is never, because it can never be, a simple matter of either/or. Much as it is, in this instance, never a choice, as such, between Black and Derrida. It is, rather, a persistent, relentless, unending negotiation between "I only have one language" and "it is not mine," on the El Biar/Paris end, and "It is your own," on the Plainfield, New Jersey, end.

The "Proper Grammar" of Dis-comfiture

It is, of course, entirely plausible to render this apparent dichotomy as a conflict. There could be little argument against such a presentation. However, what is being posited here is the authority, if you will, of disenfranchisement. If language is beyond our—or all, for that matter—possession, what can be done with, in the name of, (a) language that always, and always a priori, dispossesses the speaker? What kind of speaking does dis-comfiture, and dis-comfiture alone, make possible? Are we to shout from the rooftops, "Dis-comfit yourselves, all speakers, you have nothing to lose but what you have already lost: your comfort in and with language"?

Or are we, to coin a phrase, to confront the matter in a Black register? That is, are we to address the question of record: What is the "proper grammar" of and for dis-comfiture? And to pose this question is to run the risk, we must surely intuit, of undermining the very project on which Joe Black stakes his grammatical self. After all, we cannot—indeed, we must not—know in advance what grammar will be proper to dis-comfiture, what creativity will be required, what liberties will have to be taken with "proper grammar."

Under these conditions, it will be difficult to remain faithful to the teacher from Plainfield, New Jersey. The least we can do is to ask that he keep his most treasured linguistic possession, his fidelity to "proper grammar," close—close to us in order that we might have some historical memory of what and why "proper grammar" means to l'autre, this particular other who also once pitched for a living. In doing so, however, we must never forget that while our Black other always wanted to be a pitcher until history denied him that opportunity (a history undone by Jackie Robinson), Joe Black educated himself in order to teach, and, finally, it was the teacher—who insisted on correct pronunciation, who asked of tous les autres (qui a demandé à tous les autres)—who gave us a legacy brimming with intellectual and political demand. No wonder, then, that the teacher long outlived the pitcher, no matter that it was this self-same pitcher who, memorably, became the first black pitcher to win a World Series game.

If, for no other reason, we attend to the specter of "proper grammar," if, for no other reason, we keep it in our thinking, then we must do so in order that we keep faith with the speaking that was Joe Black. After all, the integrity of Black's struggle, like that of Derrida, resides in his capacity to use the difficulty that is his and our relationship with language to reach far beyond his determination to advocate for "mere" "grammar."

It is for this reason that education, my son, should be a right. I stand foursquare behind that commitment.

However, and this may be my shortcoming, I will never fail to regard it as a privilege. A privilege for and to which I will always be responsible. Because of this, I can never take access to educational institutions for granted. I might even regard it with too much reverence. The upshot of my reverence, however, is that I always approach it with seriousness. And pleasure, because what a thing it is to learn.

This is your world, the one your mother and I have made, are making, for you. The life of college professors in a small college town in upstate New York. A world dominated by books, popular culture, universities, and linguistic facility; a world where Martin Heidegger, Liverpool F.C., the Chicago Cubs, Joel Embiid (you are a 76ers fan; you do further harm to my already traumatized Knicks self), and Russell Wilson (you are also nominally a Seahawks fan, both because it is your sister's team and because of Wilson, a mixed-race quarterback) are all equal. Well, all equal after Liverpool, that is. This is the world in which you are coming of age.

Your maternal grandfather is a retired (and much revered) college teacher, your maternal grandmother is a retired librarian, your paternal grandmother is an avid reader, your mother and I are teachers too, your older brother is a writer, your younger brother is an adept, college-bound student, and your sister has an insatiable appetite for travel. Nip, this is your world, one for which I hold you responsible.

A world of books and learning, a world in which language and learning matter.

You are gifted linguistically, a smart phrase always at the ready. Discipline that propensity so that you might deploy it astutely. It is through language, Nip, that we are in the world. It is a sign of egkrateia—it speaks your ability to master the world. It matters that you acquire this skill, because this world that Trump is making has every intention of mastering you. That is, it is intent on your subjugation.

In all of this, find a language that is your own, a language that can bear the weight of your being/Being.

I have always understood this challenge, to make a language that can bear the weight of Dasein, as Heideggerian in nature. According to Heidegger, German and Greek are the only languages that can bear thought; that is, these are the only languages in which we can do philosophy.

It wouldn't hurt to prove Heidegger wrong. But I am not asking for that. All I want is that you take care with language so that you have always to hand, or as often as possible, the facility, fluency, and sense of the moment to command language.

For my part, I am trying here to command "another kind of writing." But only so that you can acquire "another way of thinking." Your way of thinking, of "thinking thinking," as you are prone to tease me, is what you should always keep in the forefront of your thinking.

In the face of difficulty, sometimes in the face of injustice, sometimes when fortune smiles on you, do not seek relief from difficulty—always, before all else, think your place in the world, think who you are in the world, think what the world gives you, often fortuitously, when you least expect it, and, in turn, what the world will take from you, often with no good reason.

I want Ezra to confront the question of who he is as the founding question of his existence. I want him to be troubled by this question, troubled as it applies to matters of race, troubled as it applies to the issue of adoption, troubled as to what it means to have to confront the possibility of "passing." I want him to be troubled by this question so that he will be required to grapple with it, to live with it as a permanent or intermittent form of discomfiture. I want the question to keep him up at night, to disturb his sleep in the small hours of the morning. I want him to approach all the important questions in his life in this way. Better still, I want him to live in expectation of the question. The question, or the questions that derive from the question, as a source of infinite intellectual possibility. I want him to be, simultaneously, prepared for the question(s) and yet always taken entirely by surprise by it. I want him to trust nothing so much as his capacity to think. I want him to take joy in thinking. To think is always, and before all else, to refuse answers that reveal themselves too easily.

> *I will not resort to Rudyard Kipling's best-known poem and ask, Nip, that you "treat these two imposters just the same." "If" only, as it were.*
>
> *And so I urge discernment and discrimination. In that spirit, "treat" each "imposter" you encounter on her, his, or their own merits. Judge them in terms of who they are, or in terms of who it is they present themselves to you as.*
>
> *I am asking much of you, my son, perhaps more than you have to offer.*
>
> *I know, however, that this will not surprise you because you are well aware that I would always rather err on that side. I ask for more with only the slightest apology.*
>
> *At a certain point, however, it will be up to you to decide how much it is you will ask of yourself. That, Nip, will be a crucial moment. It could as easily be a decisive one. (It often is, my son, it could not be otherwise.)*
>
> *In the moment of decision, I have for you a singular hope (a word you like, "singular," a word over which we have tussled, you and I—the difference between "single" and "singular"). It is my hope that you will be haunted, and haunted again, troubled, unsettled, maybe even a little angry and put off, by what it is I have written in your name here. Your name, titular it appears here, on the cover page:* An Essay for Ezra.
>
> *Because of you, I must think of how it is I critique Trump as I would not have had to were you not in this world. Because of Trump, I must think of how it is I care for you, love you, and impart what it is I know to you as I would not have had to were he not in the position he is in.*
>
> *Because of you, I now understand "terror" differently, contemplating what it might mean to live not "in terror of" but "for terror," in its Hegelian and Heideggerian formulations.*
>
> *You have made of "terror" a gift to me.*

No wonder, then, that I want Ezra to strive for—achieve, if at all possible—a Socratic "mastery" over himself. In Plato's *Phaedo*, a dialogue that takes place literally hours before Socrates's death, Socrates explains to his interlocutor Simmias why it is important to achieve "mastery" over not just "certain pleasures" but all of them.

Most important, Socrates describes the process of acquiring virtue (and, or, through, "wisdom"), a process that depends on not mistaking virtue for that which passes itself off as virtue:

> My good Simmias, I fear that this is not the right exchange to attain virtue, to exchange pleasures for pleasures, pains for pains and fears for fears, the greater for the less like coins, but that the only valid currency for which all these things should be exchanged is wisdom. With this we have real courage and moderation and justice and, in a word, true virtue, with wisdom, whether pleasures and fears and all such things be present or absent. When these are exchanged for one another in separation from wisdom, such virtue is only an illusory appearance of virtue.[42]

It is the binary mode of discursive and political "exchange" that Socrates insists must be broken. "Pain" cannot be dialectically bound to "pain," similarly for "fear." The very logic that so intimately connects "pleasures" to "pleasures," that is the cycle that must be disrupted in order to arrive, first, at "virtue," itself only a way station on the road to "wisdom." In order to achieve "wisdom," "real courage" will be required. That is, it will not suffice, by any means, to follow that line of advocacy that insists on being inextricably bound in a dialectical relation. An action of self-mastery (named, as is so often the case with Socrates, "moderation" here) and "real courage" will be necessary to attain "justice," a "justice" that does not rely solely on itself, that is dependent on more than merely the instruments of "justice," but a "justice" that enables the acquisition of "wisdom."

We are, of course, free to quibble that "wisdom" is hardly what identity politics advocates are in search of (although, one suspects, it would neither go amiss nor be dismissed out of hand, as such). However, if we grant that what Socrates is undoing is the dialectic, and that his intended target is the dialectic as the hegemonic currency, to mix metaphors, the "wisdom" becomes something politically useful (Brechtian, in Jameson's argument) rather than merely an exercise in philosophical exegesis. "Wisdom," then, is that mode of thinking that will not succumb to what is current, to that form of discourse that produces the "illusory appearance of virtue." "Wisdom" is what stands definitively against the "illusory."

The manner in which "wisdom" is presented (are we witnessing a dissembling or the truth?) and the "Form" that "wisdom" assumes are crucial, appropriately, because it is in the *Phaedo* that Socrates delineates his "theory of Form" more fully and carefully than anywhere except the *Republic*. The "Form" matters because, as in his discussion with Simmias and Cebes about how it is that we come to acquire knowledge (and the function of the—immortal—soul in this acquisition), both Cebes and Socrates recognize that "for us learning is nothing other than recollection."[43] (For Socrates, Cebes's assertion is, true to form, phrased as a question to Simmias, "What we call learning is recollection?" It is, however, a crucial distinction, as will be argued shortly.) It would be entirely explicable to prioritize the role of "recollection" over "learning" in this discussion about the immortality of the soul. It is, after all, precisely because of the soul's immortality that it is possible to access that knowledge that is immemorially stored within it, that knowledge that can be "recollected" into a "Form" that allows us to live a "virtuous" life. The knowledge is, in this rendering, extant, and it is simply—to grossly misstate the matter—up to us to bring it back, to reach for it in that "virtuous" archive.

Here it might be instructive to employ the Socratic method—proceeding through the question—as a means of resituating the work of "learning." Socrates's question to Simmias is, of course, not a question as such. It stands as its own form of assertion. However, Socrates's form (of sourcing knowledge, so to speak) provides the occasion for thinking the relationship between "recollection" and "learning." At the very least, we can say, "recollection" as such is by no means a visceral response to knowledge. We do not automatically know how to recollect. Instead, it is always necessary for us to "learn" how to "recollect." How we do that comes, of course, with its own set of questions. To begin with, what is it in us that inclines us toward "recollection"? How do we know we are "recollecting"? How, and this is important in light of Socrates's warning against simulation, can we be sure of what it is we are "recollecting"? How do we reassemble, into/as a body of knowledge, that which we have "recollected"? How do we arrange, in what order, that which is now available to us through "recollection"?

As such, we could say that in affirming the importance of pedagogy, Socrates opens the way for the anthropology of "recollection." Again, however, we come to anthropology through the imperative to "learn." Always, of course, on the grounds—as Socrates urges us—of discernment, of making decisions about how it is we work with a body of knowledge; how, we could say, we handle the knowledge that the soul offers us for and through "recollection." To "learn," then, as itself constituting a very particular mode of intellectual labor.

> *Still and all, only you can decide if my bequest is a blessing or a curse. Or both; or, by turns, one and then the other. Or, maybe, neither, which I rather hope will not be the case. I offer this essay, as you well know, with love. I have no choice but to trust you with this bequest, with all its good intentions. I ask your indulgence—forgive me for all its imperfections.*
>
> *Paradoxically, it is my hope that the terror of Trump, which has so dominated your life since November 2016, can be put to good pedagogical use. It is my hope that the terror that Trump is will terrify you at an intellectual level. It is my hope, because I love you, that the terror of Trump will forever make you allergic to all modes of unthinking affirmation. We know, you, your mother, and me, that white essentialism, white nationalism, white supremacy, will stop at nothing. We know that it can kill people, white as well as black, but black in disproportionate numbers.*
>
> *It is because I love you, Nip, that I want so desperately to make this bequest to you. It is the greatest gift that I can give you.*

All of this, of course, is complicated by the fact that in certain moments Ezra will simply be vulnerable because he is black. And because he is black he will be, with no cause except racism, exposed to the violence of the world in ways that his white friends, his mother, his grandfather, the white girl he might be dating, are not. That is the force of the contradiction that he must confront. It is this inevitable moment for which he must prepare himself. That is the moment, Jane and I know, for which we can never adequately prepare him. In that way, his vulnerability and ours are shared, but by no means equally. As important, we are trying to explain to Nip that Trump is simply the latest incarnation of a racist American polis. Trump is merely the intensification of an old American predilection. The latest, but by no means the last, chapter in a long story. Fortunately for Nip, he has enough memory of the Barack Obama presidency. He has the broad—if not deep—sense that his way of moving in the world, his understanding of who he is, could be, was, just a few short years ago, different. Nip recalls Obama with a wistful fondness—"I wish Obama were still president," he remarks longingly. It helps Nip, of course, that like him Obama is the son of a white American mother and an African father. Like his, a white midwestern mother, to boot. Kansas and Iowa, respectively.

This inclining, this "training," if you will, of Ezra for discrimination is no mean task. This is his "doctrinal apprenticeship." Obama, as Nip well knows, is the exception—theirs is a fortuitous similarity, part of the African-American's presidency coinciding with the years in which our son has been growing up. Discrimination, in its etymological sense, will require Nip, crucially, for him, to refuse the temptation of essentialism of any stripe. For Ezra a critique of essentialism must begin with his own self-designation. That is, he must frame, he must phrase, his assertion, "I am black," or "I am African-American," not in the declarative but rather undertake to think who he is as a question: "What claim am I making when I pronounce myself 'black' or 'African-American'?" It must proceed from there into an inquiry about how his insistence on his blackness is in-/commensurate with how the world apprehends him. Black in relation to what? To whom? As such, his inquiry will have to include a series of questions about how this locates him in relation to his mother, his maternal grandparents, and his brothers, all of whom are white.

Nip will have to decide if a distinction exists between his maternal family and his paternal one (coloured South Africans, a racial designation that continues to have sociopolitical effects in the post-apartheid state)—will their geopolitical distance apart mean that there will be different levels of intimacy that he can achieve? Should such a question even present itself? He will have to ask himself about his linguistic habits, one of which is to suggest, generally in humorous moments (when we're kidding around or listening to music), that "Daddy and I can use the N-word, but you can't, Mommy." Whether or not to enfranchise himself (and me) linguistically, and disenfranchise his mother, is, we try to tell him (if not in quite these terms), a political decision.

Nip, can you learn to "despise" that language, that privileged position you understand yourself to have in relation to a particular racially historicized vocabulary, that you "love"?
The thing-in-itself: Ding an sich: love.

This is a political decision for which Nip is responsible. For which he is responsible to himself, to Jane, to me. What, we are all trying to figure out, are the effects of Nip's (and my) linguistic enfranchisement? We are of course not the first family to confront this issue, but it is nonetheless an issue we must address because it, a priori, has the effect of determining (delimiting) who in the household can, in very particular instances, use what words in relation to whom. It might be only one word, it might be several, but even if it is only one word, it is an important one and a term freighted with an ugly political history.

"But I'm not a nigga either . . ."

Dave Chappelle explains that "on network television they have a department called 'Standards and Practices.' This is a department that tells you what you can and cannot say on television. And if you're doing your job well you should never hear from them.

"But if you're making 'Chappelle's Show' you'll hear from these motherfuckers all the time. . . ."

Rene: "The sketches are fantastic."

David: "Then why am here?"

Rene: "Because, David, you can never say the word 'faggot' on our network."

"I said, 'Alright, I'll take it out.'

"As I was leaving, it occurred to me. 'Hey Rene, quick question . . . Why is it that I can say the word 'nigga' with impunity but I can't say the word 'faggot?'"

Rene: "Because, David, you are not gay."

"I said, 'Well, Rene, I'm not a nigga either.'"[44]

And yet Chappelle uses this word, indiscriminately, in his sketches, designating anything from another black person to a friend who is white to a white crack addict to . . . well, just about everyone. "Nigga" is Chappelle's repeated self-description.

On this count Chappelle's logic is simultaneously inarguable and unacknowledged self-indictment. Chappelle is absolutely right in refusing Rene's essentialist implication, which bears traces of Chappelle's "alphabet people" critics. Rene's logic, following the calculus of identity politics, is that because Chappelle is black he is free—and he alone, in this conversation, we presume—to use the word "nigga." To do so repeatedly, and "with impunity."

On the other hand, however, if, as Chappelle does, you give the word "nigga," or "nigger," farceuristic life, repeatedly, if you invoke it so routinely as to make its usage entirely unremarkable, why *would you—as if it were a revelation—get your hackles up when that self-presentation attaches itself to you bureaucratically, as it were? Bureaucratically, in the form of Rene feeling entirely free to remind you of who you are—a "nigga." You really shouldn't be surprised, should you, David? You opened the door to this, didn't you?*

You are the word you keep alive. You are—as the other, to the white bureaucrat—the self-designation you keep in circulation.

Reaping what you sow . . . We all know what that parable promises, don't we, David?

In this encounter, what Chappelle comes, literally, face-to-face with is the impossibility of a politics of circumscription.

Implicitly, Chappelle understands his politics of language to be operative. He, alone, can dispense the word "nigga." Forgetting, all the while, that Rene has in her bureaucratic arsenal a force infinitely more powerful: the Word ("Law") that is white authority.

In giving permission for the farceur to give life to the word, the Word reveals how the word is entirely free to hoist itself by its own petard.

The joke's on you, David. Not on Rene. On you.

And you did everything to set up the joke.

You can't get out of this one. You can't just up and walk away, dropping your mike and declaring, "I'm out."

A Socratic Ethics

Can Ezra censure his mother if he and I are free to invoke the term? How does the economy of racially circumscribed domestic circulation work if not through a perverse form of racial "disenfranchisement"? The N-word is of course a term with which Nip is familiar through popular culture—the internet, the music he hears (Chance the Rapper is a big favorite and is moderate in his deployment of the term; Travis Scott is another, and the term's invocation is a matter of habit to him), give him a certain license to use the term. As such, whether or not the term should continue to be used, not only by African-Americans but by anyone at all, is the subject of a debate that is long-standing. After all, the economy of discourse is such that (racially inflected) delimitation or prohibition is almost impossible to impose once a term has been put into circulation, regardless of who instigates it or who the community of origin might be.

When there is no thinking, the "state of language" will become ominous. We must pay attention to what it is the language as such is reaching toward. The "state of Trump's language" is what aspires to be the "language" and, as such, the "ideology" of the "state." What Trump says, and how his support staff and partisans act in response, inscribes the desire for full synchrony between the "state" of white "language" and the political desires of white "bodies." Nothing divides them. This is Barthes turned to nightmarish ends. Let us apostrophize it as "Charlottesville," as, in Trump's words, "There are good people on both sides."

Discrimination, One Last Time

In his dissembling, Trump demonstrates his inability to discriminate. We understand perfectly well why it is he is recuperating white supremacists. These supremacists are his ideological kin, conceived narrowly and expansively. Understood narrowly, only some of Trump's ideological kin share, in strictly cultural-economic terms, his class; in broader terms, however, this is big-tent white supremacism—copious and accommodating enough to include college-educated white suburban women (minivan-driving "soccer moms"), Wall Street corporate types (happy to lower their taxes), and unskilled white men, from upstate New York to the Mississippi Delta, angry at the specter of a world passing them by. Come one, come all, white supremacists of all stripes are welcome.

Trump's intellectual deficiency, or his cynicism, or his ability to rally white xenophobes, his capacity to instill terror, is only part of the problem. It is, as I have argued, a significant set of problems. However, what matters at least as much to me is that you, Ezra, will apprehend "terror" in its full complexity. That you will recoil from and resist Trump's brand of terror, and that you will, in the very same breath, keep Kojève's, Hegel's, and Heidegger's injunctions close. That you will make out of Trump's terror a thing of Hegelian-Heideggerian thought. In order that you might be/*Be* in the world as a *Being* of thinking. That you might, as it were, fight terror with terror.

> What I have really tried to explain to you, Nip, is that Trump is not the only political figure, for which read "constituency of white racists," unable to master the work of discrimination.
> Perhaps, more than anything, I am asking you to learn the skill—Foucault's "art," and Machiavelli's too, if in lesser measure—of what

it means to think your place in the world. To acquire the discipline so that you not only viscerally understand that—God knows it is obvious—there are certainly not "good people on both sides" but can also explicate, to yourself, why it is that some of these people are constitutively "bad."

In truth, caring for yourself might require you, as much as anything else, to know who they are.

I am not, much as I learn from James Baldwin, asking you to love them. That is your decision.

I am, however, asking you to, insofar as it is possible, know them.

That act, of striving to know them, that act, my son, is what allows you to rise to the level of thinking.

Once more, to interpose myself into Foucault's notion of care of the self: knowing the self is possible only if the self cares for itself enough to think itself.

Begin there, Ezra, this is my last request. Begin with thinking how it is you care for yourself, care for your place in the world, care for the care of those about whom you care. Begin there and I might, as far as it is possible (and I doubt that it is very far, but you must allow me this, I am your father), be able to trust you just an iota more to the future.

Regardless, it is all, it is the most, I can do. Would that I were able to do more.

I cannot. I now understand, as I will often in the days, months, and years to come, that there is only so much I can do. That is, in moments I can help, in other moments I will be nigh on helpless.

And, so, Nip, I have to, I must, much as I do not want to, my son, I must . . .

I must trust you to the future.

Here I follow Audre Lorde:

> *we seek beyond history*
> *for a new and more possible meeting*

In so doing, I am trusting you. And, in trusting you, I am trusting what it is your mother, your siblings, your grandparents have given you: that a "new and more possible meeting" might present itself to you, in your lifetime, through and because of how it is you live your life.

Nip, like James Baldwin, you will be left to testify on your own behalf.

In this spirit of precarity (living in a history that is an indifferent actor; history as an often inexplicable force; history as, one hopes, holding always within itself, often at the least expected moments, the unfolding of the event) and confidence (in you, in what is in you, in your ability and determination to meet what this history throws up, throws at you), my son, I trust you to the future.

Trusting you to the future is a sign of my helplessness. I submit, with no great pleasure and often in bad faith, to contingency.

However, trusting you to the future may also be the only gift of worth, of any possible worth, that I have to offer you.

In all probability I am giving you a gift that is not mine to give—a "new and more possible meeting."

But I insist on making the gift.

A gift addressed to you, written, titularly, in your name.

But signed, again and again, in mine. Signed, and underscored: "terror."

Postscript

November 7, 2020

> Rather an end with terror than terror without end!
> —Marx, "The Eighteenth Brumaire of Louis Bonaparte"

It was Jane who suggested it. That we gather in front of the TV when Joe Biden was declared the winner in the 2020 U.S. presidential election. Ironic, because of Nip, Jane, and me, Jane is the least enamored of electoral politics. Three glasses in hand, she secured a bottle of sparkling apple cider to celebrate.

At 11:15 a.m. on November 7, 2020, we duly took our seats to watch CNN. Nine minutes later, CNN anchor Wolf Blitzer announced Biden's victory. We raised our glasses. We didn't cheer.

Relief.

Relief. That is all we felt.

On the CNN desk Blitzer turned first to David Axelrod, former Obama adviser, and then to Gloria Borger, senior political commentator, before inviting Van Jones, African-American political commentator and veteran of the Obama White House, to speak. Barely in control of himself, Jones, visibly moved, gave shaking voice to the relief we felt in our household that morning:

> It's easier to be a parent this morning.
> It's easier to be a dad.
> It's easier to tell your kids character matters.
> Telling the truth matters.
> Being a good person matters.[1]

Ezra watched Jones but did not say anything.

As soon as Jones was finished speaking, Jane asked him how he felt having just watched a black man break down on national TV in relief. Nip turned silent, unwilling to engage.

Ezra is twelve now. Five foot ten and a half and inching ever upward, it seems. He wears a size 11 sneaker.

On the equivalent occasion four years ago he was devastated.

On this morning, he got up from the couch, raised himself to his full height, and left the room.

He had other things on his mind. And what they were he would not say.

A rare enigmatic moment from our normally irrepressible and intensely voluble son.

I wonder if perhaps he knows the continued threat that faces him. After all, some seventy-four million Americans voted for Trump.

Relief, respite, is not the end of terror.

The choices Marx offers are hardly ideal. To perish at the hands of terror is preferable to unending terror.

Hard to argue with Van Jones, though. November 7, 2020, was indeed a "good day."

Ezra, as far as I can glean, was already preparing himself for the days to come. Who knows what they might yield?

Accept the relief that the moment offers and ready the preadolescent black self for what is to come.

Acknowledgments

I began this essay less than twelve hours after Donald Trump won the 2016 presidential election. I wrote simply because I had to, because I had to find a way to speak to Ezra. In a frenzied thirty-six hours I wrote almost seventeen thousand words. Now, three and a half years later, especially in the wake of George Floyd's killing, it feels as if I never really stopped writing this essay; as if the need for me to speak to Ezra presents itself ever and anew with a fresh urgency. Mercifully, I added the final touches on the eve of Trump's defeat.

Over the course of the writing, I have been fortunate in my editor, Doug Armato. Doug gave me the latitude to find my way to a writing. I tried first this form then that one, knowing that I could, no matter my hesitation, abandon my writing into his keeping. Doug helped me write this essay in ways that I am sure he would prefer not to know about. Nonetheless, his insights, his thoughtfulness, his carefully chosen words, were, as they always are, invaluable. I thank him especially for being able to see, and to bring my attention to, the "whole" of my project. Doug is always on hand to help me "see"—in Heidegger's sense—what I am trying to do. And has been able to do so, I hasten to add, for almost two decades now.

In the process of working toward that moment when I could finally abandon the essay (we abandon our projects, we are never done with them, or them with us), I once again relied on my friendships with John Drabinski and Jeff Nealon. In the most difficult moments, when the harshest questions presented themselves, Jeff and John were supportive. What is more, they were both funny in doing so. I have immense regard for their work; I am glad that I am able to count on them in the moment of record. I remain, happily, in their debt.

In the past decade and a half or so, I have found in (Fr.) Robert Caserio a generous interlocutor, a sharp mind, a resolute disposition, and a catholic appetite for reading. Without fail, he will point me in one direction or another, suggest this text or that. His magnanimity of spirit is outdone only by his capacity for helping me keep faith in whatever project it is I am working on. As always, Eminence, my thanks.

I would be unable to navigate the world of high tech without Ms. Renee Milligan and Ms. Donna Pinnisi. No doubt I test their patience. I am tempted to apologize but that would be out of character. The best I am willing to offer is a grudging thanks.

I am grateful to Tim Campbell, colleague, friend, fellow Knicks sufferer, who read the drafts with a lucid and a kind eye.

My thanks to our older son, Alex, for taking me, not once but twice, to a live comedy show in Minneapolis.

I can only say to 'Trane, no thanks for annoying me no end.

To my daughter, Bug: I could not be prouder of you, Kiddo. You remind me every day what a remarkable human being you are.

My thanks to Steve and Mary for making Minneapolis, without fail, hospitable.

Over the past sixteen years, I have had many an occasion to express my gratitude to Ron and Peg Juffer. Once more, thanks for those basketball games in the gym, granddad, and those daily nine holes on the Landsmeer golf course in Orange City. Once more, no one makes a better strawberry-pretzel dessert, grandma.

Once more, *gracias*, Juanita. *Lo siento.* Your reservations, I know, are many. Your example as parent, teacher, and committed political actor remains a steadfast beacon to me (and Ingrid too).

Por Izzy, mi guapa perra. Thanks for taking me on a walk every morning.

Finally, to Nip, self-proclaimed "complicated kid." That you are, son, that you are. And more power to you for being "complicated." You are wonderfully talented as a musician (guitar, keyboards, percussion, a little trumpet). Your basketball skills came as a wonderful surprise in the 2019–20 season. It is something to see the joy you take in the game, although I'd really appreciate you laying off my woeful Knicks. I find your musical repertoire nothing short of astounding. I find it inexplicable that as a twelve-year-old you like, in no particular order, Breakbot, the Ink Spots, Frank Sinatra, Cannonball Adderley, Bill Evans, Miles Davis, Keith Jarrett, Chance the Rapper, and Travis Scott. As much as anything, however, it was an honor to watch you improvise, on that one unforgettable Tuesday morning (January 21, 2020), on your guitar.

I love you, Nip, always.

Ithaca, St. Paul, Orange City

Notes

1. November 2016

1. "Transcript: Donald Trump's Taped Comments about Women," *New York Times*, December 17, 2019, https://www.nytimes.com; emphasis added.

2. Glenn Kessler, Salvador Rizzo, and Meg Kelly, "President Trump Made 19,127 False or Misleading Claims in 1,226 Days," *Washington Post*, June 1, 2020, https://www.washingtonpost.com.

3. See Michael Inwood, *A Heidegger Dictionary* (Malden, Mass.: Blackwell, 1999). Heidegger, for his part, distinguishes—emphatically—between the two renderings, preferring *verstehen* (which he also sometimes renders as *ver-stehen*) to *Verstand*; he considers the latter to be vulgar because of its ability to "flatten out" the meaning of the term. It is also important to recognize that while Heidegger sets great store by Reason, he also critiques Reason as being an object to thought.

4. Of course, we are bound to apprehend "common sense" in its Gramscian formulation: that is, a language, with all its tropes, conceits, and metaphors and in all its idioms, in which power (or hegemony) is inscribed so as to gloss the articulation of power as that which incarnates the "common" in order to diffuse (into everyday language) the effects of how language does its political work. (In this regard, Gramsci's most faithful interpreter remains Stuart Hall.)

5. *Ver-stehen*, obviously, is a neologism—an awkward, ungainly one at that—invented out of two extant terms to articulate what it is Chappelle's critique in *8:46* conveys.

6. Inwood, *Heidegger Dictionary*, 234.

7. The "thing" is invoked here in the sense that Michel Foucault deploys it in his critique of Machiavelli's *The Prince*. In this context Foucault renders the "thing"—"government as the government of things"—as that "art" of government that determines or shapes relations between state power and the "objects" on which that power acts, on which power has the ability to act. Michel Foucault, *Security, Territory, Population: Lectures at the Collège de France 1977–1978*, trans. Graham Burchell (New York: Palgrave Macmillan, 2007), 97.

8. "Christopher Dorner's Manifesto, in Full" (redacted), February 2013, LAist, posted June 12, 2020, https://laist.com.

9. "*8:46,* Dave Chappelle," YouTube, posted June 11, 2020, https://www
.youtube.com.

10. Alexandre Kojève, *Introduction to the Reading of Hegel: Lectures on
the "Phenomenology of Spirit,"* ed. Allan Bloom, trans. James H. Nichols Jr.
(Ithaca, N.Y.: Cornell University Press, 1969), 27.

11. This condition is well known to black America, a recognition that
grounds W. E. B. Du Bois's charge to future generations in his 1958 autobiography. A committed communist by the end of his life, Du Bois had
exiled himself to Ghana, embraced the Soviet Union, and denounced the
liberal democracy of the United States. America's capacity to do harm in
the world led Du Bois to the conclusion that there was only one possible
salvation for the nation: "Our children must rebuild it." W. E. B. Du Bois,
*The Autobiography of W. E. B. Du Bois: A Soliloquy on Viewing My Life from
the Last Decade of Its First Century* (New York: Oxford University Press,
2007), 295. And they must "rebuild it" not as a representative democracy
but as a communist society. Representative democracy had not only failed
black Americans but also fomented racism and succeeded in preventing
a radical, antiracist working-class unity from emerging in the United
States. Du Bois's charge, however, no matter its urgency, rings hollow. It
rings hollow because generation after generation of black Americans have
taken up this work, only to find themselves repeatedly cast as Sisyphus.

12. In this regard, among other contributions, Abigail Cerra's work
is significant. See her op-ed, bylined only "former Minneapolis public
defender," "Consider What Would Have Happened to George Floyd If
He Had Survived," MN Injustice, accessed March 9, 2021, https://www
.mninjustice.org/op-ed; and Jennifer Mayerle, "Practice of 'Coaching'
Minneapolis Police Officers Questioned by Conduct Oversight Commis-
sion," CBS Minnesota, August 25, 2020, https://minnesota.cbslocal.com.
I highlight Cerra's recent work because most of it has focused on police
practices and judicial underwriting of those practices in Minneapolis. See
also Alex S. Vitale's argument on the colonialist, racist history of policing
in *The End of Policing* (London: Verso, 2017).

13. "Christopher Dorner's Manifesto."

14. This name, I hope to suggest in a future project, can and must take
its cue from "utopia." That is, the name committed to ending the domi-
nation of the state, capitalism, and representative democracy as the first
and only horizon of possibility in which humans are able to *be.*

15. CHAZ, founded in the wake of and in response to George Floyd's
murder, lasted from the first week of June 2020 to July 1, 2020. It included
the barricading of the Seattle Police Department's East Precinct. After the
authorities shut it down, the protesters moved to other zones in the city.

16. See Jacques Derrida's work on the Shoah, *Cinders,* trans. Ned Luk-
acher (Minneapolis: University of Minnesota Press, 2014); and his most
sustained reflection on his early life—as a Jew—in Algeria, *Monolingualism
of the Other; or, The Prosthesis of Origin,* trans. Patrick Mensah (Stanford,
Calif.: Stanford University Press, 1998). I take up the issue of Derrida's

complicated relationship to Algeria in the final chapter of my book *The Burden of Over-representation: Race, Sport, and Philosophy* (Philadelphia: Temple University Press, 2018).

17. Jacques Derrida, *On Cosmopolitanism and Forgiveness*, trans. Mark Dooley and Michael Hughes (London: Routledge, 2001), 57.

18. Again, see Vitale's *End of Policing*. See also Radley Balko, *Rise of the Warrior Cop: The Militarization of America's Police Forces* (New York: Public Affairs, 2014); Jeff Pegues, *Black and Blue: Inside the Divide between the Police and Black America* (Amherst, N.Y.: Prometheus Books, 2017); and Kristian Williams, *Our Enemies in Blue: Police and Power in America* (Oakland, Calif.: AK Press, 2015).

19. Kristy Parker, "Prosecute the Police," *The Atlantic*, June 13, 2020, https://www.theatlantic.com.

20. Angela J. Haverty and Earl Smith, *Policing Black Bodies: How Black Lives Are Surveilled and How to Work for Change* (New York: Rowman & Littlefield, 2018), ix.

21. See Jennifer E. Cobbina, *Hands Up, Don't Shoot: Why Protests in Ferguson and Baltimore Matter, and How They Changed America* (New York: New York University Press, 2019).

22. Cobbina, 3.

23. Cobbina, 27.

24. Trump settled the case without admitting wrongdoing. In *The Making of Donald Trump* (Brooklyn: Melville House, 2016), David Cay Johnston points to Trump's history of settling without acknowledging wrongdoing—this practice extends from housing discrimination to shady business dealings with figures in the New York–area underworld.

25. The young men's sentences were vacated and they were awarded a $41 million settlement for wrongful conviction and imprisonment.

26. I address this issue in the introduction and the opening chapter of my work on football, *Long Distance Love: A Passion for Football* (Philadelphia: Temple University Press, 2007), and in the chapters on C. L. R. James and Stuart Hall in *What's My Name? Black Vernacular Intellectuals* (Minneapolis: University of Minnesota Press, 2003).

27. Roland Barthes, *Camera Lucida: Reflections on Photography*, trans. Richard Howard (New York: Hill and Wang, 2010), 119.

28. Roland Barthes, *Roland Barthes by Roland Barthes*, trans. Richard Howard (New York: Hill and Wang, 2010), 145.

29. Martin Heidegger, *What Is Called Thinking?*, trans. Fred D. Wieck and J. Glenn Gray (New York: Harper & Row, 1968), 4.

30. Heidegger, 4.

31. In the most reductive fashion, forging an "unsubstantiated" relationship between Heidegger's philosophy and his support for National Socialism is the interrogative force that drives Hugo Ott's biography *Martin Heidegger: A Political Life*, trans. Allen Blunden (New York: Basic Books, 1993). By "unsubstantiated" I mean that at no point does Ott engage Heidegger's philosophical work. His charge against Heidegger rests

entirely on unverified logic, official documents (correspondence with other figures, memos from Heidegger's time as rector of Freiburg), and insinuation.

32. Toni Morrison, *Beloved* (New York: Alfred A. Knopf, 1987), dedication.

33. Michael Van Sickler, "Video of Villages Man Chanting 'White Power' Retweeted, Then Deleted, by Trump," *Tampa Bay Times*, June 28, 2020, https://www.tampabay.com.

2. Martin Luther King and White People

1. I delineate the concept of "the burden of over-representation" in my 2018 book of the same title.

2. Martin Luther King Jr., "The Power of Nonviolence," in *I Have a Dream: Writing and Speeches That Changed the World*, ed. James Melvin Washington (New York: Harper One, 1992), 31.

3. For information on the speech in which Washington made this statement, see "Booker T. Washington (1856–1915): Speech to the Atlanta Cotton States and International Exposition," October 18, 1895, American RadioWorks, https://american radioworks.publicradio.org. Of course, what Washington overlooked—or would not allow himself to acknowledge—was that in the United States the "social" is indissociable from institutional (that is, political) power and that his dream of a separate and distinct black socius was unsustainable in an America dominated by the enfranchised white majority. On the signal importance of the franchise, Du Bois writes: "The power of the ballot we need in sheer self-defence,—what else shall save us from a second slavery? Freedom, too, the long-sought, we still seek,—the freedom of life and limb, the freedom to work and think." W. E. B. Du Bois, *The Souls of Black Folk* (1903; repr., Boston: Bedford Books, 1997), 43. However, it is in Du Bois's chapter "Of Mr. Booker T. Washington and Others" that King (and Ezra) finds greater resonance about the shared responsibility for the abject political condition of the Negro. Critiquing Washington for his economically driven accommodationism with white authority, Du Bois argues, "His [Washington's] doctrine has tended to make the whites, North and South, shift the burden of the Negro problem to the Negro's shoulders and stand aside as critical and rather pessimistic spectators, when in fact the burden belongs to the nation, and the hands of none of us are clean if we bend not our energies to righting these great wrongs" (72). Du Bois's "pessimism" figures not as the Gramscian precondition for political action ("pessimism of the intellect, optimism of the will"), but as the political indictment of white America: "pessimism" as the privilege of the perpetrator. And, like all privilege, it is a "pessimism" unearned, and, as such, it is unethical. Du Bois, however, does not halt his call to responsibility there. All Americans are charged with the huge task of "righting these great wrongs," because—and this is the heart of his indictment as much as it constitutes the "nationalizing" of political responsibility—there is no room for a Pon-

tius Pilate in fin de siècle America because the "hands of none of us are clean if we bend not our energies" where there is work to be done. The American national project is, in Du Bois's calculus, a zero-sum game. It is, literally, a case of all or nothing: the nation must be equal for all, or it will destroy itself in upholding its race-based inequality. Democracy, like sovereignty, is indivisible.

4. King as speaking a Du Boisian truth, not (only) to power but to a nation that had historically (willfully) failed African-Americans, once with the bureaucratic ineptitude, insufficient political will, and wide-scale mismanagement that was Reconstruction (Du Bois takes particular aim at the Freedmen's Bureau in *The Souls of Black Folk*) and again with the red-baiting that was the McCarthy era, that historical moment in which the United States clamped down on freedom of expression and freedom of political association. That second failure proved intolerable to Du Bois, driving him into self-imposed exile in Ghana, where he died, on August 27, 1963, in the capital city of Accra.

5. Emmanuel Levinas, *Otherwise Than Being, or Beyond Essence,* trans. Alphonso Lingis (Pittsburgh: Duquesne University Press, 2008), 8.

6. America's oldest burden, of course, is the genocidal violence committed against the indigenous populations.

7. Du Bois, *The Souls of Black Folk,* 34.

8. I borrow "valences," of course, from the title of Fredric Jameson's wonderfully erudite work, *Valences of the Dialectic* (New York: Verso, 2009).

9. It is important to note that for Adorno "negation" should not be (too easily) equated with the "negative." Rather, "negation" ("negative dialectics") must be apprehended as the condition from which thinking begins: "Dialectics is the consistent sense of nonidentity. It does not begin by taking a standpoint. My thought is driven by its own inevitable insufficiency." Theodor W. Adorno, *Negative Dialectics,* trans. E. B. Ashton (New York: Continuum, 2005), 5.

10. Fredric Jameson, "Wagner as Dramatist and Allegorist," in *The Ancients and the Postmoderns: On the Historicity of Forms* (New York: Verso, 2015), 38.

11. King, "The Power of Nonviolence," 31.

12. Martin Luther King Jr., "Our God Is Able," in *Strength to Love* (Boston: Beacon Press, 1981), 111.

13. Martin Luther King Jr., "On Being a Good Neighbor," in *Strength to Love,* 29.

14. See Fredric Jameson, "An American Utopia," in *An American Utopia: Dual Power and the Universal Army,* ed. Slavoj Žižek (New York: Verso, 2015).

15. King, "On Being a Good Neighbor," 28.

16. V. I. Lenin, "The Dual Power," in *Lenin Collected Works,* vol. 24, trans. Isaacs Bernard (Moscow: Progress Publishers, 1964), Marxists Internet Archive, https://www.marxists.org.

17. Martin Luther King Jr., "Love in Action," in *Strength to Love,* 33.

18. Jameson, "Wagner as Dramatist and Allegorist," 33.

19. Martin Luther King Jr., "The Man Who Was a Fool," in *Strength to Love*, 68; Martin Luther King Jr., "A Knock at Midnight," in *Strength to Love*, 59.

20. Bess Levin, "Trump Claims Teaching Kids about Racism Is 'Child Abuse,' Wants It Abolished from Schools and Replaced with a 'Patriotic Education,'" *Vanity Fair*, September 17, 2020, https://www.vanityfair.com.

21. Recent revelations also expose Nixon, egged on by Henry Kissinger, denouncing Indians in the most pejorative terms. See "'Scavengers, Sexless, Suck-up Experts': NYT Contributor Scoops Deeply Racist Kissinger-Nixon Remarks on Indians," *Tribune* (India), September 4, 2020, https://www.tribuneindia.com.

22. Walter Benjamin, "On the Concept of History," trans. Dennis Redmond, Marxists Internet Archive, https://www.marxists.org.

23. Adorno's exact phrasing is "The semblance and the truth of thought entwine." Adorno, *Negative Dialectics*, 5.

24. Martin Luther King Jr., "I Have a Dream" (speech, National Mall, Washington, D.C., August 28, 1963), American Rhetoric, https://www.americanrhetoric.com.

25. Adorno, *Negative Dialectics*, 17.

26. *Random House Webster's Unabridged Dictionary*, 2nd ed. (New York: Random House, 2001), s.v. "profound."

27. Martin Heidegger, "Epilogue: Letter to a Young Student," in *Language, Poetry, Thought*, trans. Albert Hofstadter (New York: Harper & Row, 1971), 186. See also Karl Barth, *The Theology of John Calvin*, trans. Geoffrey W. Bromiley (Grand Rapids, Mich.: William B. Eerdmans, 1995).

28. Near the end of his life, Malcolm X shifted his position from focusing on the multiple transgressions of the "white devils" (the Nation of Islam's rhetoric) to proposing that the racism endured by African-Americans should be understood as a violation of human rights and, as such, a matter for consideration by the United Nations—an ideological trajectory that began within the separatist Nation of Islam and progressed to an appeal to the global community.

29. Adorno, *Negative Dialectics*, 17. Derrida argues that the biblical Abraham (who figures in all three monotheisms) is a figure of radical irresponsibility. Commanded by God to sacrifice his son, Isaac, Abraham is utterly irresponsible to his wife, to his family, to his community, to everyone except God, whom he obeys to the point of filicide. As such, Abraham is "irresponsible," in any conventional sense, to everyone. "Irresponsibility," as conceived by Derrida, stands not in opposition to "responsibility" but instead marks the highest form of fidelity: the strictest adherence to God's command. See, among his other works, Jacques Derrida, "Force of Law: The 'Mystical Foundations of Authority,'" in *Deconstruction and the Possibility of Justice*, ed. Drucilla Cornell, Michel Rosenfeld, and David Carlson (London: Routledge, 1992); and Jacques Derrida, *The Gift of Death*, trans. David Wills (Chicago: University of Chicago Press, 1996).

30. Martin Luther King Jr., "Loving Your Enemies," in *Strength to Love,* 47.

31. King, "Love in Action," 33.

32. Martin Luther King Jr., "I Have a Dream," in Washington, *I Have a Dream,* 103.

3. The Farceur

1. Jacques Derrida, "At This Very Moment in This Work Here I Am," in *Psyche: Inventions of the Other,* vol. 1, ed. Peggy Kamuf and Elizabeth Rottenberg (Stanford, Calif.: Stanford University Press, 2007), 152.

2. Derrida, *On Cosmopolitanism and Forgiveness,* 59.

3. Is it the fear of all being made equal that girds so much of Carl Schmitt's work? Is Schmitt's argument for sovereignty the hedge against the prospect of a Jamesonian utopian?

4. "George Wallace and the Segregation Strategy of 1968," History Community, Tapatalk, October 14, 2019, https://www.tapatalk.com/groups/thehistorycommunity.

5. Dave Chappelle, *Sticks & Stones,* Netflix, August 26, 2019, https://www.netflix.com.

6. I first came across the phrase in John Snow's *Cricket Rebel: An Autobiography* (London: Hamlyn, 1972), in which Snow tells the story of how his teammate Basil D'Oliveira went around the night after England beat Australia stubbing his forefinger into Australian chests, proclaiming, "We stuffed you" (95). The phrase stayed with me because D'Oliveira is Cape Town–born and, like me, designated "coloured," and as such was denied the right to represent the country of his birth.

7. "Charlton Heston; From My Cold Dead Hands, Long Version," YouTube, posted April 26, 2008, https://www.youtube.com.

8. See Christina Walker, "10 Years. 180 School Shootings. 356 Victims," CNN, July 2019, https://www.cnn.com.

9. Ben Garrett, "Gun Show Laws by State and the Gun Show Loophole," ThoughtCo, updated January 2, 2021, https://www.thoughtco.com.

10. "*Chappelle's Show,* Reparations for Slavery," YouTube, posted September 5, 2015, https://www.youtube.com.

4. Deracializing MLK

1. Abraham Lincoln, "First Inaugural Address, March 4, 1861," in *Abraham Lincoln: Great Speeches* (Mineola, N.Y.: Dover, 2012), 61.

2. C. L. R. James, *Beyond a Boundary* (Durham, N.C.: Duke University Press, 1993), 93.

3. In March 2021, Hamilton's total wins increased to ninety-six when he triumphed in the season-opening Bahrain Grand Prix.

4. G. W. F. Hegel, *Phenomenology of Spirit,* trans. A. V. Miller (New York: Oxford University Press, 1977), 2.

5. Dave Chappelle, *Equanimity & the Bird Revelation,* Netflix, December 31, 2017, https://www.netflix.com.

6. Chappelle.

7. Jameson, "Wagner as Dramatist and Allegorist," 34.

8. Jameson, 34.

9. Morrison, *Beloved,* 3.

10. Du Bois, *The Souls of Black Folk,* 37.

11. Heidegger, *What Is Called Thinking?,* 38, 39.

12. Heidegger, 50.

13. *Random House Webster's Unabridged Dictionary,* s.v. "discrimination."

14. Hegel, *Phenomenology of Spirit,* 112.

15. Jameson, "An American Utopia," 76.

16. The link between self and other, sometimes framed as "precarity" and at others labeled "intersubjective," to name but two, is a difficulty taken up most assiduously, with varying emphasis, in the work of Judith Butler. See, in this regard, Butler's *Precarious Life: The Powers of Mourning and Violence* (New York: Verso, 2006) and *Undoing Gender* (New York: Routledge, 2004), in which she writes (in the spirit of Hegel's "recognition"): "It is not the simple presentation of a subject for another that facilitates the recognition of that self-presenting subject by the Other. It is, rather, a process that is engaged when subject and Other understand themselves to be reflected in one another, but where this reflection does not result in a collapse of the one into the Other (through an incorporative identification, for instance) or a projection that annihilates the alterity of the Other" (131).

17. Heidegger, *What Is Called Thinking?,* 50.

18. In Hegel's critique of the self we can see the first iterations of what will become Michel Foucault's "care of the self" in *The Hermeneutics of the Subject: Lectures at the Collège de France 1981–1982,* trans. Graham Burchell (New York: Picador, 2005). For his part, Foucault takes his cue from Plato's *Alcibiades,* a dialogue that enables Foucault to raise not only the question of responsibility to the other but also the question of the difficulty of the relationship of "self" to "itself." How, in Foucault's terms, is it possible for the self to care for what is (ostensibly) already constitutive of that self?

19. Adorno, *Negative Dialectics,* 408.

20. Adorno, 408.

21. This is what being-with, to stretch the conceptual limits and to welcome the always troubled haunting that is Martin Heidegger, this is what *Mitsein,* means. To be-with commences an impossible struggle, one undertaken with political determination but always without philosophical success, because any inclining toward always complicates the attempt—that is, all attempts—to distinguish self from the other. The tendency toward dialectic reasoning, to establish other as (political) foil, is precisely what Heidegger resists in his distinction between "polemics" and "thinking." "Any kind of polemics," Heidegger argues, "fails from the outset to assume the attitude of thinking. The opponent's role is not the

thinking role. Thinking is thinking only when it pursues whatever speaks *for* a subject." Heidegger, *What Is Called Thinking?*, 13. As such, the "opponent" serves only as a straw figure who can better—or best—"illuminate" the (rhetorical) claims that the self wants to advance. "Thinking," on the other hand, seeks only to establish—understand, come to terms with—what, how, and certainly why it is that the subject speaks. Heidegger's phrasing is allusive, "whatever speaks for a subject," but it no doubt turns on the question of how it is that the "subject" "says" what it "says." Thinking, then, as, in one measure, depending on the precision with which it is the "subject" speaks.

22. Levinas is keen to dispense with "otherwise than being" as that which is not transcendence, but he never quite succeeds in dispensing with transcendence; it is perhaps, we might speculate, best that Levinas does not manage to entirely overcome transcendence.

23. Jean-Luc Nancy, *The Speculative Remark (One of Hegel's Bon Mots)*, trans. Céline Suprenant (Stanford, Calif.: Stanford University Press, 2001), 19.

24. Adorno, *Negative Dialectics*, 43.

25. Adorno, 43.

26. Adorno, 43.

27. Adorno, 18.

28. Here it is necessary to acknowledge that what is proposed as "dialectics"—the autoconstitutive possibility of and for thinking—bears closely on what Derrida names "autoimmunity."

29. Adorno, *Negative Dialectics*, 19.

30. Adorno, 31.

31. Foucault, *The Hermeneutics of the Subject*, 127.

32. Foucault, 127.

33. Foucault, 129.

34. Foucault, 129.

35. As if to prove this point, Rapinoe was honored with the Ballon d'Or ("Golden Ball," awarded to the best player in the world over the previous year) in November 2019. See Simon Kuper, "Megan Rapinoe Takes Home 2019 Ballon d'Or but Is So Much More Than the Best Player in Women's Soccer," ESPN, December 2, 2019, https://www.espn.com.

36. Unless, that is, Nip grasps "base" as a Jamesonian articulation: "base-and-superstructure not as a full-fledged theory in its own right, but rather as the name for a problem, whose solution is always a unique, ad hoc invention." Fredric Jameson, *Late Marxism: Adorno, or, The Persistence of the Dialectic* (New York: Verso, 1909), 46.

37. *Merriam-Webster*, s.v. "sublate," accessed March 10, 2021, https://www.merriam-webster.com.

38. Adorno, *Negative Dialectics*, 17.

39. Adorno, 43.

40. Adorno, 45.

41. Jameson, *Late Marxism*, 17.

42. On the condition that we take Nietzsche's concept in its Deleuzian formulation. That is, "eternal return of the same" is not about the "cyclical" (repetition; inevitable repetition) but turns entirely on difference. See Gilles Deleuze, *Difference and Repetition,* trans. Paul Patton (New York: Columbia University Press, 1994), esp. "Conclusion."

43. Claire Colebrook, "Hypo-hyper-hapto-neuro-mysticism," *Parrhesia,* no. 18 (2003): 1, http://www.parrhesiajournal.org/parrhesia18/parrhesia18_colebrook.pdf.

44. Colebrook, 1.

45. Colebrook, 1.

46. Adorno, *Negative Dialectics,* 406, 408.

47. Colebrook, "Hypo-hyper-hapto-neuro-mysticism," 1.

48. Hegel, *Phenomenology of Spirit,* 2.

49. Karl Marx and Friedrich Engels, *The Communist Manifesto,* trans. Samuel Moore (New York: International Publishers, 1948), 12.

50. Derrida, "At This Very Moment," 155.

5. Haunting

1. To which we might add "pass" or "passing" in a third sense. That is, "passing" as heteronormative. See, in this regard, Jay Prosser's critique *Second Skin: The Body Narratives of Transsexuality* (New York: Columbia University Press, 1998).

2. Adorno, *Negative Dialectics,* 38.

3. Jameson, *Late Marxism,* 42; Adorno, *Negative Dialectics,* 18.

4. Arthur Nortje, "Dogsbody Half-Breed," in *Dead Roots* (London: Heineman, 1973), 104.

6. And So I Turn to James Baldwin

1. Arthur Nortje, "Waiting," in *Dead Roots,* 90.

2. James Baldwin, "Princes and Powers," in *Nobody Knows My Name* (1961; repr., New York: Vintage International, 1993).

3. James Baldwin, *No Name in the Street* (1972; repr., New York: Vintage International, 2000), 28.

4. In his work on Édouard Glissant, John Drabinski makes the point that "creole" is best understood and applied within the context of the Caribbean. Outside that space, its purchase can too easily be drawn into question. See John E. Drabinski, *Glissant and the Middle Passage: Philosophy, Beginning, Abyss* (Minneapolis: University of Minnesota Press, 2019).

5. Danzy Senna, *Caucasia* (New York: Riverhead Books, 1998), 408.

6. James Baldwin, *The Fire Next Time* (1963; repr., New York: Vintage International, 1993), 6.

7. Baldwin, 4.

8. "Dave Chappelle on Ohio's Heroin Crisis," YouTube, posted October 26, 2019, https://www.youtube.com.

9. Baldwin, 8.

10. It is important to note that throughout his life, Baldwin viewed David Baldwin as his father. In this regard, "stepfather" is invoked only in a technical sense—as in, not biological.

11. King, "The Power of Nonviolence," 32.

12. In this regard, see James's Epistle 2:14–25, in which the apostle delineates "Faith through Works," his core philosophical intervention into scripture.

13. Wendell Berry, "Christianity and the Survival of Creation," in *Wendell Berry: Essays 1993–2017*, ed. Jack Shoemaker (New York: Literary Classics of the United States, 2019), 29. In this essay, Berry acknowledges his debt, as a Christian, to Buddhism.

14. Baldwin, *The Fire Next Time*, 47.

15. King, "Love in Action," 44.

16. Vladimir Jankélévitch, *Forgiveness*, trans. Andrew Kelley (Chicago: University of Chicago Press, 2005), 2.

17. Gilles Deleuze and Félix Guattari, *What Is Philosophy?*, trans. Hugh Tomlinson and Graham Burchell (New York: Columbia University Press, 1994), 2.

18. Deleuze and Guattari, 1.

19. We know that self-mastery is integral to "sovereignty" from Plato's Socratic dialogues *Alcibiades* and the *Phaedo*. For an expansive critique of this relation, see Foucault, *The Hermeneutics of the Subject*.

20. Derrida, *On Cosmopolitanism and Forgiveness*, 59.

21. Jankélévitch, *Forgiveness*, 6.

22. King, "I Have a Dream," in Washington, *I Have a Dream*, 102.

23. Jankélévitch, *Forgiveness*, 5.

24. Martin Heidegger, *The Fundamental Concepts of Metaphysics: World, Finitude, Solitude*, trans. William McNeill and Nicholas Walker (Bloomington: Indiana University Press, 1995), 172.

25. Heidegger, 172.

26. Deleuze and Guattari, *What Is Philosophy?*, 2.

27. Deleuze and Guattari, 3.

28. Deleuze and Guattari, 3.

29. Deleuze and Guattari, 3.

30. Jankélévitch, *Forgiveness*, 5.

31. Martin Luther King Jr., "Transformed Nonconformist," in *Strength to Love*, 19.

7. Do Not a Tarantula Be

1. Baldwin, *The Fire Next Time*, 9.

2. Baldwin, 9.

3. Heidegger, *What Is Called Thinking?*, 4.

4. See Bruce Robbins, *The Beneficiary* (Durham, N.C.: Duke University Press, 2017). Using literature, especially the work of George Orwell, Robbins

argues for a historical self-consciousness about the multifarious—and often nefarious—ways in which we all derive measurable benefits from the
machinations of global capital. This, for Robbins, raises the question of our
responsibility in relation to the ways in which capital functions.

5. Baldwin, *The Fire Next Time*, 5.

6. Baldwin, 10.

7. King, "I Have a Dream," in Washington, *I Have a Dream*, 102.

8. "Bagger Vance"

1. Friedrich Nietzsche, *Thus Spake Zarathustra*, trans. Thomas Common (New York: Modern Library, 1909), 67.

2. Nietzsche's critique of "virtue," however, is complicated, because
for all his derogation of virtue, he recognizes its value. Somewhat piously,
he acknowledges this, saying, "I do not even teach that virtue is its own
reward," after which he goes on to further sing its praises when he reminds us that virtue survives neglect. Nietzsche, 103. In the main, however, Nietzsche has little appetite for anything resembling that which is
sanctimonious and goes by the name of "virtue."

3. Nietzsche, 96.

4. Nietzsche, 36.

5. Nietzsche, 74.

6. Adorno, *Negative Dialectics*, 17.

7. Adorno, 17.

8. "Cyrene" also refers to a philosophical school started by a follower
of Socrates, Aristippus, in that part of the ancient world. The Cyrenians'
philosophy bore a close resemblance to that of the Epicureans.

9. Adorno, *Negative Dialectics*, 19.

10. Adorno, 19.

11. Adorno, 22.

12. King, "The Power of Nonviolence," 33.

13. Adorno, *Negative Dialectics*, 41.

14. Theodor Adorno, *Minima Moralia: Reflections from the Damaged
Life*, trans. Dennis Redmond (Middletown, Del.: Prism Key Press, 2011), 72.

15. Karl Marx, "The Eighteenth Brumaire of Louis Bonaparte," in *The
Marx-Engels Reader*, 2nd ed., ed. Robert C. Tucker (New York: W. W. Norton,
1978), 596.

16. Karl Marx, *Capital*, vol. 1, *A Critique of Political Economy*, ed. Friedrich
Engels, trans. Samuel Moore and Edvuard Aveling (Mineola, N.Y.: Dover,
2011), 26.

17. Marx, 26.

18. Adorno, *Negative Dialectics*, 5.

19. Nietzsche is clear as to the constitution of such perverse privilege: "the love which not only beareth all punishment, but also all guilt."
Nietzsche, *Thus Spake Zarathustra*, 72. The capacity of such a "love" to
"bear" both "punishment" and "guilt" marks it as an indulgence, available

only to those with the requisite historical wherewithal to endure a condition that links the two despite their seeming disparity.

20. Adorno, 5–6.

21. In a discussion that ranges from Hegel's "spirit" to the "unconscious," Adorno declares the "subject as the subject's foe." Adorno, 10. In this section of *Negative Dialectics*, titled "The Antagonistic Entirety," Adorno gives considered attention to the contradiction and, in so doing, hones in on what may very well be the most profound truth of the contradiction: the contradiction is what makes you (the "subject") "antagonistic" to yourself. Still the "subject," as such, but now no longer the "subject" as such because the "subject" has been made to see itself as in conflict, at its deepest core, with itself. This, needless to say, raises the possibility of the "subject" as "entirely" incompatible with itself. The contradiction that sustains the dialectic could not be more powerfully and poignantly rendered than this: the "subject" as enemy to the "subject." The self as unbearable to itself, the self in conflict with itself to the point of self-destruction, although because of the force of the contradiction it is no longer possible to assert with any confidence that such an act, self-destruction, as routinely understood, is even possible. The self as always laboring under the possibility of self-indictment. Or, in Adorno's intense philosophical phrasing, "dialectics is the ontology of the wrong state of things" (11). That is, a "state of things" in need of correction. All the more so if the "subject" as such is, as it were, at stake, or the first point (origin) of the "wrong."

22. Adorno, 6.

23. Adorno, 6.

24. Fredric Jameson, "Narrative Bodies: The Case of Rubens," in *The Ancients and the Postmoderns*, 15.

25. This opacity is offered by a Lukács in philosophical retreat for his nondoctrinal argument on the dialectic in *History and Class Consciousness*. Attacked by Leninist "philosophy," Lukács offers history (counterposed to consciousness) as the "*second nature* of social reality," as quoted in Maurice Merleau-Ponty, *Adventures of the Dialectic*, trans. Joseph Bien (Evanston, Ill.: Northwestern University Press, 1973), 66. Sympathetic to Lukács, Merleau-Ponty warns that "naïve realism, as it has always done, ends in skepticism" (67).

26. Adorno, *Negative Dialectics*, 408.

27. Jameson, *Late Marxism*, 52.

28. Jameson, 52.

29. Thomas Babington Macaulay, "Machiavelli," in *Niccolò Machiavelli's The Prince: On the Art of Power*, by Niccolò Machiavelli (London: Watkins, 2007), 217.

30. See, in this regard, how a defense of this position amounts to an argument that is utterly devoid of argument—a series of essentialized race-based assertions. There is, of course, a reason for this argument sans argument: no sustainable defense can be mounted. The following newspaper opinion piece provides an example of precisely the sort of

nonargument that must be avoided: John McWhorter, "The 'Ax' versus 'Ask' Question," *Los Angeles Times,* January 19, 2014. https://www.latimes.com.

31. Roger Kahn, *The Boys of Summer* (New York: Harper Perennial, 2006), 280.

32. Kahn, 288.

33. Martin Heidegger, "Building Dwelling Thinking," in *Language, Poetry, Thought,* 146.

34. Heidegger, 151.

35. Heidegger, 157.

36. Derrida, *Monolingualism of the Other,* 8.

37. Still others prefer to call it "headhunting." And not without good reason.

38. William Shakespeare, *Twelfth Night,* 1.1.1–2.

39. Derrida, *Monolingualism of the Other,* 1.

40. Derrida, 1.

41. In my earlier work *The Burden of Over-representation,* I discuss Derrida's experience of being born enfranchised (by the Cremieux of 1840, which recognized Jews as French citizens) and then losing that status in the course of Marshall Pétain's Vichy government in the chapter titled "I Think I Saw Jacques Derrida at the 2010 World Cup in South Africa." For this reason, I will not elaborate that argument here beyond what is absolutely necessary.

42. Plato, *Phaedo,* trans. G. M. A. Grube (Indianapolis: Hackett, 2010), 17.

43. Plato, 22.

44. "Dave Chappelle Stand-Up Comedy Clip Funny 'N-Word and F-Word,'" YouTube, posted November 18, 2019, https://www.youtube.com.

Postscript

1. Video in Patrick Ryan and Morgan Hines, "Joe Biden Election Victory; CNN's Van Jones Breaks Down in Tears; Meghan McCain, More Media Figures React," *USA Today,* November 7, 2020, https://www.usatoday.com.

Index

Grant Farred is author of *Martin Heidegger Saved My Life*; *In Motion, At Rest: The Event of the Athletic Body*; and *What's My Name? Black Vernacular Intellectuals,* all published by the University of Minnesota Press.